UNDERSTANDING
MUHAMMAD

A Psychobiography of Allâh's Prophet

Ali Sina

Preface
By Ibn Warraq

r. Ali Sina was born in Iran. Some of his relatives were Ayatollahs. Like most educated Iranians he believed that Islam was a humanistic religion that respected human rights. But Dr. Sina was also blessed with an enquiring mind, a rationalistic spirit that questioned, probed, and looked at the evidence unflinchingly. What he slowly discovered about the real Islam shook him morally and intellectually, and what is more, made him realize, long before September 11, 2001, that unless someone spoke the truth about the faith he was born into, the world would be faced with a system of thought and belief that would destroy not just the West, but civilization as a whole. Since his epiphanous moment when he discovered the inhuman nature of this religion, Dr. Sina has dedicated his life to discussing, criticizing, exposing the unacceptable aspects of Islam on his widely quoted website Faith Freedom International.

The West can make use of defectors, like Dr. Sina, from Islam (apostates) in the way the West used defectors from communism.

As I wrote in *Leaving Islam,*[1] there are very useful analogies to be drawn between Communism and Islam, such as the ones Maxime Rodinson[2] and Bertrand Russell have pointed out between the mindset of the communists of the 1930s and the Islamists of the 1990s and 21st century. As Russell said, "Among religions, Bolshevism [Communism] is to be reckoned with Mohammedanism rather than with Christianity and Buddhism. Christianity and Buddhism are primarily personal religions, with mystical doctrines and a love of contemplation.

---

[1] Ibn Warraq. *Leaving Islam. Apostates Speak Out.* Amherst: Prometheus Books. p.136
[2] Maxime Rodinson: *Islam et communisme, une ressemblance frappante*, in Le Figaro [Paris, daily newspaper], 28 Sep. 2001

Understanding Muhammad

Mohammedanism and Bolshevism are practical, social, unspiritual, concerned to win the empire of this world."[3] Hence the interest in the present situation and its haunting parallels with the communism of the western intellectuals in the 1930s. As Koestler said, "You hate our Cassandra cries and resent us as allies, but when all is said, we ex-Communists are the only people on your side who know what it's all about."[4] As Crossman wrote in his introduction, "Silone [an ex-Communist] was joking when he said to Togliatti that the final battle would be between the Communists and ex-Communists. But no one who has not wrestled with Communism as a philosophy and Communists as political opponents can really understand the values of Western Democracy. The Devil once lived in Heaven, and those who have not met him are unlikely to recognize an angel when they see one."[5]

Communism has been defeated, at least for the moment, Islamism has not, and perhaps the final battle will be between Islam and Western Democracy. And these ex-Muslims, to echo Koestler's words, on the side of Western Democracy, are the only ones who know what it's all about, and we would do well to listen to their Cassandra cries.

We who live in the free West and enjoy freedom of expression and scientific inquiry should encourage a rational look at Islam, should encourage Quranic criticism. Only Quranic criticism can help Muslims to look at their Holy Scripture in a more rational and objective way, and prevent young Muslims from being fanaticized by the Quran's less tolerant verses. It is the civic duty of all individuals living in the West to inform themselves about Islam. But if they only consult the works available in the megastores, they will find apologists of Islam. It is only by going through the meticulously documented and impeccably argued website of Dr. Sina and his team of writers that we would be able to obtain a more just appraisal of Islam. Now, of course, we have Dr. Sina's book which I urge all responsible citizens whose critical faculties have not been lulled into confusion and befuddlement by oft-repeated slogans about Islam being a religion of peace to read carefully. Thanks to the courageous efforts of independent scholars like Dr. Ali Sina, there can no longer be any excuse for remaining ignorant about a religion that may annihilate all that you cherish and hold worth defending.

Ibn Warraq is the author of **Leaving Islam, What the Koran Really Says, The Quest for the Historical Muhammad, The Origins of the Koran** *and* **Why I Am Not a Muslim**, *the book that inspired many Muslims to awake and question their cherished faith.*

---

[3] B.Russell, *Theory and Practice of Bolshevism*, London, 1921 pp .5, 29, 114
[4] A.Koestler, et al, *The God That Failed*, Hamish Hamilton, London, 1950, p.7
[5] Ibid. p16

About the Author

li Sina is a Canadian of Iranian descent. He received his watered down Islamic education at school during a time when Iran was secular and Islamic revivalism, although simmering beneath the surface, had not yet erupted. Back then, few actually knew the reality of it. He left Iran before the Islamic Revolution in his mid-teens to continue his higher studies in Europe, where he learned about freedom of thought and democracy. Democracy is a concept alien to the Muslim psyche – to the extent that there is no equivalent terminology for it in Arabic or in other languages spoken by Muslims. If they have no word for it, it follows that they cannot conceive it. For Muslims, the rule belongs to Allah.

After studying the history of the western philosophy and seeing how it had evolved to eventually give birth to Enlightenment, Ali Sina concluded that what ailed the Muslim world is lack of freedom of thought. However, it was only when he read the Qur'an from cover to cover for the first time that he realized the main cause of the backwardness of Muslims is Islam.

"After reading the Qur'an, I was in shock," says Ali Sina. "I was shocked to see the violence, hate, inaccuracies, scientific errors, mathematical mistakes, logical absurdities, grammatical solecisms and dubious ethical pronouncements in the book of God." After a period of guilt, confusion, disillusionment, depression and anger, he accepted the conclusion that the Qur'an was not a book of God, but satanic verses, a hoax, and the product of a sick mind. The experience was like awakening and realizing that what he had been so intensely experiencing thus far was just a dream.

After studying the sacred Islamic texts, the *hadith* (traditions) and the *Sira* (the biography of Muhammad), Ali Sina became convinced that the ills afflicting the Muslim world are caused by Islam and that this religion is a serious threat to mankind. It was then that he decided to launch his counter-jihad. He believes that reforming Islam is impossible. That Islam is like a brittle stone. You can't mold it, but you can smash it into pieces and pulverize it. Muslims are aware of its vulnerability and that is why they are so intolerant of criticism. "Islam is like a house of cards," he says, "sustained by lies; all it takes to demolish it is to challenge one of those lies holding it together. It is a tall building, erected on quicksand; once you expose its foundation, the sand will wash away and this mighty edifice will fall under its own weight. When asked whether Islam has a future, his response is: "Yes! It belongs in the dustbin of history."

Ali Sina predicts that Islam will be nothing but a bad memory in a few short decades and that many of us would see the end of it in our own lifetime. "I must admit, I was hesitant making such a statement because I knew many would dismiss it as unrealistic and even foolhardy. Yet the more I thought about it, the more certain I became. Today, many others are also seeing the inevitability of the death of Islam. The whisperings of criticism of Islam are being heard everywhere, both by those who were born within Islam and by others. It is becoming increasingly clear that the problem is not with Muslims and how they interpret Islam but with Islam itself," he says.

Ali Sina believes that Muslims are the primary victims of Islam. "My objective is not just to expose the dangers of Islam, but also to rescue Muslims from this web of lies. I want to save them from blowing up themselves and the world, to realize that mankind is one family, and help them come back to the human race, to prosper and live in peace. I want help establish the unity of Mankind, not by introducing yet another doctrine, which always ends up dividing mankind further, but by exposing and removing the chief doctrine of hate in the world," he says.

There are many disillusioned Muslims who are confused and can find no answers anywhere. They are ready to leave Islam but they don't know where to turn. They need answers and a support group. Faith Freedom International meets that need. The Internet, because it allows anonymity, is an ideal place for apostates to meet, exchange ideas, clear each other's doubts, share experiences, support and affirm one another. Islam would have imploded a long time ago if thinking Muslims had the opportunity to question Islam without fearing for their lives. Islam has survived so far only because it has suppressed all criticisms.

Faithfreedom.org is read by millions of people across the world. It has become the meeting ground for those who are concerned about the threat of Islam and want to know what drives some Muslims to this much hate and savagery. Faith Freedom International has grown to become a movement, a grassroots movement of ex-Muslims. Its aims are (a) to unmask Islam and show that it is an imperialistic ideology akin to Nazism, but disguised as religion, and (b) to help Muslims leave it, end this culture of hate caused by their "us" vs. "them" ethos and embrace the human race in amity. Faith Freedom International has been defined "a quiet global revolution in the making." Many new apostates are made daily and they in turn are becoming soldiers in the struggle of light against darkness and their numbers are growing exponentially. What started as a trickle has become a torrent. "What a wonderful way to wage this war where the enemy becomes your friend and best ally," says Ali Sina.

Jim Ball, Sydney's No. 1 overnight broadcaster writes: "Ali Sina is the Iranian ex-Muslim behind the website faithfreedom.org. Along with other former Muslims such as Ibn Warraq, Sina is spearheading what may be the first organized movement of ex-Muslims in Islamic history, made possible during the past ten to fifteen years by Muslim immigration to the West and the growth of the Internet....It is no exaggeration to say that if the likes of Ali Sina, Ibn Warraq and Wafa Sultan prevail in the face of the traditional death penalty for leaving Islam, then Islam will never again be the same."

Ali Sina is a Secular Humanist and a World Federalist.

Understanding Muhammad

Acknowledgment

I owe thanks to many people who helped me write this book. They corrected my English and provided valuable criticism. Unfortunately I can't name them. This would most likely put their lives in peril and I also do not know their real names. Even though they remain anonymous, I am immensely indebted to them.

I also would like to thank the wonderful friends who volunteered their time to take full control of the operation of faithfreedom.org, as site administrators, editors and moderators of its forums. This allowed me to have time to work on this book.

The fight against Islamic terrorism is fought by unsung heroes. These people give their time and talent to awaken the world to the danger of Islam. They ask nothing in return and remain anonymous.

Ali Sina
April, 2008

Contents

Introduction

fter the 9/11 attack on America, a distraught American mother told me that her son, aged 23, had converted to Islam at 14. He had married a Muslim woman whom he had never seen before in an arranged marriage by his Imam (Islamic cleric), and now, with a baby, he wanted to go to Afghanistan to fight for the Taliban killing American soldiers and become a "martyr." She also said that a few years earlier he told her that once Islam takes over America, he would not hesitate to behead her, should the order come to slay the unbelievers.

****

Samaira Nazir, a bright and well educated 25-year-old British national of Pakistani descent was stabbed to death. Her throat was slashed by her thirty – year-old brother and her seventeen-year-old cousin at her parents' home. Samaira had dishonored her family by falling in love with an Afghan man they thought was of lower caste and had rejected suitors lined up to meet her in Pakistan. In April 2005 she was summoned to the family home and ambushed by everyone. A neighbor witnessed seeing her trying to escape while her father grabbed her by the hair, pulled her back into the house and slammed the door. She was heard screaming, "You are not my mother anymore!" which indicates that her mother was also involved in her cold-blooded murder. Her nieces, aged two and four were made to watch the whole proceeding as the neighbors heard them screaming. The amount of blood on the children suggested that they were only feet from the attack. The family was educated and well to do.

****

Muhammad Ali al-Ayed, a 23-year-old Saudi millionaire's son living in America, one August evening, in 2003, called Sellouk, his old Jewish Moroccan friend and suggested they get together. The two had drinks at a bar before going to Al-Ayed's apartment about midnight. There he took a knife, stabbed and nearly decapitated his friend. Al-Ayed's roommate told police the two "were not arguing" before Al-Ayed killed Sellouk. The reason for this cold-blooded murder was "religious differences," said Ayed's attorney.

****

Mohammad Taheri-azar was a 25-year-old Iranian graduate from the University of North Carolina. One day in March 2006, he rented a SUV and drove it slowly onto the campus. Then he suddenly accelerated into the college crowd with the intent to kill as many people as he could. He hit nine people and injured six of them.

****

Sanao Menghwar and his wife, a Hindu couple residing in Karachi, Pakistan, were traumatized one November evening in 2005, when upon returning from work they discovered that all their three daughters were missing. After two days of futile searching, they found out that their daughters had been kidnapped and forced to convert to Islam. The police arrested three Muslim youths in connection with the crime, who were later granted bail by a court because they were minors. The girls remain missing.

"Kidnapping Hindu girls like this has become a normal practice. The girls are then forced to sign stamped papers stating that they've become Muslims," says Laljee, a Hindu resident of Karachi. "Hindus here are too frightened to vent their anger — they fear victimization," he added.

Many Hindu girls meet similar fates in Pakistan. They are abducted, forced to convert to Islam and forced to marry a Muslim man while their parents are denied the right to see or talk to them. "How can a Muslim girl live and maintain contact with kafirs (infidels)?" remarked Maulvi Aziz, the cleric representing a Muslim kidnapper in another case that was taken to the court.

When a Hindu girl is converted to Islam, hundreds of Muslims take to the streets and chant religious slogans. The cries of the parents fall on the deaf ears of authorities. The unfortunate girls are then threatened that if they recant Islam

Introduction

they would be executed as apostates. Often lawyers avoid taking up these cases, fearing a backlash from the extremists.

****

In October 2005, three girls were walking through a Cocoa plantation near the city of Poso in Indonesia. The girls attended a private Christian school. They were attacked and beheaded by a group of Muslims. Police said the heads were found some distance from the bodies and one of the heads was left outside a church. The Muslim militants have targeted central Sulawesi Province and believe that it could be turned into the foundation stone of an Islamic state. In 2001 and 2002, Muslims attacked the Christians in that province. The fighting drew Islamic militants from all over Indonesia and resulted in the death of more than 1,000 Christians.

****

Muriel Degauque was a 38-year-old Belgian woman who, according to a neighbor who knew her since childhood, was an "absolutely normal" little girl who liked to go for sled rides when it snowed. She converted to Islam when she married a Muslim man. Later she traveled with her husband through Syria to Iraq, where she blew herself up in an attack on an Iraqi police patrol on November 9, 2005. Five policemen were killed outright and a sixth officer and four civilians were seriously injured.

****

These acts are insane, but the irony is that none of the perpetrators were insane. They were "absolutely normal" people. What motivated them to commit these heinous crimes? The answer is Islam. Such occurrences are daily events in the Islamic world. Everywhere Muslims are busy killing people for what they believe.

Why? What makes sane people commit such evil? Why are Muslims, as a lot, so angry with others, so at war with the world that they are often quick to resort to violence? Millions of Muslims riot, protest, and kill completely innocent people anytime, anywhere, when someone says something about Muhammad. This kind of behavior is not rational. Yet the perpetrators are completely sane people. How can we explain this paradox?

To understand this we must understand that Muslims are expected to be like, and to think like, their prophet. As such, their attitudes, beliefs, thoughts and actions come to reflect his personality and mind. Since Muhammad is the model for all that is righteous in Islam, it is expected that they emulate him in every way, to do what he did and to think the way he thought. The result of this is that Muslims, as a whole, by virtue of taking on the life of Muhammad, leave behind their own, forsaking their humanity and to a large degree, their individuality. As they come to inhabit the narcissistic bubble universe of their prophet, and to the extent that they follow his examples, they become extensions of him. Muslims are twigs from the tree of Islam and the root of that tree is Muhammad. They share his character, his attitude and his mindset. You could say each Muslim is a mini Muhammad of a sort. Therefore, to understand Muslims, individually as well as collectively, we must first come to know and understand Muhammad.

As a subject, Muhammad is one very few like to engage. Muslims get offended if anyone slights their prophet. Any comment, no matter how innocuous, can elicit opprobrium. Though they may allow you to criticize his followers, they do not tolerate any criticism of the prophet himself.

It is not possible to make a thorough evaluation of the psychological profile of someone centuries after his death. However, there is a wealth of information about the details of the life of Muhammad and his sayings that are recorded meticulously. Many of these accounts are embellished by exaggeration and are full of hyperbole. It is to be expected that believers would elevate the status of their prophet, falsely attribute miracles to him and make him look saintly. In the biography of Muhammad, however, we also find thousands of accounts that do not portray him as a holy man, but rather, depict him as vile, ruthless, cunning, and even as a sexual pervert. There is no reason to believe these stories are fabrications. It would not be characteristic of believers to portray their prophet as a villain. So if such stories exist, narrated by his companions, those who believed in him and loved him, in such a large numbers, it is likely that they are true.

Traditions that are diffusely recurrent are called *mutawattir*. These traditions have come down to later generations through a large number of chains of narrations, involving diverse transmitters. It is virtually impossible that all these people, living in different localities and espousing (at times radically) different views, would come together, to fabricate the exact same lie and attribute it to their prophet.

Availing ourselves of these stories, called hadith, and the Qur'an, a book believed by every Muslim to be the verbatim word of God, we shall peer into Muhammad's mind, as we try to understand him and to figure out why he did what he did. I will quote the opinions and theories of various psychologists and

Introduction

psychiatrists, and compare what Muhammad did with what these experts of the mind say. The sources I quote are all experts in psychopathology. What they say is accepted as commonsense and is shared by the majority of professionals in their field.

This book is not so much intended to be a psychoanalysis of a man who lived 1400 years ago as it is an attempt to unravel his mystique. Muhammad is an enigma to many and particularly to his followers who accept the myth, and embrace the image, while refusing to see past it. His conduct was ungodly, yet he gave all indications that he truly believed in his cause. How could such a man, so vengeful, so ruthless, and so depraved, have such charisma as to leave spellbound not only his companions, but billions of people for so many centuries?

Michael Hart, in his book, *The 100: A Ranking of the Most Influential Persons in History*, places Muhammad at the very top of his list, followed by Isaac Newton, Jesus Christ, Buddha, Confucius and St. Paul. Hart's list does not take into consideration whether the influences these people exerted were positive or negative. In his list are also other tyrants, such as Adolph Hitler, Mao Ze Dong and Joseph Stalin. The list even includes Niccolò Machiavelli. How could a man like Muhammad, so devoid of humanity, become the most influential person in history? As this book attempts to show, the answer to this question has more to do with human psyche than it does with Muhammad the person.

There is no other cause for which more blood has been shed than Islam. According to some historians, in India alone, more than 80 million people were massacred by the sword of Islam. Millions were killed in Persia, Egypt and in all other countries that were attacked by marauding Muslims, both during their conquests and in the centuries that followed. It continues today.

Muslims often brag, "We love death more than you love life." They have proven it in thousands of terrorist attacks in recent years. How can one man have so much influence over so many people, even to cheerfully die for him and not hesitate to sacrifice their own children in his cause? Why nine out of ten on-going conflicts worldwide involve Muslims, who comprise only one fifth of humanity? Taken as a statistical average, this means that Muslims, as a group, are a whopping 36 times more likely to resort to violence for conflict resolution than the rest of humanity. How can this be?

Islam is the brainchild of Muhammad. Muslims read his words in the Qur'an and hadith and follow his examples in every detail of their lives. To them, he is the best part of creation, the most perfect human being and the example to follow. They believe that if he did something, no matter how egregious, that must be the right thing. No question is asked and no value judgment is allowed.

This book presents two theses. The first is that Muhammad suffered from narcissistic personality disorder. The second is that he was affected by temporal lobe epilepsy. He may have had other mental disorders as well, but these two conditions of personality and brain explain the entire phenomenon known as Muhammad. This book proves with overwhelming evidence that Muhammad was disturbed. Though he believed in his cause and was sincere in his claim, yet he could not differentiate the imaginary from the real. His contemporaries and those who knew him better, called him *majnoon* (lunatic, crazy, possessed by jinns). They unfortunately succumbed to his brute force and their voices of sanity were silenced. New discoveries of the human brain have finally vindicated them. But we should keep in mind, that despite psychological disorder, a narcissist is fully aware he is lying and despite that he is the first to believe in his own lies.

There are several books in the market critical of Muhammad that give the account of his violence and perverse character, however few of them explain what went in his mind. This book aims to do just that.

Although this book is not addressed to Muslims, it is mainly for them I have written it. As a Persian proverb says, I spoke to the door so the wall can hear. Enough has been said about Muhammad being a looter, a mass murderer, a marauding gangster, a pedophile, an assassin, a lustful womanizer, and what not. Muslims hear all that, and continue believing in him without blinking. Oddly, some of them even claim that after they read my articles on the Internet, their "faith in Islam grew." They have accepted Muhammad as a superior being and the "Mercy of God among mankind." They do not judge him by the standards of human morality and conscience. On the contrary, they believe that it was he who set the standards. For them, right and wrong, good and evil are not determined by the Golden Rule, a concept that is alien to the Muslim psyche, but by *halal* (permitted) and *haram* (forbidden), wanton religious values that have no basis in logic, ethics, or morality. Muslims are genuinely incapable of questioning Islam. They dismiss every doubt and consider things that are incomprehensible as "test" of God. To pass that test and to prove their faith, all they have to do is believe in every nonsense and absurdity unquestioningly.

Chapter One

Who Was Muhammad?

Your Lord has not forsaken you, nor does He hate you. The future will be better for you than the past. And soon your Lord will give you so that you wilt be content. Did He not find you an orphan and give you shelter? Did He not find you wandering and guide you? Did He not find you in need and enrich you? (Q. 93:3-8)[6]

 et us begin with Muhammad's story. Let us examine his life. Who was he and what was his thinking? In this chapter we will briefly go through the salient points in the life of a man, whom over a billion people literally worship. In fact Islam is nothing but Muhammadanism. Muslims claim that they worship no one but Allâh, but since Allâh was only Muhammad's alter ego, his other alias and invisible sock puppet, in practice, it's Muhammad whom they worship and that

---

[6] Qur'an Sura 93: Verses 3-8 (Translations of the Qur'an in this book are either by Yusuf Ali or by Shakir.) My work is not about the sacred scriptures of Islam, but it is based directly on them. The passages I cite are taken from the Qur'an and the Hadith. The Qur'an purports to be not the work of any human, but the very words of Allâh himself, from beginning to end. The Ahadith (plural for Hadith) are short, collected anecdotes and sayings about Muhammad regarded by Muslims as essential to the understanding and practice of their religion. It is not necessary for me, in this book, to discuss the innumerable questions raised by the Qur'an and the Hadith, their translation into other languages, or the disputes over subtle nuances in those texts. For purposes of this book, the passages I cite will mostly speak for themselves. I have taken them from widely accepted sources.

Understanding Muhammad

is exactly what Muhammad intended. Islam is the personality cult of Muhammad. We will read his words as they were dictated in the Qur'an, claimed by him to be the words of God, and see him through the eyes of his companions and wives. We will take a look at how he rose from a derelict preacher to become a de facto ruler of all of Arabia in just a decade, how he divided people in order to control them, how he instilled sedition and hate and roused some to wage war against others and how he used raids, rape, torture, and assassination to cast terror in the hearts of his victims and subdue them. We will learn about his genocides and his penchant for deception as a strategy, the very strategy used by Muslim terrorists today. After understanding Muhammad you will come to see that the terrorists are doing exactly what their prophet did.

The Birth and Childhood of Muhammad

In the year 570 A.D., in Mecca, Arabia, a widowed young woman, Amina, gave birth to a boy whom she called Muhammad.[7] Though Muhammad was her only child, Amina gave him to a Bedouin woman, to be raised in the desert when he was only six months old.

Some wealthy Arab women sometimes hired wet nurses for their infants. This freed them from nursing and allowed them to have another child right away. More children meant higher social status. But that was not the case with Amina who was a widow with only one child to care for and not wealthy. Abdullah, Muhammad's father, died six months before his birth. Also, this practice was not really that common. In fact Khadijah, the first wife of Muhammad, who was the wealthiest woman of Mecca, had three children from her previous marriages and bore six more to Muhammad. She raised them all on her own. [8]

Why would Amina give away her only child to be raised by someone else?   There is too little information on Muhammad's mother for us to understand her and the decision she made.

---

[7] Acording to one tradition (that I have not been able to verify its authenticity) Muhamamd's original name was Qutham. He was also known as Halabi. He changed his name to Muhammad (praised one) at the age of fifty-three, when he migrated to Medina.

[8] Muhammad had four daughters and two sons. His male children, Qasim and Abd al Menaf (named after deity Menaf) died in infancy. His daughters reached adulthood and married, but they all died young. The youngest daughter, Fatima, was survived by two sons. She outlived Muhammad by only six months.

Who Was Muhammad?

An interesting piece of information that sheds some light on her psychological makeup and her relationship with her new born child is that Amina did not breastfeed Muhammad. After his birth, the infant was given to Thueiba, a maid of his uncle Abu Lahab, (the very man whom Muhammad cursed in Sura 111 of the Qur'an, along with his wife) to be nursed. Why Amina did not nurse her child is not mentioned. All we can do is to speculate. Was she depressed by the fact that she had become a widow at such a young age? Did she think the child was an impediment to the possibility of remarriage?

A death in the family can cause chemical changes in the brain that can lead to depression. Other factors that may increase a woman's chances of depression are: living alone, anxiety about the fetus, marital or financial problems and the young age of the mother. Amina had just lost her husband, she was alone, poor, and young. Based on how much we know about her, she was a good candidate to suffer from depression. Depression may interfere with the mother's ability to bond with her growing baby. Also, depression during pregnancy can place the mother at risk for having an episode of depression after delivery (postpartum depression).[9]

Some research suggests that depression in pregnant women can have direct effects on the fetus. Their babies are often irritable and lethargic. These newborns may grow into infants who become slow learners, and emotionally unresponsive, with behavior problems, such as aggression. [10]

Muhammad grew up among strangers. As he grew, he became aware that he did not belong to the family with whom he was living. He must have wondered why his own mother, whom he visited twice a year, did not want him.

Halima, Muhammad's wet nurse, six decades later recounted that at first she did not want to take Muhammad for he was an orphan of a poor widow with little means. Eventually she accepted him because she did not find a child from a wealthy family, and because her own family desperately needed the extra income even though it was not much. Did this reflect in the way she cared for the child? Did Muhammad feel unloved in his foster family's home during those crucial formative years when a person's character is shaped?

---

[9] Studies have shown that the newborns of the mothers with prepartum and postpartum depressive symptoms had elevated cortisol and norepinephrine levels, lower dopamine levels, and greater relative right frontal EEG asymmetry. The infants in the prepartum group also showed greater relative right frontal EEG asymmetry and higher norepinephrine levels. These data suggest that effects on newborn physiology depend more on prepartum than postpartum maternal depression but may also depend on the duration of the depressive symptoms. ncbi.nlm.nih.gov

[10] www.health.harvard.edu/newsweek/Depression_during_pregnancy_and_after_0405.htm

Understanding Muhammad

Halima reported that Muhammad was a solitary child. He would withdraw to an imaginary world and converse with friends that no one could see. Was this the reaction of a child who did not feel loved in the real world and made up one in his mind in which he could find refuge and be loved?

Muhammad's mental health became a matter of concern to his wet nurse who, when he reached the age of five, took him back to Amina. Not having found a new husband yet, Amina was reluctant to take the child back, until Halima told her about Muhammad's strange behavior and his fantasies. Ibn Ishaq has recorded Halima's words:

> His [Halima's own son] father said to me, 'I am afraid that this child has had a stroke, so take him back to his family before the result appears.'... She [Muhammad's mother] asked me what happened and gave me no peace until I told her. When she asked if I feared a demon had possessed him, I replied that I did.[11]

It is normal for children to see monsters under their beds and talk to imaginary friends. But Muhammad's case must have been exceptionally alarming. Halima's husband said, "I am afraid that this child has had a stroke." This information is significant. Years later, Muhammad spoke of his strange childhood experiences:

> Two men in white clothes came to me with a golden basin full of snow. They took me and split open my body, then they took my heart and split it open and took out from it a black clot which they flung away. Then they washed my heart and my body with that snow until they made them pure.[12]

What is certain is that impurities of the mind don't appear as a clot in the heart. Apart from the fact that children are sin-free, sins cannot be removed

---

[11] Sirat Ibn Ishaq, page 72: Ibn Ishaq (pronounced Is-haq, Arabic for Isaac) was a Muslim historian, born in Medina approximately 85 years after Hijra (704. died 768). (Hijra is Muhammad's immigration to Medina and the beginning of the Islamic calendar), He was the first biographer of Muhammad and his war expeditions. His collection of stories about Muhammad was called "Sirat al-Nabi" ("Life of the Prophet"). That book is lost. However, a systematic presentation of Ibn Ishaq's material with a commentary by Ibn Hisham (d. 834) in the form of a recension is available and translated into English. Ibn Hisham, admitted that he has deliberately omitted some of the stories that were embarrassing to Muslims. Part of those embarrassing stories were salvaged by Tabari, (838–923) one of the most prominent and famous Persian historians and a commentator of the Qur'an.

[12] W. Montgomery Watt: Translation of Ibn Ishaq's biography of Muhammad (p. 36)

with surgery and snow is not a good cleanser. This whole story is a fantasy or a hallucination.

Muhammad was now reunited with his mother, but this union did not last long. A year later Amina died. He did not speak of her much. When Muhammad conquered Mecca, fifty five years after her death, he visited his mother's tomb at Abwa, a place between Mecca and Medina where she was buried and wept. He told his companions:

> This is the grave of my mother; the Lord has permitted me to visit it. And I sought leave to pray for her, but it was not granted. So I called my mother to remembrance, and the tender memory of her overcame me, and I wept. [13]

Why would God not allow Muhammad to pray for his mother? What had she done that she did not deserve to be forgiven? Unless we believe that God is unjust, this certainly does not make sense. Obviously God had nothing to do with it. It was Muhammad who could not forgive his mother, even half a century after her death. He probably remembered her as an unloving cold woman, was resentful of her and had deep emotional wounds that were never healed.

Muhammad then spent two years in the house of his grandfather, who, mindful of him being an orphan, lavished his grandson, the only remnant of his deceased son Abdullah, with excessive love. Ibn Sa'd writes that Abdul Muttalib gave the child so much attention that he had not given any of his sons.[14] Muir writes in his biography of Muhammad: "The child was treated by him with singular fondness. A rug used to be spread under the shadow of the Ka'ba, and on it, the aged chief reclined in shelter from the heat of the sun. Around the carpet, but at a respectful distance, sat his sons. The little Muhammad was wont to run close up to the patriarch, and unceremoniously take possession of his rug. His sons would seek to drive him off, but Abdul Muttalib would interpose saying: 'Let my little son alone.' He would then stroke him on the back, as he delighted in watching his childish prattle. The boy was still

---

[13] Tabaqat Ibn Sa'd p. 21. Ibn Sa'd (784-845) was a historian, student of al Waqidi. He classified his story in eight categories, hence the name Tabaqat (categories). The first is on the life of Muhammad (Vol. 1), then his wars (Vol. 2), his companions of Mecca (Vol. 3), his companions of Medina (Vol. 4), his grand children, Hassan and Hussein and other prominent Muslims (Vol. 5), the followers and the companions of Muhammad (Vol. 6), his later important followers (Vol. 7) and some early Muslim women (Vol. 8). The quotes from Tabaqat used in this book are taken from the Persian translation by Dr. Mahmood Mahdavi Damghani. Publisher *Entesharat-e* Farhang va Andisheh. Tehran, 1382 solar hijra (2003 A.D.).
[14] Tabaqat Volume 1, page 107

under the care of his nurse, Baraka, but he would ever and anon quit her, and run into the apartment of his grandfather, even when he was alone or asleep." [15]

Muhammad remembered the preferential treatment he received from Abdul Muttalib. Peppering it with his imagination, he later said that his grandfather used to say, "Let him alone for he has a great destiny, and will be the inheritor of a kingdom;" and would tell Baraka, "Beware lest you let him fall into the hands of the Jews and Christians, for they are looking out for him, and would injure him!"[16] However, no one remembered those comments, for none of his uncles readily accepted him when he made his claim, except Hamza, who was of his own age. Abbas also joined his cause, but only after Muhammad's star had risen and he was at the gate of Mecca ready to invade it.

Alas, fate was not clement to Muhammad. Only two years after living in the household of his grandfather, the old patriarch died at the age of eighty-two and the boy came under the guardianship of his uncle Abu Talib.

The orphan child felt bitterly the loss of his loving grandfather. As he followed his bier to the cemetery of Hajun, he was seen weeping; and years later, he retained a fond memory of him.

Abu Talib faithfully discharged the trust. "His fondness for the lad equaled that of Abdul Muttalib," writes Muir. "He made him sleep by his bed, eat by his side, and go with him whenever he walked abroad. And this tender treatment he continued until Muhammad emerged from the helplessness of childhood." [17] Ibn Sa'd quotes Waqidi who narrated that Abu Talib, although not wealthy, took care of Muhammad and loved him more than his own children.

Because of the devastating psychological blows during his childhood, Muhamamd feared abandonment and must have been emotionally traumatized. This becomes evident from an incident that took place when he was 12 years old. One day, Abu Talib decided to go to Syria for a business trip. He intended to leave the child behind. "But when the caravan was ready to depart, and Abu Talib about to mount his camel, his nephew was overcome by the prospect of so long a separation and clung to his protector. Abu Talib was moved, and carried the boy along with him."[18] This degree of attachment to his uncle is a clue that Muhammad was in constant fear of losing his loved ones.

---

[15] The Life of Muhammad by Sir. William Muir [Smith, Elder, & Co., London, 1861] Volume II Ch. 1. P. XXVIII

[16] *Katib al Waqidi*, p. 22

[17] Tabaqat Vol I. P 108,

[18] The Life of Muhammad by Sir. William Muir Vol. II Ch. 1. P. XXXIII

Who Was Muhammad?

Despite this great affection, and even though Abu Talib remained a staunch defender of him throughout his life – doting on him even more than he did his own children – Muhammad proved to be an ungrateful nephew in the end. When the aging uncle was in his deathbed, Muhammad visited him at his bedside. All the sons of Abdul Muttalib were also present. Thinking always of the well-being of his nephew, Abu Talib made an earnest plea to his brothers to protect Muhammad, who was now 53 years old. They promised to do so, including Abu Lahab, whom he had cursed. After that Muhammad requested his uncle to convert to Islam.

Muhammad was cognizant that his followers were mostly meek and lowly. To boost his prestige he needed someone of stature to embrace his cause. Ibn Ishaq narrates: "Whenever men came together at the fairs, or the apostle heard of anyone of importance coming to Mecca, he went to them with his message."[19] The chroniclers also tell us that Muhammad rejoiced immensely when Abu Bakr and then Omar enlisted in his cause. The conversion of Abu Talib would have elevated his prestige among his uncles and the Quraish, the tribe that resided within Mecca and were custodians of the Ka'ba, giving him the credibility and status he so desperately craved. Instead, the dying man smiled and said he would rather die in the faith of his forefathers. Thus, with his hopes dashed, Muhammad walked out of the room murmuring: "I wanted to pray for him, but Allâh stopped me from doing so."[20]

It is difficult to believe that God would stop his prophet from asking forgiveness for the man who raised him, protected him all his life, and sacrificed so much for him. This would lower God to a level that would render him unworthy of worship. The sacrifices Abu Talib and his family made for the sake of Muhammad were immense. This man, while yet incredulous of his nephew's claim, stood like a rock against his opponents, shielding him from any possible harm, and for 38 years remained his most stalwart supporter. Despite that Muhammad proved to be an ungrateful man. When Abu Talib refused to convert to Islam, he felt so rejected that he could not bring himself even to say a prayer at his death. Bukhari reports:

Narrated Abu Said Al-Khudri, that he heard the Prophet when somebody mentioned his uncle (i.e. Abu Talib), saying, 'Perhaps my intercession will

---

[19] Sirat, Ibn Ishaq page. 195
[20] Life of Muhammad, Muir Vol 2 p.195

be helpful to him on the Day of Resurrection so that he may be put in a shallow fire reaching only up to his ankles. His brain will boil from it.,[21]

Muhammad's youth was relatively eventless and not noteworthy enough for him to talk about and for his biographers to recount. He was shy, quiet and not very sociable. Despite the fact that he was cared for and even spoiled by his uncle, Muhammad remained sensitive to his status as an orphan. The memories of his loveless and lonely childhood haunted him for the rest of his life.

Years passed. Muhammad remained a loner, a recluse in his own world, distant and even aloof from his peers. Bukhari[22] says Muhammad was "shyer than a veiled virgin girl."[23] He remained so for the rest of his life, insecure and timid, something he tried to compensate for by puffing himself up, with pomposity and self-aggrandizement.

Muhammad did not engage in any important occupation. At times he would attend sheep, a profession mostly reserved for girls and deemed unmanly by the Arabs. The pay was meager and he depended on his impoverished uncle for his sustenance.

Marriage to Khadijah

Finally, at the age of 25, Abu Talib secured for Muhammad a job, to work as a trustee for a wealthy merchant woman, a relative, named Khadijah. Khadijah was a comely forty-year-old successful merchant and a widow. Muhammad made one trip to Syria in her service, selling her merchandise and buying what she had ordered. Upon his return, Khadijah fell in love with the young Muhammad and, through a maid, proposed marriage to him.

Muhammad was a needy man, both financially and emotionally. For him the marriage with Khadijah was a blessing. In her, he could find the mother he

---

[21] Bukhari Volume 5, Book 58, Number 224:

[22] Abu Abdullah Muhammad Bukhari (c. 810-870) was a collector of hadith also known as the *sunnah*, (collection of sayings and deeds of Muhammad). His book of hadith is considered second to none. He spent sixteen years compiling it, and ended up with 2,602 hadith (9,082 with repetition). His criteria for acceptance into the collection were amongst the most stringent of all the scholars of ahadith and that is why his book is called Sahih (correct, authentic). There are other scholars, such as Abul Husain Muslim and Abu Dawood who worked as Bukhari did and collected other authentic reports. Sahih Bukhari, Sahih Muslim and Sunnan Abu Dawood are recognized by the majority of Muslims, particularly Sunnis, as complementing the Qur'an.

[23] Bukhari: Volume 4, Book 56, Number 762:

had craved as a child, as well as the financial security that allowed him to never work again.

Khadijah was more than willing to take care of all her young husband's needs. She found her happiness in giving, caring, and in self-sacrifice.

Muhammad was not fond of work. He preferred to withdraw from the world and retreat into his own thoughts. Even as a child, he avoided the company of other children and did not play with them. He would often spend his time alone in a pensive mood. He did not know how to be happy or have fun. He hardly laughed, and if he did, he covered his mouth. From this, and following the tradition of their prophet, Muslims do not regard laughing to be pious.

In his secluded imaginary world, Muhammad was no longer the cast-off, unwanted child that he had come to see himself as during the early years of his life, but rather loved, respected, praised, and even feared. When reality became hard to bear and his loneliness overwhelmed him, he would escape into fantasy, where he could be anyone or anything he wanted to be. He must have discovered this realm at a very young age, when he was living with his foster family, and spending lonesome long days alone in the desert. This idyllic and comforting world of fantasies was to remain his refuge for the rest of his life. It became as real to him as the real world, only more pleasing. Leaving his wife at home with six children to take care for, Muhammad would retreat to caves around Mecca to spend his days secluding himself from the world, wrapped in his own thoughts and sweet reveries.

Mystic Experience

One day, at the age of forty, after having spent many days in a cave by himself, Muhammad had a strange experience. He started having rhythmic muscle contractions, abdominal pains, as if someone was squeezing him violently, fasciculation (muscle twitching), involuntary movement of head and lips, sweating, and rapid heartbeat. In this agitated state he heard voices and claimed to have had a vision of a ghost.

He ran home terrified, shivering and sweating. "Cover me, cover me," he pleaded with his wife. "O Khadijah, what is wrong with me?" He told her everything and said, "I fear that something may happen to me." He thought he had become possessed by demons again. Khadijah reassured him and told him not to be afraid, that he was visited by an angel and was chosen to be a prophet.

Understanding Muhammad

After his encounter with the ghostly figure, identified by his wife as Gabriel, Muhammad was convinced of his prophetic rank. This suited him well and fulfilled his desire for grandiosity. He began preaching his message.

What was his message? The message was that he had become a messenger and people had to believe in him. As the result they had to respect him, love him, obey him and even fear him. After 23 years of preaching, the core message of Muhammad remained the same. Islam's main message is that Muhammad is a messenger and that people must obey him. Beyond that, there is no other message. Failure to recognize him as such entails punishment, both in this world and the next. Monotheism, which is now the main argument of Islam, was not originally part of the message of Muhammad.

After he taunted the Meccans for years by insulting their religion and gods, they refused all dealings with him and his followers, who at his instruction, emigrated to Abyssinia. Eventually, to appease the Meccans, Muhammad was compelled to compromise. Ibn Sa'd narrates:

> One day the Prophet was in a gathering around the Ka'ba and was reading to them the sura an-Najm (sura 53). When he came to the verses 19-20 that read, '*Have you then considered the Lat and the Uzza, and Manat, the third, the last?*' Satan placed the following two verses in the mouth of the Prophet. '*They are pretty, and there is hope in their intercession.*'[24]

These words pleased the Quraish and they ended their boycott and hostility. This news reached the Muslims in Abyssinia who joyously returned to Mecca.

After a while, Muhammad realized that by acknowledging the daughters of Allâh as deities he had undermined his own position as the sole intermediary between Allâh and people, making his new religion indistinguishable from pagan beliefs and therefore redundant. So he retracted and said the two verses acknowledging the daughters of Allâh were satanic verses. He then replaced them with *"What! For you the males and for Him the females! This indeed is an unjust division!"*[25] Meaning, how dare you attribute daughters to God, when you yourselves pride in having sons? Females are deficient in intelligence and it is unbefitting for Allâh to have daughters. This division is very unfair.

Some of Muhammad's followers left him on this account. To justify this flip-flop and regain their confidence, he claimed that all other prophets were

---

[24] Tabaqat Volume I, page 191
[25] Qur'an, 53:19-22

16

also fooled by Satan, who inspired them with demonic verses that deceptively seemed to come from God.

> And we did not send before you any messenger or prophet, but when he desired, the Satan made a suggestion respecting his desire; but Allâh annuls that which Satan casts, then does Allâh establish His communications, and Allâh is all Knowing, Wise. So that He may make what Satan casts a trial for those in whose hearts is diseased. (Q.22:52-53)

Muhammad wrote these verses because several of his followers, realizing that he was making the Qur'an up as situation dictated, left him. What these verses essentially say, to put it even more bluntly, is that even when I, Muhammad, goof and you catch me with my pants down, it is still your fault because your heart is diseased.

Thirteen years passed, and no more than seventy or eighty people rallied around him. His wife, who not only attended to his needs, but also admired, flattered, and idolized him in a servile way was his first follower. Her social standing convinced a few other average people such as Abu Bakr, Othman and Omar to join his cause too. Apart from these few, the rest of Muhammad's followers were a bunch of slaves belonging to the dignitaries of the Quraish, and a few disaffected youths.

The Myth of Persecution

Muhammad's call in Mecca was received with indifference. The Meccans, like most non-Muslims of today, were tolerant of all religions. Religious persecution in those lands was unheard of. Polytheistic societies are generally tolerant by nature. They were offended when Muhammad insulted their gods. Despite that, they did not harm him.

Muhammad encouraged his followers to leave Mecca. Naturally the Meccans did not like that idea. The Muslim families were upset, as were the masters of slaves who had converted to Islam. Some of the slaves were caught while trying to escape and were beaten. That was not, of course, religious persecution. The Meccans were simply trying to protect what they considered to be their property. For example, when Bilal was caught, his master, Umaiyah, beat him and put him in chains. Abu Bakr paid his price and he was set free. He was being punished for trying to escape, causing a financial loss to his owner and not for his beliefs. There are also stories of Muslims being beaten by their family members for converting to Islam. A hadith narrates that Omar, prior to his own conversion, had tied up his sister forcing her to leave Islam.[26] Omar was an intolerant and strict man, both before and after his conversion. These stories can hardly be classified as religious persecutions. In the Middle East individualism is an alien concept. What you believe and what you do is everyone's business. Women in particular cannot make their own decisions. Even today, Muslim women can be honor-killed if they decide to marry a man of their choice without the consent of their families.

There is a story of persecution about a woman known as Summayyah. Ibn Sa'd is the only historian who says Summayyah suffered martyrdom in the hands of Abu Jahl. Al-Bayhaqi relying on Ibn Sa'd writes, "Abu Jahl stabbed her in her private parts."[27] If this martyrdom had really occurred it would have been trumpeted forth by every biographer and would have been reported in innumerable traditions. This is just an example of the kind of exaggeration that Muslims have been fond of making from the beginning.

In fact, the same biographer also claims that Bilal was also the first martyr. He long survived the alleged persecutions, came back to Mecca when that town was conquered by Muhammad and chanted the Azan from the roof top of Ka'ba. He died a natural death.

Some Islamic sources claim that Summayyah, her husband Yasir, and their son Ammar were persecuted in Mecca. However, Muir has shown that after Yasir died of natural causes, Summayyah married the Greek slave Azraq and had a child called Salma.[28] How then are we to understand that she died under persecution? Azraq belonged to Taif, and was one of the slaves who, at the siege of that city (some fifteen years later), fled over to Muhammad's camp. It is natural to conclude that Summayyah, after Yasir's death, married Azraq and lived at Taif and that the story of her persecution and martyrdom is an Islamic fairy tale.

Muhammad was not against slavery. Later, when he came to power, he forced thousands of free people into slavery. However, his order to leave Mecca was disrupting the social order and causing sedition. Because of that and his constant taunting of their religion, he became a *persona non grata* among his people, the Quraish. Yet at no time were he and his followers persecuted

---

[26] Sahih Bukhari *Volume 5, Book 58, Number 207*

[27] Al-Dalaa'il, 2/282

[28] Sir William Muir: The Biography of Mahomet, and Rise Of Islam. Chapter IV page 126

Who Was Muhammad?

because of their faith. Muslims make many baseless claims. Polytheists generally don't give a hoot about what others believe. They are pluralistic by their very nature. Ka'ba housed 360 idols, each a patron of a different tribe. There were Jews, Christians, Zoroastrians, Sabeans (an extinct monotheistic faith) and all sorts of religions in Arabia, whose followers were freely practicing their religions. There were other prophets also preaching their faiths. Religious intolerance in Arabia began with Islam.

There is no evidence of any persecution against Muhammad and Muslims in Mecca. Nonetheless, Muslims make such claims because Muhammad has made that claim. Muslims will not doubt anything Muhammad has said. Astonishingly, even some non-Muslim historians who are not sympathetic to Islam have fallen into that trap and have echoed this untruth. Muhammad claimed victimhood, when in reality he was the victimizer. Muslims do the same. Everywhere it is Muslims who are killing, oppressing and persecuting, and yet they are the ones who cry loudest claming to be victims and oppressed. To understand this phenomenon we must understand the psychology of Muhammad and his followers. This we shall do in the next chapter.

As the matter of fact it was Muhammad who preached intolerance even when still in Mecca. Muslims often quote Sura 109 as evidence that Muhammad preached tolerance. This Meccan sura reads:

1. Say : O ye that reject Faith!
2. I worship not that which ye worship,
3. Nor will ye worship that which I worship.
4. And I will not worship that which ye have been wont to worship,
5. Nor will ye worship that which I worship.
6. To you be your Way, and to me mine

Maududi, Qutb and many other Muslim scholars know better. They do not see this sura as an indication of tolerance. Maududi in his interpretation of the Quran writes:

> If the Surah is read with this background in mind, one finds that it was not revealed to preach religious tolerance as some people of today seem to think, but it was revealed in order to exonerate the Muslims from the disbelievers religion, their rites of worship, and their gods, and to express their total disgust and unconcern with them and to tell them that Islam and kufr (unbelief) had nothing in common and

there was no possibility of their being combined and mixed into one entity. Although it was addressed in the beginning to the disbelieving Quraish in response to their proposals of compromise, yet it is not confined to them only, but having made it a part of the Quran, Allah gave the Muslims the eternal teaching that they should exonerate themselves by word and deed from the creed of kufr wherever and in whatever form it be, and should declare without any reservation that they cannot make any compromise with the disbelievers in the matter of Faith. That is why this Surah continued to be recited when the people to whom it was addressed as a rejoinder, had died and been forgotten, and those Muslims also continued to recite it who were disbelievers at the time it was revealed, and the Muslims still recite it centuries after they have passed away, for expression of disgust with and dissociation from kufr and its rites is a perpetual demand of Faith.[29]

Immigration to Medina

Having to care for numerous children, while having to deal with a self-absorbed husband, Khadijah neglected her business, so that by the time she died, the family was impoverished. Shortly after Khadijah's death, Muhammad's other supporter, his uncle and guardian Abu Talib, also died. Deprived of these two close powerful allies, and ignored by the Meccans, he decided to immigrate to Medina, where he had received pledges of allegiance by some of its inhabitants. He ordered his followers to go first. Some of them were reluctant. He told them that if they didn't, they would "find their abode in Hell."[30]

Muhammad himself stayed behind. Then, one night, he claimed Allâh told him his enemies were about to attempt to hurt him. He then asked his loyal friend Abu Bakr to secretly accompany him to Medina. The following verse is about that intimation:

Remember how the Unbelievers plotted against you [Muhammad], to keep you in bonds, or slay you, or get you out (of your home). They deceive, and Allâh too deceives; but the best of deceivers (*makerin*) is Allâh. (Q.8:30)

---

[29] http://www.usc.edu/dept/MSA/quran/maududi/mau109.html
[30] Qur'an, 4:97: "When angels take the souls of those who die in sin against their souls, they say: 'In what (plight) were ye?' They reply: 'Weak and oppressed were we in the earth.' They say: 'Was not the earth of Allâh spacious enough for you to move yourselves away?' Such men will find their abode in Hell, - What an evil refuge!"

Who Was Muhammad?

As this Qur'anic verse suggests, it appears that Allâh is guessing what the Meccans were plotting. Doesn't this verse reveal the fears of a paranoid Man? Muhammad lived among the Meccans for thirteen years, taunting them and insulting their religion, just as Muslims today insult the religion of everyone else, and yet they tolerated him. Except for Muhammad's own claim, there is no historical evidence they ever tried to harm him.

In history written by Muslims themselves, there is no evidence of persecution against Muhammad. The elders of the Quraish, vexed at his insults, repaired to his aged uncle Abu Talib and said, "This Nephew of yours, has spoken opprobriously of our gods and our religion, and has abused us as fools, and given out that our forefathers were all astray. Now, avenge us yourself of our adversary (seeing that you are in the same case with ourselves), or leave him to it that we may take our satisfaction."[31]

This is hardly the language and approach of persecutors. This is a plea, an ultimatum to Muhammad to stop abusing their gods. Compare that to the actions of today's Muslims when their prophet is portrayed in a few cartoons. Muslims rioted; and, in far away places such as Nigeria and Turkey, killed nearly one hundred people who had nothing to do with those cartoons, and yet the Quraish tolerated numerous insults against their gods for thirteen years.

The night Muhammad escaped to Medina, in the company of his loyal friend Abu Bakr, marks the beginning of the Islamic calendar. In Medina, he found Arabs who were less sophisticated than the Meccans. An added advantage was that they were ignorant of his background and character, to which the Meccans were privy. As a result, they were more receptive to his message.

Muhammad was not the first Arab prophet. Several other pretenders from other parts of Arabia were his near contemporaries. The best known was Musailama, who started his prophetic calling a few years before Muhammad, but unlike the prophet of Islam, he was successful in his own town and among his own people. Interestingly, a woman called Sijah was also a claimant to that title, and she too had a sizable following among her own people. Both of these prophets were preaching monotheism. There is convincing evidence that, prior to Islam's dominance in Arabia, women there were much more respected and had more rights there than at any time since. None of these other prophets, however, resorted to violence in order to expand their religions or to rob people. They did not want to conquer territories and build empires, but rather, in the tradition of the Biblical prophets, were solely interested in preaching and in

---

[31] Sir William Muir, *Life of Muhammad,* Vol. 2, chap. 5,. p. 162.

inviting people to worship God. Muhammad was the only prophet-warrior of Arabia. The above-mentioned prophets were not antagonistic with each other. They cooperated and did not fight over dominance.

The Medinan Arabs accepted Muhammad readily, not because of the profundity of his teachings, which basically, as stated above, consisted only in telling people to believe in him, but because of their rivalry with the Jews. Medina was essentially a Jewish town. The Jews, by virtue of their faith, considered themselves to be "chosen people." They were also wealthier and more educated than the Arabs and, as a result, were envied by them. Most of Medina was owned by the Jews. This city was a Jewish town. *Kitab al-Aghani*[32] traces the first settlement of the Jews in Medina back to the time of Moses. However, in the 10th century book *Futuh al-Buldan (The Conquest of The Towns),* Al Baladhuri writes that, according to the Jews, a second Jewish immigration took place in 587 BC, when Nebuchadnezzar, the king of Babylon, destroyed Jerusalem and dispersed the Jews throughout the world. In Medina, the Jews were merchants, goldsmiths, blacksmiths, artisans, and farmers, whereas the Arabs were laborers and mostly worked for the Jews. They came to Medina at least a thousand years after the immigration of the Jews, i.e. in 450 or 451 A.D., when a great flood in Yemen forced various Arab tribes of the Saba region to migrate to other parts of Arabia. These tribes came to Medina in the fifth century as economic refugees. Once they converted to Islam, they banished and massacred their hosts and took over their city.

After gaining a foothold in Yathrib, later called Medina, the Arabs started to raid and rob the Jews. Jews in return said what any oppressed people would: when their Messiah comes, he will take their revenge. When these Arabs heard Muhammad claiming to be a messenger of God and proclaiming himself to be the one foretold by Moses, they thought by accepting him and converting to Islam they would outrival the Jews.

Ibn Ishaq narrates: "Now Allâh had prepared the way for Islam in that they lived side by side with the Jews, who were people of the Scriptures and knowledge, while they themselves were polytheists and idolaters. They had often raided them in their district, and whenever bad feeling arose, the Jews used to say to them, 'A prophet will be sent soon. His day is at hand. We shall follow him and kill you by his aid;.... So when they heard the apostle's message, they

---

[32] A collection of poems in many volumes compiled by Abu al-Faraj Ali of Esfahan. It contains poems from the oldest epoch of Arabic literature down to the 9th cent. It is an important source of information on medieval Islamic society.

said one to another: 'This is the very prophet of whom the Jews warned us. Don't let them get to him before us!'"[33]

It is ironic that Judaism and its messianic belief should become the strength of Islam. Without it, Muhammad may have never had any followers and Islam would have died like most cults do.

Again, there is little or no evidence to support Muhammad's claim that Meccans persecuted Muslims. This claim is unquestioningly repeated by both Muslims and some non-Muslim historians. The anger and animosity toward Muslims was reaction to Muhammad's own behavior. This in no way resembles any persecution we see of Muslims today, or persecution of followers of other faiths by Muslims. It was Muhammad, not the Meccans, who ordered Muslims to leave their homes. He enticingly promised:

> To those who leave their homes in the cause of Allâh, after suffering oppression, we will assuredly give a goodly home in this world; but truly the reward of the Hereafter will be greater. If they only realized (this)! (Q.16:41)

The immigrants had no source of income. How was Muhammad to deliver this promise and give "goodly homes" to those who, at his behest, had forsaken their homes? They had become poor and relied on the charity of the Medinans for sustenance. Muhammad was about to lose his credibility. His followers were whispering their discontent. Some started to defect from his camp. His response to all this was another threatening verse:

> They [the unbelievers] long that you should disbelieve even as they disbelieve, that you may be upon a level (with them). So choose not friends from them till they forsake their homes in the way of Allâh; if they turn back (to enmity) then take them and kill them wherever you find them, and choose neither friend nor helper from among them. (Q.4:89)

How can we reconcile these friendship prohibitions and threats with the claim that the Meccans had driven Muhammad and his followers out of their homes? In this verse, Muhammad is telling his followers to kill those Muslims who defect and want to return to Mecca. This is reminiscent of the reverend Jim Jones' "Jonestown" compound in Guyana, where he ordered his men to shoot anyone attempting to escape. All of this was designed to isolate his followers so he could better control and indoctrinate them. When one is separated from

---

[33] Sirat Ibn Ishaq, P.197

family and friends, and joins a cult where everyone is bewitched, it becomes difficult to think or question the authority of the leader.[34]

Divide and Rule

Despite his frantic threats that divine punishment awaited those who would abandon him, Muhammad had to find a way to provide a source of livelihood for his followers. To solve this problem, he told them to rob the Meccan caravans. He asserted that the Meccans had driven them out of their homes and so it was lawful for them to plunder them.

> Permission (to fight) is given to those upon whom war is made because they are oppressed, and most surely Allâh is well able to assist them. Those who have been expelled from their homes without a just cause except that they say: Our Lord is Allâh. (Q.22:39-40)

Meanwhile, he issued many Qur'anic verses prodding his followers to fight the non-believers.

> O Prophet! Rouse the believers to the fight. If there are twenty amongst you, patient and persevering, they will vanquish two hundred: if a hundred, they will vanquish a thousand of the unbelievers: for these are a people without understanding. (Q.8:65)

Muhammad justified these attacks by playing what today we call the victim card, much as his followers do today. He claimed that unbelievers had

---

[34] Jalal al-Din al-Suyuti says: "A group of people from Mecca accepted Islam and professed their belief; as a result, the companions in Mecca wrote to them requesting that they emigrate too; for if they don't do so, they shall not be considered as those who are among the believers. In compliance, the group left, but were soon ambushed by the nonbelievers (Quraish) before reaching their destination; they were coerced into disbelief, and they professed it." [Jalal al-Din al-Suyuti "al-Durr al-Manthoor Fi al- Tafsir al-Ma-athoor," vol.2, p178;]
Suyuti writes that in one hadith Allâh's Apostle said, "There is no Hijra (i.e. migration) (from Mecca to Medina) after the Conquest (of Mecca), but Jihad and good intention remain; and if you are called (by the Muslim ruler) for fighting, go forth immediately."
This shows that prior to the conquest of Mecca, emigration from that town was one of the requisites for Muslims. This is additional evidence of the fact that Muslims were coerced by Muhammad to abandon their homes, while their families did everything they could to keep their loved ones from following this man.
Jalal al-Din al-Misri al-Suyuti al-Shafi`i al-Ash`ari, also known as Ibn al-Asyuti (849-911) was the mujtahid imam and renewer of the tenth Islamic century. He was a hadith master, jurist, Sufi, philologist, and historian. He authored works in virtually every Islamic science.

been oppressing believers and waging war against them. In reality, he initiated the hostilities, by raiding the Meccans' caravans and killing them as soon as he had enough men believing in him and willing to do his bidding.

The contradiction is obvious. In one verse Muhammad urges his followers to immigrate to Medina and threatens those who might be thinking of staying behind with murder and hell. In other verses he falsely claims that Muslims have been expelled without just cause and refers to them as "those against whom war is made."

The following Arabic proverb: *Darabani, wa baka; Sabaqani, wa'shtaka.* "He struck me, and started crying; then he went ahead of me and charged me with beating him!" perfectly illustrates Muhammad's modus operandi. His followers play the same dirty game to this day. This strategy made Muhammad dazzlingly successful. He roused sons against their fathers, turned brothers against brothers, and undermined tribal alliances, corroding the fabric of the society. Using this tactic, he eventually brought all of Arabia under his domination.

Do not assume that there is something about Arabs that makes them susceptible to stupidity. Even today, Westerners converting to Islam become just as inimical to their own people and countries as those Arabs did 1400 years ago. John Walker Lindh converted to Islam and went to Afghanistan to fight for Al-Qaeda against America. Joseph Cohen was an orthodox Jew who converted to Islam; and today he says that killing Israelis, including their children, is legitimate.[35] Yvonne Ridley, the BBC journalist who sneaked into Afghanistan in 2001 and was captured by the Taliban, converted to Islam upon her release, and now hates her own country so much she calls it "the third most hated country of the world" (after Israel and America supposedly). She supports suicide bombings, calling them "martyrdom operations," and has called the notorious terrorist Abu Musab al-Zarqawi, who had killed thousands of Iraqis in a campaign of violence in Iraq and had also masterminded the bombing in Jordan that killed 60 and injured 115 persons in a wedding ceremony, "a hero." As for the Chechen terrorist leader Shamil Basayev, the mastermind of the Moscow theatre hostage crisis and the Beslan school massacre, he is "a martyr whose place in Paradise is assured," says Ridley.[36] Inciting hatred worked for Arabs and all those who now call themselves Muslims, and it will work for others too.

---

[35] http://www.youtube.com/watch?v=BJLsdydjSPo
[36] *Daily Muslims*, July 12, 2006

Promise of Heavenly Rewards

Several verses of the Qur'an exhort Muslims to carry out raids on innocent people and loot them, for reward in this world and in the next. "Allâh promises you much booty that ye will capture." (Q. 48:20) To placate the conscience of those who might have felt some guilt about what they were doing, Muhammad made his Allâh say: "Enjoy what you took in war, lawful and good."[37]

Many Muslim atrocities throughout the centuries were inspired by this and similar verses. Amir Tîmûr-i-lang, also known as Tamerlane (1336-1405), was a ruthless man who became emperor through banditry. In an autobiographical memoir, *The History of My Expedition against India*, he wrote:

My principal object in coming to Hindustan (India) and in undergoing all this toil and hardship has been to accomplish two things. The first was to war with the infidels, the enemies of Islam; and by this religious warfare to acquire some claim to reward in the life to come. The other was a worldly object; that the army of Islam might gain something by plundering the wealth and valuables of the infidels: plunder in war is as lawful as their mothers' milk to Muslims who war for their faith, and the consuming of that which is lawful is a means of grace. [38]

Even if we assume that those eighty or so Muslims who emigrated were indeed forced out by the Meccans, how would this justify the raids on the caravans? The goods in those caravans did not necessarily belong to the people who allegedly exiled the Muslims. Is anyone who thinks they are being

---

[37] Qur'an, 8:69. See also Qur'an, 8:74: "Those who believe, and adopt exile, and fight for the Faith, in the cause of Allâh as well as those who give (them) asylum and aid, - these are (all) in very truth the Believers: for them is the forgiveness of sins and a provision most generous." One who is not familiar with Muhammad's style of writing (actually, of reciting, as he was illiterate) may wonder how the order to loot people can be reconciled with the command to fear Allâh. However, those who read the Qur'an in Arabic notice that the verses rhyme, and Muhammad often added words or phrases that are out of place, such as 'fear Allâh,' 'Allâh is most merciful,' 'He is all knowing, all wise,' etc., just to make his verses rhyme. Otherwise, it is inconceivable to fear the wrath of God and at the same time pillage and murder innocent people. By doing so—by associating God with looting, genocide and rape—Muhammad lowered the moral standards of his followers and sanctified evil. Thus pillage became holy pillage, killing became holy killing, and iniquity was sanctioned and even glorified. He assured his men that those who fight for their Faith would be rewarded, not only with the spoils of war but with forgiveness for their sins.

[38] Malfuzat-i Timuri, or Tuzak-i Timuri, by Amir Tîmûr-i-lang In the History of India as told by its own historians. The Posthumous Papers of the Late Sir H. M. Elliot. John Dowson, ed. 1st ed. 1867. 2nd ed., Calcutta: Susil Gupta, 1956, vol. 2, pp. 8-98.

persecuted in a city justified in taking his revenge on any citizen of that city? Muslims use the same logic when they bomb and kill innocent civilians. If they perceive a country as having been unfriendly towards them, they think it is okay to impose payback by killing any innocent citizen of that country. Everything Muslims do today that baffles the world is an imitation of what Muhammad did.

In Chapter 22, Verse 39 of the Qur'an, Allâh gives permission to fight. This is the very same verse with which Osama Bin Laden began one of his letters to America. Can we therefore really say that Islam has nothing to do with Islamic terrorism?

Incite to Violence

In Medina, the immigrants from Mecca were a mere handful. To be effective in his raids, Muhammad also needed the help of recent Muslim converts native in that town, whom he called "Ansar" (the helpers).

However, the Medinans had not joined Islam in order to raid caravans and wage wars. Believing in Allâh is one thing. Raiding, robbing and killing people are altogether something else. Arabs, prior to Muhammad, were not used to religious wars. Even today, there are Muslims who, though they may believe in Allâh, do not want to fight and kill for their religion. To persuade that kind of follower, Muhammad made his Allâh issue this command:

> Fighting is good prescribed for you, and you dislike it. But it is possible that you dislike a thing which is good for you, and that you love a thing, which is bad for you. But Allâh knows, and you know not. (Q. 2:216)

Soon, the Prophet's efforts bore fruit. Goaded by greed for booty and by promises of rewards in the afterlife, the Medinan Muslims joined in the banditry and looting business as well. As Muhammad's army grew and his ambition soared, the bandit decided to graduate to potentate. He encouraged his followers not only to wage war for him "in the way of Allâh" but also to pay for the expenses of those wars.

> And spend of your wealth in the cause of Allâh, and make not your own hands contribute to (your) destruction; but do good; for Allâh loves those who do good. (Q.2:195)

Understanding Muhammad

Note how Muhammad links "doing good" with looting, terror, and murder. It is by this very twisted sense of morality that Muslims are able to sacrifice their consciences and take up a sociopathic situational ethics toward other groups, one that must always be played to their advantage. However a situation benefits Muslims is considered good. Muhammad made his followers believe that subsidizing his warfare and committing such acts of terrorism for Islam were the best deeds that pleased God.

Today, Muslims who cannot fight, compensate by contributing to Islamic "charities." These "charities" are not established to build hospitals, orphanages, schools or senior housing. Rather, they are established to expand Islam, to build mosques and madrassas, train terrorists, and finance jihad. Islamic charities will aid the poor only to enlist them for their political cause. A good example of that is the huge amount of money the Islamic Republic of Iran pays to the Hezbollah of Lebanon. This, of course, is not done out of real charity. The masses of Iranians today are living in abject poverty. Those who are lucky enough to work, try to survive with a salary that amounts to no more than $100 US dollars per month. They are in dire need of food, jobs and shelter. Why then take their money and give it to the Lebanese? The idea is to make Islam taste sweet in their mouths and enlist them in the war against Israel.

When people didn't pony up enough funds for his military campaigns, Muhammad would angrily rebuke them:

> And what reason have you that you should not spend in Allâh's way? And Allâh's is the inheritance of the heavens and the earth, not alike among you are those who spent before the victory and fought (and those who did not): they are more exalted in rank than those who spent and fought afterwards; and Allâh has promised good to all; and Allâh is Aware of what you do. (Q.57:10)

Muhammad cleverly equates the money that Muslims spent on his warfare to a "loan" given to God, and promised them "goodly interest" on their money:

> Who is he that will Loan to Allâh a beautiful loan? For (Allâh) will increase it manifold to his credit, and he will have (besides) a liberal Reward. (Q.57:11)

In this way, he made his followers believe that Allâh is in debt to them for aiding Muhammad in his wars of conquest. While Muhammad made Allâh tell his followers how great will be the reward of those who finance his warfare expeditions, he did not want them to brag about their contributions and their sacrifices. Making sacrifices was to be understood as a privilege. It was the believers who had to be grateful to him for the opportunity of serving him, and not the other way round:

> Those who spend their substance in the cause of Allâh, and follow not up their gifts with reminders of their generosity or with injury, -for them their reward is with their Lord: on them shall be no fear, nor shall they grieve. (Q. 2:262)

After rousing them to wage war and instructing them to smite the necks of the unbelievers, he assured them that their "good deeds" would never be forgotten.

> So when you meet in battle those who disbelieve, then smite the necks until when you have overcome them, then make (them) prisoners, and afterwards either set them free as a favor or let them ransom (themselves) until the war terminates. That (shall be so); and if Allâh had pleased He would certainly have exacted what is due from them, but that He may try some of you by means of others; and (as for) those who are slain in the way of Allâh, He will by no means allow their deeds to perish. (Q. 47:4)

In other words, Allâh can kill the unbelievers without the help of the Muslims, but he wants Muslims to do it in order to test their faith.

Thus Muhammad depicts Allâh as a mafia godfather, a thuggish gang-leader who tests the loyalty of his henchmen by asking them to kill. In Islam, the faith of the believer is ultimately tested by their bloodthirstiness and, readiness to kill in the cause of Allâh. Then he said:

> And prepare against them what force you can and horses tied at the frontier, to frighten thereby the enemy of Allâh and your enemy and others besides them, whom you do not know (but) Allâh knows them; and whatever thing you will spend in Allâh's way, it will be paid back to you fully and you shall not be dealt with unjustly. (Q. 8:60)

Muhammad made empty promises that those who warred (with body or finances) against unbelievers and accepted him as Allâh's messenger would find rewards piled high in the afterlife. In characterizing these rewards, he was indeed most generous and extravagant. He claimed there would be all kinds of goodies and endless sexual indulgence in paradise, and warned that punishment loomed for those who were stingy in subsidizing his warfare: [39]

> Believers! Shall I point out to you a profitable course that will save you from a woeful scourge? Have faith in Allâh and His apostle, and fight for Allâh's cause with your wealth and with your persons. That would be best for you, if you but knew it. He will forgive you your sins and admit you to gardens watered by running streams; He will lodge you in pleasant mansions in the gardens of Eden. That is the supreme triumph. (Q.61:10-11)

> [In Paradise] they shall recline on couches lined with thick brocade, and within reach will hang fruits of both gardens. Which of your Lord's blessings would you deny? Therein are bashful virgins whom neither man nor jinnee will have touched before. Which of your Lord's blessings would you deny? Virgins as fair as corals and rubies. Which of your Lord's blessings would you deny? (Q.55:53-55)

> [In Paradise] theirs shall be gardens and vineyards, and high-bosomed maidens for companions: a truly overflowing cup. (Q.78:32-33)

> Believe in Allâh and His messenger, and spend out of the whereof He has made you heirs. For, those of you who believe and spend, - for them is a great Reward. (Q.57:7) [40]

These and similar verses of the Qur'an make it easy to understand why so many Islamic charities have been caught financing terrorist organizations.[41] One would think that charity and terrorism are diametrically opposed concepts, but such a distinction is not obvious to Muslims. Islamic charities are meant to

---

[39] Qur'an, Chapter 47, Verse 38: "Behold, ye are those invited to spend (of your substance) in the Way of Allâh: But among you are some that are niggardly. But any who are niggardly are so at the expense of their own souls. But Allâh is free of all wants, and it is ye that are needy. If ye turn back (from the Path), He will substitute in your stead another people; then they would not be like you!"

[40] See also Chapter 63, Verse 10.

[41] An affidavit made public in federal court in Virginia in August 19, 2003, contends that the Muslim charities gave $3.7 million to BMI Inc., a private Islamic investment company in New Jersey that may have passed the money to terrorist groups. The money was part of a $10 million endowment from unnamed donors in Jiddah, Saudi Arabia.

http://pewforum.org/news/display.php?NewsID=2563

Also on July 27, 2004, the U.S. Justice Department unsealed the indictment of the nation's largest Muslim charity and seven of its top officials on charges of funneling $12.4 million over six years to individuals and groups associated with the Islamic Resistance Movement, or Hamas, the Palestinian group that the U.S. government considers to be a terrorist organization.

http://www.washingtonpost.com/wp-dyn/articles/A18257-2004Jul27.html

promote Islam and support jihad. To us, this is terrorism; to a Muslim, it is holy war, an obligation and the most meritorious act in the sight of Allâh.

Thus, to fight in the cause of Allâh became an ordinance of Islam, binding upon all Muslims. Muhammad roused the immigrants against their own people, calling for just vengeance to be taken against them because of their alleged persecution of Muslims.

> Fight until there is no *fitnah* (mischief/dissension) and religion is wholly to Allâh. (Q. 8:39)

When some of his followers showed reluctance to make war, he coerced them to do his bidding by propitiously "revealing" new injunctions from Allâh, who warned of their dire fate if they disobeyed.

> And those who believe say: Why has not a chapter been revealed? But when a decisive chapter is revealed, and fighting is mentioned therein you see those in whose hearts is a disease look to you with the look of one fainting because of death. Woe to them then! (Q.47:20)

If these verses tell us one thing, it is that Islam is by definition belligerent. As long as people believe in Islam and think that the Qur'an is the word of God, Islamic terrorism will always win out. Those within Islam who might call for reform, tolerance, and a "dialogue between civilizations" are easily silenced by the authority of the Qur'an, so many of whose verses rouse believers to wage war against unbelievers.

> Fight then in Allâh's way; this is not imposed on you except in relation to yourself, and rouse the believers to ardor maybe Allâh will restrain the fighting of those who disbelieve and Allâh is strongest in prowess and strongest to give an exemplary punishment. (Q. 4:84)

Giving them the assurances of success:

> And Allâh will by no means give the unbelievers a way against the believers. (Q. 4:141)

And promises of celestial rewards:

Those who believed and fled (their homes), and strove hard in Allâh's way with their property and their souls, are much higher in rank with Allâh; and those are they who are the achievers (of their objects). (Q. 9:20) [42]

Muslims scholars everywhere echo this incitement to violence. Saudi Arabia's leading religious figure, the grand mufti, defended the spirit of jihad, or holy war, as a God-given right. "The spread of Islam has gone through several phases, secret and then public, in Mecca and Medina," the holiest places in Islam, said Sheikh Abdel Aziz Al Sheikh in a statement carried by the state news agency SPA. "God then authorized the faithful to defend themselves and to fight against those fighting them, which amounts to a right legitimized by God, 'This... is quite reasonable, and God will not hate it.'"[43] he said.

Saudi Arabia's most senior cleric explained that war was not Muhammad's first choice: "He gave three options: either accept Islam, or surrender and pay tax, and they will be allowed to remain in their land, observing their religion under the protection of Muslims."[44] The Grand Mufti is right. Violence against non-Muslims was only a last resort, if they refused to convert or surrender peacefully to the armies of Islam. This is no credit to Muhammad. Few armed robbers resort to violence if their victim peacefully cooperates. Criminals only use violence if they are resisted.

In an Internet based debate that I held with Mr. Javed Ahmed Ghamidi, arguably the most prominent Pakistani Islamic scholar, through his student Dr. Khalid Zaheer, Mr. Ghamidi wrote: "The possibility of killings mentioned in the Qur'an are either meant for those who were guilty of murder, or causing mischief on earth, or those who were declared unworthy of living in this world any more after they had denied the clearly communicated and understood message from God." Mr. Ghamidi is a moderate Muslim. However, he knows his religion well and knows that those who reject Islam are "unworthy of living in this world any more" and must be put to death.[45]

---

[42] See also Qur'an, 8:72, "Those who believed and those who suffered exile and fought (and strove and struggled) in the path of Allâh, - they have the hope of the Mercy of Allâh: And Allâh is Oft-forgiving, Most Merciful." and

Qur'an Chapter 8, Verse 74: "Those who believe, and adopt exile, and fight for the Faith, in the cause of Allâh as well as those who give (them) asylum and aid, - these are (all) in very truth the Believers: for them is the forgiveness of sins and a provision most generous."

[43] http://metimes.com/articles/normal.php?StoryID=20060918-110403-1970r

[44] Ibid.

[45] http://www.faithfreedom.org/debates/Ghamidip18.htm

Who Was Muhammad?

Raids

Muslims often speak with pride about Muhammad's "battles." It is a pride based on illusions. Muhammad avoided battles. He preferred ambushes and raids, which allowed him to take his victims by surprise and massacre them while they were unprepared and unarmed.

During the last ten years of his life, after he moved to Medina and felt strong amongst his followers, Muhammad launched 74 raids.[46] Some of them amounted to little more than assassinations, while others were expeditions of thousands of men. He participated in 27 of them. These are called *ghazwa*. The wars he ordered his men to wage but did not himself take part in are called *sariyyah*. Both *ghazwa* and *sariyyah* mean raid, ambush, and sudden attack.

Bukhari narrates a hadith from Abdullah bin Ka'b who said, "Whenever Allah's Apostle wanted to make a Ghazwa, he used to hide his intention by apparently referring to different Ghazwa."[47]

When Muhammad took part in a war, he would always stay behind his troops, protected by his special entourage. Nowhere in the authentic biographies of Muhammad, do we read that he ever fought personally.

In one of the battles, a war known as *the Sacrilegious War*, fought in Mecca, Muhammad attended upon his uncles. Now nearly twenty years old, his efforts were confined to gathering up the arrows discharged by the enemy during the ceasefires and handing them to his uncles. As Muir explains: "Physical courage, indeed, and martial daring, are virtues which did not distinguish the prophet at any period of his career."[48]

Muhammad and his men ambushed towns and villages without warning, descended upon unarmed civilians, cowardly butchered as many of them as they could, and took as spoils of war the vanquished community's herds and livestock, their weaponry and their entire belongings, as well as their wives and children. The raiders sometimes ransomed the women and children for money, or kept/sold them as slaves. The following is an account of one of these raids as recorded in the Islamic annals:

> The Prophet had suddenly attacked Banu Mustaliq without warning while they were heedless and their cattle were being watered at the places of water. Their fighting men were killed and their women and children were taken as captives; the Prophet

---

[46] Tabaqat, Vol. 2, pp. 1-2.

[47] Sahih Bukhari Volume 5, Book 59, Number 702:

[48] William Muir, Life of Muhammad Volume II, Chapter 2, Page 6.

got Juwairiya on that day. Nafi said that Ibn Omar had told him the above narration and that Ibn 'Omar was in that army.[49]

In this war, says the Muslim chronicler, "600 were taken prisoners by the Muslims. Among the booty there were 2,000 camels and 5,000 goats."[50]

The world is shocked when Muslim terrorists kill children and the Muslim apologists are quick to announce that killing children in Islam is prohibited. The truth is Muhammad allowed killing children during night raids.

> It is reported on the authority of Sa'b b. Jaththama that the Prophet of Allâh (may peace be upon him), when asked about the women and children of the polytheists being killed during the night raid, said: They are from them.[belong to them][51]

The objective of Muhammad's raids was primarily to loot. A number of sources considered authoritative by virtually all Muslims attest that in order to win, the Prophet took advantage of the element of surprise:

> Ibn 'Aun reported: I wrote to Nafi' inquiring from him whether it was necessary to extend (to the disbelievers) an invitation to accept (Islam) before meeting them in fight. He wrote (in reply) to me that it was necessary in the early days of Islam. The Messenger of Allâh (may peace be upon him) made a raid upon Banu Mustaliq while they were unaware and their cattle were having a drink at the water. He killed those who fought and imprisoned others. On that very day, he captured Juwairiya bint al-Harith. Nafi' said that this tradition was related to him by Abdullah b. Omar who (himself) was among the raiding troops.[52]

To justify such dastardly attacks on civilians, Muslim historians have often accused their victims of conspiring against Islam. However, there is no reason to believe that any Arab tribe would have benefited by invading the Muslims, who had become a strong group of bandits. Contrary to this claim, many tribes adopted policies of appeasement vis-à-vis Muslims by signing peace treaties with Muhammad in order to stay safe. Those treaties were later broken by the prophet when he became powerful.

---

[49] Sahih Bukhari, Vol. 3. Book 46, Number 717
[50] Ibid.
[51] Sahih Muslim Book 019, Number 4321, 4322 and 4323:
[52] Sahih Muslim Book 019, Number 4292:

Who Was Muhammad?

The loot did not just bring wealth to his marauding gang. It also provided them with sex slaves. Juwairiya was a beautiful young woman whose husband was slain, who fell to the lot of a Muslim. Aisha, Muhammad's favorite and youngest wife (who, according to Muslim sources was six years old when the fifty-one year old Muhammad married her, and nine when he consummated the marriage) accompanied Muhammad on this expedition and later narrated:

> When the prophet—peace be upon him—distributed the captives of Banu Almustaliq, she (Juwairiya) fell to the lot of Thabit ibn Qyas. She was married to her cousin, who was killed during the battle. She gave Thabit a deed, agreeing to pay him nine *okes* of gold for her freedom. She was a very beautiful woman. She captivated every man who saw her. She came to the prophet - peace be upon him -, to ask for his help in the matter. As soon as I saw her at door of my room, I took a dislike to her, for I knew that he would see her as I saw her. She went in and told him who she was, the daughter of al-Harith ibn Dhirar, the chief of his people. She said: 'You can see the state to which I have been brought. I have fallen to the lot of Thabit, and have given him a deed for ransom, and I have to come to ask your help in the matter.' He said: 'would you like something better than that? I will discharge your debt, and marry you.' She said: 'Yes.' 'O then it is Done!' the messenger of Allâh replied.[53]

This account should end any argument about the real motive behind Muhammad's multiple marriages. He and his men murdered Juwairiya's husband in an unprovoked raid. She was the daughter of the chief of Bani Mustaliq and a princess in her own right. She was reduced to slavery and became the possession of one of Muhammad's marauding thugs. However, because of her beauty, the holy Prophet offered to "set her free" under the condition that she marry him. Is that freedom? What other choice did she have? Even if Muhammad did actually set her free, where could she go?

Muslim apologists insist that most of Muhammad's wives were widows. One could thus get the impression that he married them out of charity. What they leave out is that these "widows" were young and beautiful, and they had become widows through him. Juwairiya was 20 years old at the time and Muhammad was 58. Islamic chroniclers admit that Muhammad did not marry women unless they were young, beautiful, and childless. Except for Sauda, who was in her thirties when Muhammad

---

[53] http://66.34.76.88/alsalafiyat/juwairiyah.htm

married her so she could take care of his children, and according to a hadith he stopped sleeping with her after he got prettier and younger women,[54] all his wives were in their teens or early twenties and this is when he was in his fifties and sixties. The historian Tabari[55] tells us that Muhammad did not marry women who had children or were not young and beautiful. Tabari narrates that Muhammad solicited Hind bint Abu Talib, his own cousin, to marry him, but when she told him that she had a child, he desisted. Another woman was Zia'h bint Aamir. Muhammad asked someone to solicit her for marriage. She accepted, but when he was told of her age, he changed his mind.[56]

A Muslim named Jarir ibn Abdullah narrated that once Muhammad asked him, "Have you got married?" He replied in the affirmative. Muhammad then asked, "A virgin or a matron?" He replied, "I married a matron." Then Muhammad said, "Why have you not married a virgin, so that you may play with her and she may play with you?"[57]

Women for the messenger of Allâh were only sex objects. They had no more rights than chattel. Their function was to give pleasure to their husbands and birth to their children.

Rape

Muhammad allowed his men to rape the women captured in raids. However, after capturing the women, Muslims faced a dilemma. They wanted to have sex with them but also wanted to return them for ransom and therefore did not want to make them pregnant. Some of these women were already married. Their husbands had managed to escape when taken by surprise and were still alive. The raiders considered the possibility of coitus interruptus (withdrawing from intercourse prior to ejaculation). Unsure of the best course of action, they went to Muhammad for counsel. Bukhari reports:

> Abu Saeed said: 'We went out with Allâh's Apostle for the Ghazwa of Banu Al-Mustaliq and we received captives from among the Arab captives and we desired

---

[54] Aisha has narrated that Sauda gave up her (turn) day and night to her in order to seek the pleasure of Allâh's Apostle (by that action). [Bukhari Volume 3, Book 47, Number 766]

[55] Muhammad ibn Jarir al-Tabari (838–923) was one of the earliest, most prominent and famous Persian historians and exegetes of the Qur'an, most famous for his *Tarikh al-Tabari* and *Tafsir al-Tabari*.

[56] *Persian Tabari*, Vol. IV, page 1298.

[57] Bukhari *Volume 3, Book 34, Number 310:*

women and celibacy became hard on us and we loved to do coitus interruptus. So when we intended to do coitus interruptus, we said, 'How can we do coitus interruptus before asking Allâh's Apostle who is present among us?' We asked (him) about it and he said, 'It is better for you not to do so, for if any soul (till the Day of Resurrection) is predestined to exist, it will exist.[58]

Notice that Muhammad does not forbid raping women captured in war. Instead, he indicates that when Allâh intends to create anything, nothing can prevent it. In other words, not even the absence of semen can prevent it. So Muhammad is telling his men that coitus interruptus would be futile and ill-advised because it would be an attempt to thwart the irresistible will of Allâh. Muhammad does not say a word against the forced insemination of these captive females. In fact, by criticizing coitus interruptus, in effect he supported forced insemination.

In the Qur'an, Muhammad's god made it legal to have intercourse with slave women, the so-called "right hand possessions," even if they were married before their capture.[59]

---

[58] Bukhari, Volume 5, Book59, Number 459. Many other canonical hadiths recount how Muhammad approved intercourse with slave women, but said coitus interruptus was unnecessary because if Allâh willed someone to be born, that soul would be born regardless of coitus interruptus. See the following:

Bukhari 3.34.432: "Narrated Abu Saeed Al-Khudri: that while he was sitting with Allâh's Apostle he said, 'O Allâh's Apostle! We get female captives as our share of booty, and we are interested in their prices, what is your opinion about coitus interruptus?' The Prophet said, 'Do you really do that? It is better for you not to do it. No soul that which Allâh has destined to exist, but will surely come into existence.'"

Sahih Muslim is another source considered factual and accurate by virtually all Muslims. Here is Sahih Muslim 8.3381: "Allâh's Messenger (may peace be upon him) was asked about 'azl, (coitus interruptus) whereupon he said: The child does not come from all the liquid (semen) and when Allâh intends to create anything nothing can prevent it (from coming into existence)."

Muslims also consider Abu Dawood highly accurate and factual. Here is Abu Dawood, 29.29.32.100: "Yahya related to me from Malik from Humayd ibn Qays al-Makki that a man called Dhafif said that Ibn Abbas was asked about coitus interruptus. He called a slave-girl of his and said, 'Tell them.' She was embarrassed. He said, 'It is alright, and I do it myself.' Malik said, 'A man does not practise coitus interruptus with a free woman unless she gives her permission. There is no harm in practicing coitus interruptus with a slave-girl without her permission. Someone who has someone else's slave-girl as a wife does not practice coitus interruptus with her unless her people give him permission.'"

See also Bukhari 3.46.718, 5.59.459, 7.62.135, 7.62.136, 7.62.137, 8.77.600, 9.93.506 Sahih Muslim 8.3383, 8.3388, 8.3376, 8.3377, and several more.

[59] Qur'an, 4:24: "Also (prohibited are) women already married, except those whom your right hands possess: Thus hath Allâh ordained (Prohibitions) against you."

Qur'an, 33:50): "O Prophet! We have made lawful to thee thy wives to whom thou hast paid their dowers; and those whom thy right hand possesses out of the prisoners of war whom Allâh has assigned to thee."

Qur'an, 4:3: "If ye fear that ye shall not be able to deal justly with the orphans, marry women of

Torture

Ibn Ishaq narrates the story of the conquest of Khaibar. He reports that Muhammad, without warning, attacked this fortress town, inhabited by Jews and killed many unarmed people as they were fleeing. Among those captured was Kinana. Ibn Ishaq states:

> Kinana al-Rabi, who had the custody of the treasure of Banu Nadir, was brought to the apostle who asked him about it. He denied that he knew where it was. A Jew came (Tabari says 'was brought') to the apostle and said that he had seen Kinana going to a certain ruin every morning early. When the apostle said to Kinana, 'Do you know that if we find you have it (the treasure) I shall kill you?' He said, 'Yes.' The apostle gave orders that the ruin was to be excavated and some of the treasure was found. When he asked him about the rest (of the treasure?) he refused to produce it, so the apostle gave orders to al-Zubayr Al-Awwam, 'Torture him until you extract what he has.' So he kindled a fire with flint and steel on his chest until he was nearly dead. Then the apostle delivered him to Muhammad b. Maslama and he struck off his head, in revenge for his brother Mahmud.[60]

On the same day that Muhammad tortured to death the youthful Kinana, he took his seventeen year old wife Safiya to a tent for sexual intercourse. Two years earlier, the Prophet had beheaded Safiya's father along with all the males (except those who had not yet begun pubescence) of the Jewish tribe Bani Quraiza. Ibn Ishaq writes:

> The apostle occupied the Jewish forts one after the other, taking prisoners as he went. Among these were Safiya, the wife of Kinana, the Khaibar chief, and two female cousins; the apostle chose Safiya for himself. The other prisoners were distributed among the Muslims. Bilal brought Safiya to the apostle, and they passed the bodies of several Jews on the way. Safiya's female companions lamented and strewed dust on their heads. When the apostle of Allâh observed this scene, he said, 'Remove these she-devils from me.' But he ordered Safiya to remain, and threw his *reda* [cloak] over her. So the Muslims knew he had reserved her for his own. The

---

your choice, two or three or four; but if ye fear that ye shall not be able to deal justly (with them), then only one, or (a captive) that your right hands possess, that will be more suitable, to prevent you from doing injustice."

[60] Sirat Rasul Allâh, p. 515.

apostle reprimanded Bilal, saying, 'Hast thou lost all feelings of mercy, to make women pass by the corpses of their husbands?'

Bukhari also has recorded a few ahadith about Muhammad's conquest of Khaibar and his rape of Safiya.

Anas said, 'When Allâh's Apostle invaded Khaibar, we offered the Fajr prayer there (early in the morning) when it was still dark. The Prophet rode and Abu Talha rode too and I was riding behind Abu Talha. The Prophet passed through the lanes of the town quickly and my knee was touching the thigh of the Prophet. He uncovered his thigh and I saw the whiteness of the thigh of the Prophet. When he entered the town, he said, 'Allâhu Akbar! Khaibar is ruined. Whenever we approach near a nation then evil will be the morning of those who have been warned.' He repeated this thrice. The people came out for their jobs and some of them said, 'Muhammad (has come).' (Some of our companions added, 'With his army.') We conquered Khaibar, took the captives, and the booty was collected.

Dihya came and said, 'O Allâh's Prophet! Give me a slave girl from the captives.' The Prophet said, 'Go and take any slave girl.' He took Safiya bint Huyai. A man came to the Prophet and said, 'O Allâh's Apostles! You gave Safiya bint Huyai to Dihya and she is the chief mistress of the tribes of Quraiza and An-Nadir and she befits none but you.' So the Prophet said, 'Bring him along with her.' So Dihya came with her and when the Prophet saw her, he said to Dihya, 'Take any slave girl other than her from the captives.'' Anas added, 'The Prophet then manumitted her and married her.'

Thabit asked Anas, 'O Abu Hamza! What did the Prophet pay her as *mahr* (dowry)?' He said, 'Her self was her *mahr* for he manumitted her and then married her.' Anas added, 'While on the way, Um Sulaim dressed her for marriage (ceremony) and at night she sent her as a bride to the Prophet.'[61]

---

[61] Sahih Bukhari, 1.8.367
In this hadith the commentator narrates how they [the Muslims] raided the city of Khaibar, during the dawn taking the population off guard. "Yakhrab Khaibar" (Khaibar is ruined) exclaimed Muhammad, as he passed from one stronghold triumphantly to another: "Great is Allâh! Truly when I light upon the coasts of any people, wretched for them is that day!
After the conquest of the town, it came time to share the booty. Dihya, one of the warriors, received Safiya as his share. Safiya's father who was the chief of the Bani Nadir had been beheaded by the order of Muhammad three years earlier. After the conquest of Khaibar, her young husband Kinana was tortured and murdered by his order too. Someone informed Muhammad that the seventeen year old Safiya was very beautiful. So Muhammad offered Dihya two girls, the cousins of Safiya, in exchange and got Safiya for himself.

There is also a hadith narrated by Anas, a companion of Muhammad, who recalled that a group of eight men from an Arab tribe came to Muhammad but they found the climate of Medina unsuitable. Muhammad prescribed camel urine as medicine and sent them to meet his camel attendant outside of the town. The men killed the camel attendant and drove away the camels. When Muhammad was informed, he sent some men to pursue them. Then he had their hands and feet cut off, ordered nails which were heated and passed over their eyes, and they were left in a rocky land to die slowly. Anas said that they asked for water, and nobody provided them with water till they died.[62]

The Arabs committed murder and theft and had to be punished, but why this much torture? Wasn't Muhammad doing exactly the same things? Where did Muhammad get his camels? Weren't they stolen? Didn't he raid and kill people to loot them?

This double standard is what has characterized the Muslim world since its inception. The concept of the Golden Rule and fairness is absent in the psyche of the Muslims. They demand all privileges in non-Muslim countries, while they deny the basic human rights to non-Muslims in countries where they are the majority. They sincerely believe this is how things should be.

Assassination

Today the world is shocked to learn that some Muslims feel that the only way to deal with the critics of Islam is to assassinate them. In 1989, Khomeini issued a fatwa (religious decree) to assassinate Salman Rushdie, because Rushdie had written a book, *The Satanic Verses*, that some believed insulted Islam. Some condemned Khomeini and accused him of being an extremist. Amazingly, many blamed Rushdie instead, for being "insensitive" to Muslims' sensitivity. On February 14, 2006, the Iranian state news agency reported that the fatwa will remain in place permanently.

Since its inception, the Islamic regime of Iran has systematically eliminated its opponents by assassinating them, whether those opponents live in Iran or in exile in other countries. Hundreds of dissidents have

---

[62] Bukhari Volume 4, Book 52, Number 261:

Who Was Muhammad?

been killed in this way, including Dr. Shapoor Bakhtiar, a true democrat and the last Prime Minister appointed by the Shah.

What most people don't know is that assassination was Muhammad's way of dealing with his opponents. Today's Muslim assassins are merely following their prophet's example.

Ka'b bin Ashraf was one of Muhammad's victims. As Muslim historians have reported, he was young and handsome, a talented poet and a chief of the Banu Nadir, one of the Jewish tribes of Medina. After Muhammad banished the Banu Qainuqa', another Jewish tribe of Medina, Ka'b became concerned about his own people's security vis-à-vis the Muslims, so he visited Mecca to seek protection. He composed poems and praised the Meccans for their bravery and honor. When Muhammad heard about this, he went to the mosque, and after the prayer, said:

'Who is willing to kill Ka'b bin Al-Ashraf who has hurt Allâh and His Apostle?' Thereupon Muhammad bin Maslama got up saying, 'O Allâh's Apostle! Would you like that I kill him?' The Prophet said, 'Yes.' Muhammad bin Maslama said, 'Then allow me to say a (false) thing (i.e. to deceive Ka'b).' The Prophet said, 'You may say it.' Then Muhammad bin Maslama went to Ka'b and said, 'That man (i.e. Muhammad) demands Sadaqa (i.e. Zakat [alms]) from us, and he has troubled us, and I have come to borrow something from you.' On that, Kab said, 'By Allâh, you will get tired of him!' Muhammad bin Maslama said, 'Now as we have followed him, we do not want to leave him unless and until we see how his end is going to be. Now we want you to lend us a camel load or two of food.' ...Muhammad bin Maslama and his companion promised Ka'b that Muhammad [bin Maslama] would return to him. He came to Kab at night along with Kab's foster brother, Abu Na'ila. Kab invited them to come into his fort, and then he went down to them. His wife asked him, 'Where are you going at this time?' Kab replied, 'None but Muhammad bin Maslama and my (foster) brother Abu Na'ila have come.' His wife said, 'I hear a voice as if blood is dripping from him.' Ka'b said, 'They are none but my brother Muhammad bin Maslama and my foster brother Abu Naila. A generous man should respond to a call at night even if invited to be killed.' ...So Muhammad bin Maslama went in together with two men, and said to them, 'When Ka'b comes, I will touch his hair and smell it, and when you see that I have got hold of his head, strip him. I will let you smell his head.' Kab bin Al-Ashraf came down to them wrapped in his clothes, and diffusing perfume. Muhammad bin Maslama said, 'I have never smelt a better scent than this.' Ka'b replied, 'I have got the best Arab women who know how to use the high class of perfume.' Muhammad bin Maslama requested of Ka'b, 'Will you allow me to smell your head?' Ka'b said, 'Yes.' Muhammad smelt it and made his companions smell it as well. Then he requested of Ka'b again, 'Will you let me (smell your head)?' Ka'b said, 'Yes.' When Muhammad got a strong hold of him, he said (to his companions), 'Get at him!' So they killed him and went to the Prophet and informed him. (Abu Rafi) was killed after Ka'b bin Al-Ashraf. [63]

The Prophet of Allâh not only encouraged assassination, he advocated deception and treachery, as well. Another victim of Muhammad's assassination operations was an old man called Abu Afak, who was said to be 120 years old. He composed poetry, some of which lamented that people had become followers of Muhammad. He wrote that Muhammad was a crazed man who arbitrarily told people what was prohibited and what was allowed, and who had caused them to surrender their intelligence and become hostile to one another. Ibn Sa'd reports this story as follows:

> Then occurred the "sariyyah" [raid] of Salim Ibn Umayr al-Amri against Abu Afak, the Jew, in [the month of] Shawwal in the beginning of the twentieth month from the hijrah [immigration from Mecca to Medina in AD 622], of the Apostle of Allâh. Abu Afak, was from Banu Amr Ibn Awf, and was an old man who had attained the age of one hundred and twenty years. He was a Jew, and used to instigate the people against the Apostle of Allâh, and composed (satirical) verses [about Muhammad].
> Salim Ibn Umayr who was one of the great weepers and who had participated in Badr, said, 'I take a vow that I shall either kill Abu Afak or die before him.' He waited for an opportunity until a hot night came, and Abu Afak slept in an open place. Salim Ibn Umayr knew it, so he placed the sword on his liver and pressed it till it reached his bed. The enemy of Allâh screamed and the people who were his followers, rushed to him, took him to his house and interred him.[64]

The only "crime" this aged man had committed was in composing satirical verses critical of Muhammad.

When Asma bint Marwan, a Jewish mother of five small children heard about this, she was so outraged that she composed a poem cursing the men of Medina for letting a stranger divide them and for allowing him

---

[63] Bukhari, 5.59.369
[64] The Kitab al Tabaqat al kabir, Vol. 2, p 31

to assassinate a venerable old man. Again Muhammad went to the pulpit and cried out:

> 'Who will rid me of Marwan's daughter?' 'Umayr bin 'Adiy al-Khatmi who was with him heard him, and that very night he went to her house and killed her. In the morning he came to the apostle and told him what he had done and he [Muhammad] said, 'You have helped Allâh and His apostle, O 'Umayr!' When he asked if he would have to bear any evil consequences, the apostle said, 'Two goats won't butt their heads about her.' [65]

After receiving praise from Muhammad for the assassination of Asma, the killer went to her children, bragged about committing the murder, and taunted those little kids and the clan of the victim.

> Now there was a great commotion among Banu Khatma that day about the affair of bint [daughter of] Marwan. She had five sons, and when 'Umayr went to them from the apostle he said, 'I have killed bint Marwan, O sons of Khatma. Withstand me if you can; don't keep me waiting.' That was the first day Islam became powerful among B. Khatma; before that those who were Muslims concealed the fact. The first of them to accept Islam was 'Umayr b. 'Adiy who was called the 'Reader' and 'Abdullah b. Aus and Khuzayma b. Thabit. The day after Bint Marwan was killed the men of B. Khatma became Muslims because they saw the power of Islam. [66]

After these assassinations, Muslims in Medina became more boastful, arrogant and imperious, as they had cast terror in the hearts of their opponents. He wanted to send the message that any opposition or criticism of him could mean death.[67] That is exactly the same modus

---

[65] From pp. 675-676 of *The Life of Muhammad* , which is A. Guilaume's translation of *Sirat Rasul Allâh.*

[66] Ibid.

[67] Ibn Sa'd narrates another version of this story: "Bint Marwan, of Banu Umayyah ibn Zayd, when five nights had remained from the month of Ramadan, in the beginning of the nineteenth month from the hijrah of the apostle of Allâh. 'Asma' was the wife of Yazid ibn Zayd ibn Hisn al-Khatmi. She used to revile Islam, offend the prophet and instigate the (people) against him. She composed verses. Umayr Ibn Adi came to her in the night and entered her house. Her children were sleeping around her. There was one whom she was suckling. He searched her with his hand because he was blind, and separated the child from her. He thrust his sword in her chest till it pierced up to her back. Then he offered the morning prayers with the prophet at al-Medina. The apostle of Allâh said to him: 'Have you slain the daughter of Marwan?' He said: 'Yes. Is there something more for me to do?' He [Muhammad] said: 'No. Two goats will not butt together about her.' This was the word that was first heard from the apostle of Allâh. The apostle of Allâh called him 'Umayr, 'basir' (the seeing)." -- Ibn Sa'd's in Kitab al-Tabaqat al-Kabir, translated by S. Moinul Haq, Vol. 2, p. 24.

operandi Muslims employ today, where the threat often only need be implied. They follow the model and example set by their prophet, who they regard as their greatest strategist. They want to create a boundary of fear so they may establish their supremacy through terror.

There is no doubt in the mind of the Muslim terrorists that this strategy works. To them, the Qur'anic injunction of "casting terror in the heart of the unbelievers"[68] seems a sure way to victory. It worked for Muhammad. He bragged, "I have been made victorious with terror."[69] It worked in Spain when the terrorists killed two hundred people by blowing up commuter trains on March 11, 2004, and in response, the Spaniards voted a socialist for government who immediately adopted a policy of appeasement vis-à-vis the Muslims.

Because of the successful precedents set by Muhammad and his ideological heirs, terrorists conclude that a terror strategy will work everywhere and every time. They will not stop unless the world falls or they are proven wrong by facing a much greater force.

The Islamic world is sick, and it would be shortsighted to deny that the cause of this sickness is Islam. Almost every crime, every act of inhumanity perpetrated by Muslims is inspired and justified through the words and the deeds of Muhammad. This is the painful truth that, sadly, so many would rather not see.

Genocide

There were three Jewish tribes living in and around Yathrib, the Banu Qainuqa', the Bani Nadir and the Banu Quraiza. As stated above, they were the original inhabitants of this town. At first Muhammad thought that because he had denounced polytheism and had embraced the Biblical prophets, the Jews would eagerly flock to become his followers. The earlier chapters of the Qur'an are full of stories about Moses and Biblical tales. Originally Muhammad had adopted Jerusalem as the *qibla* for his prayers, humbugging the Jews for their allegiance. Muslim scholar W. N. Arafat writes, "It is also generally accepted that at first the Prophet

---

[68] Qur'an 3:151 "Soon shall We cast terror into the hearts of the Unbelievers, for that they joined companions with Allâh, for which He had sent no authority: their abode will be the Fire: And evil is the home of the wrong-doers!
[69] Bukhari, 4.52.220.

Who Was Muhammad?

Muhammad hoped that the Jews of Yathrib, as followers of a divine religion, would show understanding of the new monotheistic religion, Islam."[70] However, to his dismay, the Jews, just like the Quraish, paid little heed to his calling. After his hopes were dashed and his patience vexed, he grew hostile towards them. Jews were in no hurry to abandon their ancestral faith in order to embrace Muhammad's new religion. Their rejection enraged him and he sought revenge. The assassination of Abu Afak and Asma only marked the beginning of his animosity towards the Jews. Already emboldened by his plundering of the passing caravans, Muhammad had his eyes on the wealth of the Jews in Yatrib and was looking for an excuse to make his move, to get rid of them and to lay his hands on their wealth. His anger against the Jews started showing in the Qur'anic verses that he composed, where he accused them of being ungrateful to Allâh, of killing their prophets and breaking their own laws. He even went as far as to say that because the Jews had broken the law of Sabbath, God transformed them into apes and swine.[71] To this day many Muslims are convinced that monkeys and pigs are descendants of the Jews.

Invasion of Banu Qainuqa'

The first group of the Jews to fall under the wrath of Muhammad was the Banu Qainuqa.' They lived in quarters within Yathrib named after them. They made their living as artisans, goldsmiths, blacksmiths, making household instruments and weaponry. They were not, however, skilled in the arts of soldiering and left that aspect to the Arabs, a mistake which eventually proved fatal to their existence. The Banu Qainuqa' was allied with the Arab tribe of Khazraj and supported them in their conflicts with their rival Arab tribe, the Aws.

The opportunity to invade these Jews arrived when a skirmish broke out between a handful of Jews and Muslims. A member of Banu Qainuqa' played a prank and pinned the skirt of a Muslim woman squatting in a Jeweler's shop in the B. Qainuqa' marketplace to the ground. Upon standing, her cloth tore and she was stripped naked. A Muslim man passing by, already filled with the hatred of the Jews by his prophet,

---

[70] From the Journal of the Royal Asiatic Society of Great Britain and Ireland, (1976), pp. 100-107 By W. N. Arafat

[71] Quran, 2:65, 5:60, 7:166

jumped on the Jew and killed him. The relatives of the victim then killed the Muslim in retaliation.

This was the opportunity Muhammad was looking for. Instead of trying to calm the situation, he unjustly blamed the Jews, all of them, and told them to submit to his religion or face war. The Jews answered his threats with defiance and shut themselves up in their quarters. He laid siege on them, shut off their water supply, and promised to kill them all.

In the Qur'an, verse 3:12, Muhammad reiterated his threat: "You will be defeated and gathered together to hell and worst indeed is that place to rest," while bragging how he defeated the Quraish, earlier at Badr.

After a fortnight, the tribe tried to negotiate their surrender, but Muhammad would not budge. He wanted to slay them all. Abdullah ibn Ubayy, the revered patriarch of the Khazraj, took hold of Muhammad's collar and told him that he would not allow his allies and friends to be slain with no cause. Muhammad was aware of the respect that the Khazraj had for their chief. He knew that they could rally around him and this would mean his own defeat. He pushed away ibn Ubayy while his face was blackened with rage and agreed not to massacre the Jews provided they leave the city. This story is reported by Ibn Ishaq.

> Babu Qainuqa' were the first of the Jews to break their agreement with the apostle and to go to war, between Badr and Ohod, and the apostle besieged them until they surrendered unconditionally. 'Abdullah b. Ubayy b. Salul went to him when God had put them in his power and said, 'O Muhammad, deal kindly with my clients' (now they were allies of Khazraj), but the apostle put him off. He repeated the words, and the apostle turned away from him, whereupon he thrust his hand into the collar of the apostle's robe; the apostle was so angry that his face became almost black. He said, 'Confound you, let me go.' He answered, 'No, by God, I will not let you go until you deal kindly with my clients. Four hundred men without mail and three hundred mailed protected me from all mine enemies; would you cut them down in one morning? By God, I am a man who fears that circumstances may change.' The apostle said, 'You can have them.' [72]

---

[72] Ibn Ishaq Sirat, p. 363

Who Was Muhammad?

The biographers also add that Muhammad had sullenly said "Let them go. God curse them, and God curse him also! So Muhammad pardoned their lives provided they were sent into exile."[73]

He demanded that the Banu Qainuqa' hand over all their materials, wealth and war equipage, from which he set aside one fifth for himself and distributed the rest among his men. The tribe was then banished. The Muslim historians gloat saying that these refugees entered Azru'a in Syria where they stayed for a while and soon perished.[74]

Invasion of Banu Nadir

Next it was the turn of the Banu Nadir. This was another Jewish tribe of Yathrib. After seeing what Muhammad did to the Banu Qainuqa', Ka'b Ibn Ashraf, the chief of the Banu Nadir, sought the protection of the Quraish and as explained above, he was assassinated.

There was a retaliatory war (Ohud) between the Meccans and Muslims in which the latter had lost. Muhammad needed to compensate that loss and restore the faith of his followers that Allâh had not forsaken them with more victories. Banu Nadir was an easy target.

The Pakistani Muslim historian and commentator of the Qur'an, and ideologue of today's Islamic revivalism, Maududi, narrates the story as follows: "For some time after these punitive measures [the banishment of the Qainuqa' and serial assassinations of Jewish poets] the Jews remained so terror stricken that they did not dare commit any further mischief. But later when in Shawwal, A. H. 3, the Quraish in order to avenge themselves for the defeat at Badr, marched against Medina with great preparations, and the Jews saw that only a thousand men had marched out with the Holy Prophet (upon whom be Allâh's peace) as against three thousand men of the Quraish, and even they were deserted by 300 hypocrites who returned to Madina, [The followers of Abdullah ibn Ubayy, Chief of the Khazraj] they committed the first and open breach of the treaty by refusing to join the Holy Prophet in the defence of the city although they were bound to it."[75]

---

[73] Ibid.
[74] AR-Raheeq Al-Makhtum by Saifur Rahman al-Mubarakpuri
http://islamweb.islam.gov.qa/english/sira/raheek/PAGE-26.HTM
[75] http://www.islamicity.com/mosque/quran/maududi/mau59.html

Understanding Muhammad

It is amazing that Muslims think that Jews were bound to help Muhammad wage a religious war against the Meccans, despite the fact that he had banished one of their tribes and had assassinated their chief and two poets. The war between Muhammad and the Quraish had nothing to do with the Jews, and by assassinating their people and banishing the Banu Qainuqa', Muhammad had already broken any agreement he may have had with them. And yet, to justify his treacherous acts, Muslim apologists blame the Jews for being at fault with their agreement.

Muhammad was now looking for an excuse to get rid of the Banu Nadir. They owned the best cultivated lands of Yathrib and gardens with date trees, and employed many Arabs. Accordingly, a few Muslims, who thanks to Muhammad had become full-fledged bandits, killed two men from Banu Kalb. As it happened, this tribe had signed a treaty with Muhammad that his men would not rob or kill their people in exchange for their support. The killers had mistaken the victims for members of another tribe. Now, as tradition dictated, Muhammad was obliged to pay blood money for this bloodshed. Despite all the wealth grabbed from the Banu Qainuqa', the Prophet went to the Banu Nadir and asked them that as part of their original covenant, they must also help pay this blood money. This was an outrageous demand, and Muhammad hoped that the Banu Nadir would balk and that this would give him an excuse to do with them as he did with the Banu Qainuqa'. The Banu Nadir, however, were too terrified to deny this unjust demand. They agreed to pitch in and withdrew to collect the money. Muhammad and his companions sat beneath a wall, waiting. This was not what Muhammad had in mind. He had come making the most unfair demand, hoping to get a negative reaction and act upon his devious design. Now, he needed to plot a new strategy.

Suddenly he had a new "inspiration." He stood up and without saying anything to his companions left the place and went home. Later, when his companions joined him and enquired about it, he told them the Angel Gabriel had informed him the Jews were plotting to drop a rock on his head from atop the wall beneath which they were sitting. With this excuse he started to prepare his attack on the Banu Nadir.

None of Muhammad's companions saw anyone climbing the wall or had any intimation about a plot against their lives. However, these men, having benefited financially from following him and believing everything he told them, had no reason or inclination to doubt what he was telling them then.

Who Was Muhammad?

Any rational person can see the absurdity of Muhammad's story. If the Banu Nadir really wanted and dared to kill him, they did not need to climb on a wall to throw a stone. This accusation was clearly false. Muhammad was accompanied by only a handful of his followers, Abu Bakr, Omar, Ali and perhaps one or two more. It was easy to kill them all, if that was what they had in mind.

The Prophet who believed that God is *khairul maakereen* (the best of the deceivers), (Q.3:54) was himself a cunning man. The story of Gabriel informing him of the Jews' plot against his life is as credible as the story of his visits to hell and heaven. Nonetheless his easy-to-fleece followers believed him and were so enraged by this fabrication that they rallied around him to shed the blood of the innocent people.

Maududi finishes this narrative by saying: "Now there was no question of showing them any further concession. The Holy Prophet at once sent to them the ultimatum that the treachery they had meditated against him had come to his knowledge; therefore, they were to leave Medina within ten days; if anyone of them was found staying behind in their quarters, he would be put to the sword." Maududi demonstrates a perfect example of Muslim "logic" when he simply tells the story of Muhammad's treachery as if it were the natural and normal way to behave.

Abdullah ibn Ubayy did his best to help the Banu Nadir, but by then his influence was too weak and Muhammad's men had become too blinded by their zealotry. They did not allow bin Ubayy to enter Muhammad's tent as they struck him and cut his face open.

After a few days the Banu Nadir negotiated to leave behind all their belongings for Muhammad and left town. Some of them went to Syria and some went to Khaibar to be slain only a few years later when Muhammad set his eyes on that prosperous and green Jewish fortress.

Even though Muhammad let these people go, his first thoughts were to massacre them. The following extract from Sira makes this clear.

Concerning B. al-Nadir the Sura of Exile came down in which it is recorded how God wreaked His vengeance on them and gave His apostle power over them and how He dealt with them. God said: 'He it is who turned out those who disbelieved of the scripture people from their homes to the first exile.... 'So consider this, you who have understanding. Had not God prescribed deportation against them,' which was vengeance from God, 'He would have punished them in this world,' (Q. 59: 3) i.e. with the sword, 'and in the next world there would be the punishment of hell' as well.[76]

In this siege, Muhammad ordered the cutting and burning of the trees belonging to the Banu Nadir. This kind of savagery was unprecedented even amongst the primitive Arabs. All he had to do to justify this crime was to make his imaginary friend approve of what he had done. That is easy when you have the God up your sleeve.

What you (O Muslims) cut down of the palm-trees (of the enemy), or you left them standing on their stems, it was by leave of Allâh. (Q. 59: 5)

It is easy to fathom why in the scorching desert environment, desert dwellers considered cutting trees and poisoning wells to be a capital crimes against humanity, as it went against all treaties and local customs.

A Muslim scholar, Al-Mubarkpuri, says: "The Messenger of Allâh (Peace be upon him) seized their weapons, land, houses, and wealth. Amongst the other booty he managed to capture, there were 50 armours, 50 helmets, and 340 swords. This booty was exclusively the Prophet's because no fighting was involved in capturing it. He divided the booty at his own discretion among the early Emigrants and two poor Helpers, Abu Dujana and Suhail bin Haneef. Anyway the Messenger of Allâh (Peace be upon him) spent a portion of this wealth on his family to sustain their living the year around. The rest was expended to provide the Muslim army with equipment for further wars in the way of Allâh. Almost all the verses of Sûra Al-Hashr (Chapter 59 - The Gathering) describe the banishment of the Jews and reveal the disgraceful manners of the hypocrites. The verses manifest the rules relevant to the booty. In this Chapter, Allâh, the All-Mighty, praises the Emigrants and Helpers. This Chapter also shows the legitimacy of cutting down and burning the enemy's land and trees for military purposes. Such acts cannot be regarded as phenomena of corruption so long that they are in the way of Allâh."[77]

Like Maududi, Mubarakpouri also reveals the disturbing lack of conscience and situational ethics that characterizes the *ummah*. Muslims do what their prophet did. They consider burning and looting the

---

[76] Ibn Ishaq irat, p. 438
[77] AR-RaheeQ Al-Makhtum (THE SEALED NECTAR)- Memoirs of the Noble Prophet Saifur Rahman al-Mubarakpuri - Jamia Salafia – India http://www.al-sunnah.com/nektar/11.htm

properties of non-Muslims legitimate acts of war, as they were both practiced and sanctioned by him. Based on the actions of Muhammad, it is fair to conclude that Islamic violence is unfortunately not a deviation from true Islam. Murdering, plundering, raping and assassinating are Islamic practices. Nothing is off limits when it comes to promoting the religion of Allâh.

Ironically, the Sura Al-Hashr ends by exhorting believers to be "pious," which makes it clear that piety for Muslims has an entirely different meaning. Muslim apologists say that the morality of today should not be applied to Muhammad who lived 1400 years ago. The irony is that they uphold that morality as standard and try to impose it on all mankind and for all times.

One Muslim wrote to me, *"This whole narrative has been problematic for many people because of their notions of what is morally correct and what is morally wrong. The origin of this sickness [sic] rests squarely on the Christian mentality of 'turn the other cheek,' and the 'redemptive suffering of Christ,' both of which have been sicknesses in the minds of Europe for centuries on end."* I don't believe that morality and ethics are sicknesses. They stem from human consciousness and their compass is the Golden Rule. We know the difference between right and wrong when we consider the way we would like to be treated.

Invasion of Banu Quraiza:

The last Jewish tribe of Yathrib to fall victim to Muhammad's vindictiveness was the Banu Quraiza. Soon after the Battle of the Trench (Khandaq) was over, the Meccans, fed up with Muhammad's constant raids on their caravans, came to the gates of Medina to punish him. Advised by a Persian believer, they dug trenches around the city making it difficult for Muhammad's enemies (The Confederates) to enter, causing their retreat. Muhammad set his eyes on the Banu Quraiza. He claimed that the Archangel Gabriel had visited him "asking that he should unsheathe his sword and head for the habitation of the seditious Banu Quraiza and fight them. Gabriel noted that he with a procession of angels would go ahead to shake their forts and cast fear in their hearts,"[78] writes Al-Mubarakpouri.

---

[78] Ibid. www.al-sunnah.com/nektar/12.htm

Al-Mubarakpouri continues: "the Messenger of Allâh immediately summoned the prayer caller and ordered him to announce fresh hostilities against Banu Quraiza,"[79]

It is important, in studying Islam, to note that the call to prayer was also the call to war. Muslim's riots and hooliganism always initiate from the mosques after they offer their prayers. They are most vicious during the holy month of Ramadan and on Fridays. In a sermon commemorating the Birthday of Muhammad, in 1981, the Ayatollah Khomeini said:

> *Mehrab* (Mosque) means the place of war, the place of fighting. Out of the mehrabs, wars should proceed. Just as all the wars of Islam proceeded out of the mehrabs. The prophet had sword to kill people. Our Holy Imams were quite militants. All of them were warriors. They used to wield swords. They used to kill people. We need a Caliph who would chop hands, cut throats, stone people. In the same way that the messenger of Allâh used to chop hands, cut throats, and stone people.[80]

Muhammad headed an army of three thousand infantry men and thirty horsemen of *Ansar* (Helpers) and *Muhajireen* (Emigrants). The Banu Quraiza was accused of conspiring against the Muslims with the Quraish. In reality, these Muslim historians deny this charge and say the Meccans withdrew without fighting because they did not receive support from the Banu Quraiza.

When Muhammad made his intentions known, Ali, his cousin and staunch supporter, swore he would not stop until he either stormed their garrisons or was killed. This siege lasted 25 days. Finally the Banu Quraiza surrendered unconditionally. Muhammad ordered the men to be handcuffed, while the women and children were confined in isolation. Thereupon the Aws tribe, who were allies of the Banu Quraiza, interceded, begging Muhammad to be lenient towards them. Muhammad suggested that Sa'd bin Mu'adh, a ruffian among them who had been fatally wounded by an arrow, give a verdict on the Jews. Sa'd was a former ally of the Banu Quraiza, but since his conversion to Islam he had a change of heart against them. He also blamed them for the fatal wound he received when a Meccan threw an arrow during the Battle of Trench. Muhammad knew

---

[79] Ibid.
[80] Ayatollah Khomeini: A speech delivered on the commemoration of the Birth of Muhammad, in 1981.

how Sa'd felt about the Banu Quraiza. He was, after all, his bodyguard and slept in the mosque.

Sa'd's verdict was that "all the able-bodied male persons belonging to the tribe should be killed, women and children taken prisoners and their wealth divided among the Muslim fighters."

Muhammad became pleased with this cruel verdict and said that "Sa'd (had) adjudged by the Command of Allâh."[81] He often credited Allâh for his own decisions. This time he chose Sa'd to verbalize his whims.

Al-Mubarakpouri adds that "In fact, the Jews deserved that severe punitive action for the ugly treachery they had harbored against Islam, and the large arsenal they had amassed, which consisted of one thousand and five hundred swords, two thousand spears, three hundred armors and five hundred shields, all of which went into the hands of the Muslims."

What Al-Mubarakpouri forgets to mention is that the Banu-Quraiza loaned their weapons as well as their shovels and picks to Muslims so they could dig the trench and defend themselves. Muslims will never be grateful to those who help them. They will take your help and will stab you in the back the moment they no longer need you. We shall see in the next chapter the psychology of this pathology.

Muslim historians have been quick to accuse the Banu Quraiza of the usual baseless charges to justify their massacre. They accused them of being mischievous, causing sedition, being treacherous and plotting against Islam. However no specifics exist as to the nature of those sins to warrant such a severe punishment and their total genocide. Trenches were dug in the bazaar of Medina and between 600 to 900 men were beheaded and their bodies dumped in them.

Huyai Ibn Akhtab, the chief of the Banu Nadir whose married daughter, Safiya, Muhammad took as his share of the booty when he invaded Khaibar, was among the captives. He was brought to the victor with his hands tied from behind. In an audacious defiance he rejected Muhammad and preferred death to submission to this brute man. He was ordered to kneel and was beheaded on the spot.

To determine who should be killed, the youngsters were examined. Those who had grown pubic hair were bundled with the men and beheaded. Atiyyah al-Quriaz, a Jew who had survived this massacre later recounted: "I was among the captives of Banu Quraiza. They (the Muslims) examined

---

[81] Bukhari, *Volume 4, Book 52, Number 280:*

us, and those who had begun to grow hair (pubes) were killed, and those who had not were not killed. I was among those who had not grown hair."[82]

Muhammad killed and banished several Jewish tribes, among them are B. Qainuqa', B. Nadir, B. Quraiza, B. Mustaliq, B. Jaun and the Jews of Khaibar. On his deathbed, he instructed his followers to cleanse the Arabian Peninsula of all non-believers,[83] an order that Omar, the second Caliph carried out later. He exterminated the Jews, the Christians and the pagans, forcing them to convert, leave or put them to death.

Now, enriched with the loot, Muhammad could be even generous to those who believed in him. Anas narrated: "People used to give some of their date palms to the Prophet (as a gift), till he conquered Banu Quraiza and Banu An-Nadir, whereupon he started returning their favors."[84]

There is a verse in the Qur'an that speaks about the massacre of the Banu Quraiza approving Muhammad's butcheries of their men and taking women and children as prisoners.

He caused those of the People of the Book who helped them (i.e. the Quraish) to come out of their forts. Some you killed, some you took prisoner. (Q. 33: 26)

Taqiyyah: the Holy Deception

Above we saw how Muhammad authorized his followers to lie, even to badmouth him, to win the trust of their victims in order to assassinate them. There are many other stories about Muslims feigning friendship with the non-believers, only to kill them once they are trusted.

At Hudaibiyyah, Muhammad signed a treaty with the Meccans, promising to return any of their youths and slaves that escaped and joined him. Ibn Ishaq narrates the story of Abu Basir, a Meccan, who went to Muhammad after this treaty was signed. The Meccans sent two men with a letter reminding him of his pact. Muhammad felt obliged and told Abu

---

[82] Sunan Abu-Dawud Book 38, Number 4390. Sunan Abu-Dawud is another collection of hadith regarded to be sahih.
[83] Bukhari Volume 4, Book 52, Number 288
[84] Bukhari Volume 4, Book 52, Number 176

Who Was Muhammad?

Basir: "Go, for Allâh will bring relief and a way of escape for you and the helpless ones with you." Abu Basir got the message. He returned with the emissaries. They had gone about six miles from Medina when the men stopped to rest. Abu Basir said, "Is your sword sharp, O brother?" When he said that it was, he said that he would like to look at it. "Look at it if you want to," he replied. Abu Basir unsheathed it and dealt him a blow that killed him. Then he came to Muhammad and said: "Your obligation is over and Allâh has removed it from you. You duly handed me over to the men, and I have protected myself in my religion lest I should be seduced therein." Muhammad did not punish this assassin but instructed him to go to *al-Is*, a region by the shore, on the road which Quraish were accustomed to take to Syria and rob the Caravans of the Quraish. Muhammad had signed a treaty not to waylay the caravans of the Quraish, so he found a way to go around it. Ibn Ishaq says: "The Muslims who were confined in Mecca heard what the apostle had said of Abu Basir, so they went out to join him in al-Is. About seventy men attached themselves to him, and they so harried Quraish, killing everyone they could get hold of, and cutting to pieces every caravan that passed them, that Quraish wrote to the apostle begging him by the ties of kinship to take these men in, for they had no use for them. So the apostle took them in, and they came to him in Medina."[85]

The history of Islam is replete with treachery and deceit. These men were Muslims and as such they were the responsibility of Muhammad. He, instead, washed his hands by sending them to another place to rob the Meccans. He condoned and even authorized their robberies. Despite that, Muslims claim that it were the Meccans who broke the treaty. The following is another example:

When the Meccans, along with other Arab tribes, had enough of Muhammad's raids and killings, they came together to punish him. However, unlike Muhammad, who never announced his plans and ambushed his victims with no warnings, the non-Muslims gave plenty of notice to their foe to prepare himself for the battle. This gave Muhammad enough time to dig a trench around Medina. The joint army of the Arabs, known as the confederates, had never seen such a thing. They camped outside the town wondering how to cross the trench. They asked the Banu Quraiza to assist them. Muhammad was wary of this alliance. So he devised a trick to drive a rift and distrust between the Banu Quraiza and the confederates. A man named Nu'aym had recently converted to Islam;

---

[85] This story is reported by Tabari, Vol 3, Page 1126

however he had not made his conversion known publicly. Muhammad summoned him and said, "You are only one man among us, so go and awake distrust among the enemy to draw them off us if you can, **for war is deceit.**" The following is the rest of the story as reported by Ibn Ishaq. It is long but important to read.

Nu'aym did as Muhammad told him. "He went to the B. Quraiza with whom he had been a boon companion, and reminded them of his affection for them and of the special tie between them. When they admitted that they did not suspect him, he said, 'Quraysh and Ghatafan are not like you. The land is your land, your property, your wives, and your children are in it, you cannot leave it and go somewhere else. Now Quraysh and Ghatafan have come to fight Muhammad and his companions, and you have aided them against him, but their land, their property, and their wives are not here, so they are not like you. If they see an opportunity they will make the most of it, but if things go badly they will go back to their own land and leave you to face the man in your country, and you will not be able to do so if you are left alone. So do not fight along with these people until you take hostages from their chiefs, who will remain in your hands as security that they will fight Muhammad with you, until you make an end of him.' The Jews said that this was excellent advice.

Then he went to the Quraish and said to Abu Sufyan b. Harb and his company, 'You know my affection for you, and that I have left Muhammad. I have heard something which I think it my duty to tell you of as a warning, but regard it as confidential.' When they said that they would, he continued, 'Mark my words, the Jews have regretted their action in opposing Muhammad and have sent to tell him so, saying, 'Would you like us to get hold of some chiefs of the two tribes, Quraysh and Ghatafan and hand them over to you, so that you can cut their heads off? Then we can join you in exterminating the rest of them. He has sent word back to accept their offer. So if the Jews send to you demanding hostages, don't send them a single man.'

Then he went to Ghatafan and said, 'You are my stock and my family, the dearest of men to me, and I do not think that you can suspect me.' They agreed that he was above suspicion, and so he told the same story as he had told Quraysh. [86]

The trick worked. When the Confederates asked the Banu Quraiza to join them for the attack, they brought an excuse and instead they

---

[86] Ibn Ishaq, Sirat, Battle of Trench

demanded that the Quraish leave with them a few of their men as hostage, which confirmed what Nu'aym had said. The Confederates became disheartened and left without a fight.

This deception saved Muslims from certain defeat. This has served as a lesson to Muslims, who ever since have incorporated treachery and deceit as strategies from which to deliver jihad. In one hadith we read:

> Hajaj Ibn `Aalat told: 'O Prophet of Allâh: I have in Mecca some excess wealth and some relatives, and I would like to have them back; am I excused if I bad-mouth you [to fool the non-Muslims]?' The Prophet excused him and said: 'Say whatever you have to say.'[87]

Practicing Muslims come to the West and pretend to be moderates. They say everything you want to hear but secretly plan for your destruction. They smile; are friendly and amiable; they even pretend to be patriotic. However, their only objective is to make Islam dominant. They talk the talk, but will not walk the walk.

Lying as a strategy to advance Islam is called taqiyyah, or "holy deception." Under taqiyyah, a Muslim is allowed to lie and say anything to pull the wool over the eyes of the non-Muslims and deceive them.

One of the major objectives, and a persistent tactic of those most skilled in taqiyyah, is to downplay the threat of Islam. The goal is to fool potential victims that jihad is not directed at them. In his book, *No god but God*, Reza Aslan engages in this Islamic art of deception, when he argues: "What is taking place now in the Muslim world is an internal conflict between Muslims, not an external battle between Islam and the West." He further writes: "The West is merely a bystander - an unwary yet complicit casualty of a rivalry that is raging in Islam over who will write the next chapter in its story."[88] Sorry, looks like we have built New York, Pentagon, London, Madrid and Beslan in the crossfire between Muslims. Mr. Aslan engages in the most brazen form of Islamic deception and yet, he was invited by CNN's Anderson Cooper to opine on the Pope's visit to Turkey, as if he were an unbiased observer.

---

[87] Sirah al-Halabiyyah, v3, p61,

[88]

http://www.nytimes.com/2005/05/04/books/04grim.html?_r=1&ex=1115784000&en=7961034fe8ef20c0&ei=5070&oref=slogin

A very funny taqiyyah often told by Muslim men to seduce western women is: "Women in Islam are treated like queens." I have yet to see a country whose queen is called deficient in intelligence, beaten, stoned and honor-killed.

When a practicing Muslim smiles at you, telling you how much he loves your country and how he wants to be your friend, remember the following hadith:

(Verily) we smile for some people, while our hearts curse (those same people).[89]

---

[89] Sahih al-Bukhari, v7, p102

Chapter Two

Muhammad's Personality Profile

There are literally tens of thousands of short stories about Muhammad. Many of them are forgeries, others are weak and dubious in nature, but some are believed to be *Sahih* (authentic, true) *hadith* (oral traditions). By reading these *Sahih hadith,* a fairly consistent picture of Muhammad emerges and it is possible to make an approximate evaluation of his character and psychological make-up.

The picture that emerges is that of a narcissist. In this chapter I will quote authoritative sources on narcissism and then will try to show how Muhammad fits that profile hand in glove.

Scholarship and research on the matter is limited precisely because Muslims have not and will not permit objective inquiry into the Qur'an or the life of Muhammad. However, what is written about him is not only consistent with the definition of narcissism, but also can be seen in many similar bizarre acts being committed today by Muslims themselves the world over. Thus, the personality disorder of one man has been bequeathed like an inheritance upon his followers, where one man's psychosis, spectacular in its depth of self-absorption, has been spreading to millions of his followers, rendering them, in the same way, self-absorbed, irrational, and dangerous.

It is through understanding the psychology of Muhammad, the ruthlessness and situational ethics so essential to his character, that we begin to understand why Muslims are so intolerant, so violent, so paranoid, and see themselves as victims, when they are the aggressors and the victimizers!

What is Narcissism?

The Diagnostic and Statistical Manual of Mental Disorders (DSM) describes narcissism as a personality disorder that "revolve around a pattern of grandiosity, need for admiration, and sense of entitlement. Often individuals feel overly important and will exaggerate achievements and will accept, and often demand, praise and admiration despite worthy achievements."[90]

The third and fourth editions of the Diagnostic and Statistical Manual (DSM) of 1980 and 1994 and the European ICD-10[91] describe NPD in similar language:

An all-pervasive pattern of grandiosity (in fantasy or behavior), need for admiration or adulation and lack of empathy, usually beginning by early adulthood and present in various contexts. Five (or more) of the following criteria must be met:

1. Feels grandiose and self-important (e.g., exaggerates achievements and talents to the point of lying, demands to be recognized as superior without commensurate achievements)

2. Is obsessed with fantasies of unlimited success, fame, fearsome power or omnipotence, unequalled brilliance (the cerebral narcissist), bodily beauty or sexual performance (the somatic narcissist), or ideal, everlasting, all-conquering love or passion

3. Is firmly convinced that he or she is unique and, being special, can only be understood by, should only be treated by, or associate with, other special, unique, or high-status people (or institutions)

---

[90] http://allpsych.com/disorders/personality/narcissism.html
[91] International Statistical Classification of Diseases and Related Health Problems, 10th edition, World Health Organization (1992)

Muhammad's Personality Profile

4. Requires excessive admiration, adulation, attention and affirmation, or failing that, wishes to be feared and notorious (narcissistic supply)
5. Feels entitled. Expects unreasonable or special and favorable priority treatment. Demands automatic and full compliance with his or her expectations
6. Is "interpersonally exploitative" i.e., uses others to achieve his or her own ends
7. Is devoid of empathy. Is unable or unwilling to identify with or acknowledge the feelings and needs of others
8. Is constantly envious of others or believes that they feel the same about him or her
9. Is arrogant, has haughty behaviors or attitudes coupled with rage when frustrated, contradicted, or confronted [92]

All these traits were confirmed in Muhammad. Apart from thinking he was the anointed messenger of God and the Seal of the Prophets (Q.33:40), Muhammad regarded himself as *Khayru-l-Khalq* (the Best of Creation), an "excellent example" (Q.33:21), and explicitly or implicitly hinted to be "exalted above other prophets in degrees" (Q.2:253). He claimed to be "the preferred one" (Q.17:55), to have been sent as a "Mercy to the worlds" (Q.21:107), to have been risen "to a praised estate" (Q.17:79) – a station which he said none but he would receive – and this is the Station of Intercession at the right hand of the Almighty next to his Glorious Throne. In other words, he would be the person who would advise God as to who should be sent to Hell and who should be admitted to Heaven. These are just some of Muhammad's megalomaniac claims about his own lofty station that are reported in the Qur'an.

The following two verses express vividly Muhammad's sense of self importance and grandiosity.

Truly, Allâh and His angels send praise and blessings [forever] upon the Prophet. O you who believe! Praise and bless the Prophet with utmost laud and blessing. (Q.33:56)

In order that you (O men) may believe in Allâh and His Messenger, that you may assist and honor Him, and celebrate His praise morning and evening. (Q.48:9)

---

[92] The language in the criteria above is based on or summarized from:
American Psychiatric Association. (1994). Diagnostic and statistical manual of mental disorders, fourth edition (DSM IV). Washington, DC: American Psychiatric Association.
Sam Vaknin. (1999). Malignant Self Love - Narcissism Revisited, first edition. Prague and Skopje: Narcissus Publication. ("Malignant Self Love - Narcissism Revisited" http://www.geocities.com/vaksam/faq1.html)

Understanding Muhammad

He was so impressed with himself, that he put the following words in the mouth of his sock puppet deity:

"And you (stand) on an exalted standard of character" (Q.68:4) and are "a lamp with spreading light." (Q.33:46)

Ibn Sa'd reports Muhammad saying:

Among all the people of the world God chose the Arabs. From among the Arabs he chose the Kinana. From Kinana he chose the Quraish (the tribe of Muhammad). From the Quraish he chose Bani Hashim (his clan). And from Bani Hashim he chose me.[93]

The following are some of the claims Muhammad made about himself in the hadith.

- The very first thing that Allâh Almighty ever created was my soul.
- First of all things, the Lord created my mind.
- I am from Allâh, and the believers are from me.[94]
- Just as Allâh created me noble, he also gave me noble character.
- Were it not for you, [O Muhammad] I would not have created the universe.[95]

Compare that to the words of Jesus, who when someone called him "good master," objected and said, "Why do you call me good? No one is good—except God alone."[96] Only a pathological narcissist can be so cut off from reality as to claim the universe was created because of him.

A narcissist may seem to be self-confident and accomplished. In reality he or she suffers from a great deficit of self-esteem and needs an outside supply of adulation, admiration, and greatness.

Dr. Sam Vaknin is the author of Malignant Self-Love.[97] He claims to be a narcissist himself and in part because of that, can be regarded as a uniquely qualified authority on the subject. Vaknin explains:

---

[93] Tabaqat V. 1 p. 2
[94] http://www.muhammadanreality.com/creationofmuhammadanreality.htm
[95] Tabaqat V. 1, p. 364
[96] Mark 10:18
[97] Sam Vaknin and Lidija Rangelovska, *Malignant Self Love – Narcissism Revisited* , Narcissus Publications, Czech Republic (January 4, 2007),

Muhammad's Personality Profile

Everyone is a narcissist, to varying degrees. Narcissism is a healthy phenomenon. It helps survival. The difference between healthy and pathological narcissism is, indeed, in measure. Pathological narcissism... is characterized by extreme lack of empathy. The narcissist regards and treats other people as objects to be exploited. He uses them to obtain narcissistic supply. He believes that he is entitled to special treatment because he harbors these grandiose fantasies about himself. The narcissist is NOT self-aware. His cognition and emotions are distorted... The narcissist lies to himself and to others, projecting 'untouchability,' emotional immunity and invincibility... For a narcissist everything is bigger than life. If he is polite, then he is aggressively so. His promises are outlandish, his criticism violent and ominous, his generosity inane. ... The narcissist is a master of disguise. He is a charmer, a talented actor, a magician and a director of both himself and his milieu. It is very difficult to expose him as such in the first encounter. [98]

The Cult of the Narcissist

The narcissist needs admirers. He draws an imaginary circle around himself, where he is the center. He gathers his fans and followers in that circle, rewards them and encourages their sycophantism. Those who fall outside the circle, are viewed as his enemies. Vaknin explains:

The narcissist is the guru at the centre of a cult. Like other gurus, he demands complete obedience from his flock: his spouse, his offspring, other family members, friends, and colleagues. He feels entitled to adulation and special treatment by his followers. He punishes the wayward and the straying lambs. He enforces discipline, adherence to his teachings, and common goals. The less accomplished he is in reality – the more stringent his mastery and the more pervasive the brainwashing...

The narcissist's control is based on ambiguity, unpredictability, fuzziness, and ambient abuse. [99] His ever-shifting whims exclusively define right versus wrong,

---

[98] healthyplace.com/Communities/Personality_Disorders/Site/Transcripts/narcissism.htm
[99] Ambient abuse is the stealth, subtle, underground currents of maltreatment that sometimes go unnoticed even by the victims themselves, until it is too late. Ambient abuse penetrates and permeates everything – but is difficult to pinpoint and identify. It is ambiguous, atmospheric, and diffuse. Hence it has insidious and pernicious effects. It is by far the most dangerous kind of abuse there is. It is the outcome of fear – fear of violence, fear of the unknown, fear of the unpredictable, the capricious, and the arbitrary. It is perpetrated by dropping subtle hints, by disorienting, by

desirable and unwanted, what is to be pursued and what to be avoided. He alone determines the rights and obligations of his disciples and alters them at will.

The narcissist is a micro-manager. He exerts control over the minutest details and behaviors. He punishes severely and abuses withholders of information and those who fail to conform to his wishes and goals.

The narcissist does not respect the boundaries and privacy of his reluctant adherents. He ignores their wishes and treats them as objects or instruments of gratification. He seeks to control both situations and people compulsively.

He strongly disapproves of others' personal autonomy and independence. Even innocuous activities, such as meeting a friend or visiting one's family require his permission. Gradually, he isolates his nearest and dearest until they are fully dependent on him emotionally, sexually, financially, and socially.

He acts in a patronising and condescending manner and criticizes often. He alternates between emphasizing the minutest faults (devalues) and exaggerating the talents, traits, and skills (idealizes) of the members of his cult. He is wildly unrealistic in his expectations, which legitimizes his subsequent abusive conduct...[100]

Muhammad invented a big lie that his adherents believe to be the absolute truth. The danger is that they, like the believers of Hitler's lies, are willing participants.

In the previous chapter, where we read the introduction to Muhammad, we saw how he separated his followers from their families and the level of control he exerted over their private lives. Sadly the situation has not changed much after 1,400 years. I have received many heartbreaking stories from parents who told me their daughter or son

---

constant – and unnecessary – lying, by persistent doubting and demeaning, and by inspiring an air of unmitigated gloom and doom ("gaslighting"). This definition is given by Dr. Sam Vaknin in his article "Ambient Abuse, first published in "Verbal and Emotional Abuse on Suite 101," also published in *Malignant Self Love – Narcissism Revisited*, Ibid. and at http://samvak.tripod.com/abuse10.html (date not given), (accessed June 22, 2007).

[100] "The Cult of the Narcissist" by Dr. Sam Vaknin, published in *Malignant Self Love – Narcissism Revisited*, and at http://samvak.tripod.com/journal79.html, c. Sam Vaknin, date not given (accessed June 22, 2007).

converted to Islam and is now surrounded by Muslims who have persuaded them not to visit their parents.

The Cause of the Narcissist

The Narcissist knows that direct self-promotion will be seen as repulsive and will be rejected. Instead, he presents himself as a modest, almost self-effacing person, one in the service of God, humanity or the cause, whatever the case may be. Behind this facade is however, a clear stratagem. The narcissist "bestows" on his followers a CAUSE, one so great, so august they cannot do without it. Through hype and manipulation, this cause becomes more important than the lives of the people who would be believers. So brainwashed do they become, they are willing to die, and, of course, kill for it. The narcissist encourages sacrifice – the more, the better. Then he presents himself as the axis of that cause. The cause revolves around him. It's he alone who can make it happen and lead the followers to that Promised Land. This colossal cause can't exist without the narcissist. He therefore becomes the most important person in the world.

That is how the narcissist cult leader manipulates his followers. The cause is just a means to their personal end. It could be anything. For Jim Jones, the man who led over 900 people to their mass suicide in Guyana, "social justice" was the cause, and he was the messiah of that cause.

Hitler chose National Socialism as his cause. He did not openly glorify himself, but rather the cause of "Aryanism" and the superiority of Germany. He, of course, was the indispensable inspirer and Fuehrer of that cause.

For Stalin the cause was communism. Anyone who disagreed with him was against the proletariat and had to be killed.

Muhammad did not ask his followers to worship him. In fact he claimed to be "only a messenger." Instead he demanded obedience by adroitly calling his followers to obey "Allâh and his messenger." In one Qur'anic verse, he puts the following words into the mouth of his Allâh:

> They ask you about the windfall (spoils of war). Say: The windfalls are for Allâh and the Messenger. So be careful of (your duty to) Allâh and set aright matters of your difference, and obey Allâh and His Messenger if you are believers. (Q.8:1)

Since Allâh had no use for things stolen from a bunch of Arabs, all those spoils automatically had to go to his proxy, his messenger. Since no one could see or hear Allâh, all the obedience was to Muhammad. It was he who had to be feared because he was the only intermediary of this most fearsome god of whom he was warning people. Allâh was necessary for Muhammad to dominate. Without the belief in Allâh, would his foolhardy followers have sacrificed their lives, killed people, including their own relatives, looted people's belongings and handed everything over to him? This imaginary Allâh was Muhammad's tool of domination. Allâh was Muhammad's alter ego, a convenient tool. Ironically Muhammad preached against associating partners with Allâh, when, in fact, he associated with Allâh in a manner which made them logically and practically inseparable.

Narcissists need a cause to harness their followers. The Germans did not start the war for Hitler's sake. They did it for the cause that he sold them.

Dr. Sam Vaknin writes: "Narcissists use anything they can lay their hands on in the pursuit of narcissistic supply. If God, creed, church, faith, and institutionalized religion can provide them with narcissistic supply, they will become devout. They will abandon religion if it can't."[101]

Islam was an instrument of domination. After Muhammad, others used his cult for the very same purpose. Muslims become like putty in the hands of those leaders who invoke Islam.

Mirza Malkam Khan (1831-1908), an Armenian who converted to Islam and together with Jamaleddin Afghani launched the idea of an "Islamic Renaissance" (*An-Nahda*), had a slogan of unrivaled cynicism: "Tell the Muslims something is in the Qur'an, and they will die for you."[102]

The Legacy of the Narcissist

On his deathbed, Muhammad urged his followers not to remain idle, and exhorted them to push on and continue their jihad to conquest. Genghis Khan gave a similar command to his sons on his deathbed. He told them he desired to conquer the world, but that since he could no longer do it, they should fulfill his dream. The Mongols, like Muslims,

---

[101] healthyplace.com/Communities/Personality_Disorders/Site/Transcripts/narcissism.htm
[102] Amir Taheri Neo-Islam http://www.benadorassociates.com/article/19333

were terrorizors. For the narcissist, all that matters is to win. They have no conscience. For them, lives of other humans are cheap.

In 1940, Hitler, at the age of 51, became aware of a tremor in his left hand. He usually hid it by keeping his left-hand in his pocket, by holding an object, or by cupping his right hand over his left. As the disease advanced, he stayed away from the public. He realized his death was approaching. He became more resolute, launching his attacks with a renewed sense of urgency, knowing he was in a race against time. The narcissist wants to leave a legacy.

It is a mistake to think of Islam as a religion. The religious/spiritual aspect of Islam was created later by Muslim philosophers and mystics who gave esoteric interpretations to Muhammad's asinine words. His followers molded the religion according to their penchant, and with the passage of time, those interpretations inherited the seal of antiquity and thus credibility.

If Islam is a religion, then so were Nazism, communism, Satanism, Heaven's Gate, People's Temple, Branch Davidian, etc. If we think of religion as a philosophy of life to educate, to bring forth human potential, to elevate the soul, to stimulate spirituality, to unite hearts and to enlighten mankind, then Islam surely fails that litmus test completely. Therefore, by this measure, Islam should not and cannot be regarded as a religion.

Narcissist wants to be God

For the narcissist, what ultimately matters is power. He wants to be respected, noted, and not neglected. Narcissists are lonely, insecure and shamed. Their greatest desire is to satisfy their need for the kind of respect and attention they receive as ambassadors of great causes. The cause is not really important. It is merely an excuse. Narcissists invent fictitious gods and spurious causes presenting themselves as the sole representatives of such causes. The more they glorify their false deities, the more power they can obtain for themselves.

Allâh was for Muhammad a convenient tool by which to manipulate people. Through him, he could wield unlimited authority over his followers. He became the master of their lives. There was only one God, almighty and fearsome as well as generous and forgiving, and he, Muhammad, was the one and only intermediary between Him and mankind. This made Muhammad God by proxy. Though obedience was supposed to flow from Allâh down to him, in actuality it was always Muhammad and his every whim that they were expected to satisfy. Dr. Vaknin explains this dynamic in his article "For the Love of God – Narcissists and Religion"[103]

> God is everything the narcissist ever wants to be: omnipotent, omniscient, omnipresent, admired, much discussed, and awe-inspiring. God is the narcissist's wet dream, his ultimate grandiose fantasy. But God comes handy in other ways as well.
>
> The narcissist alternately idealizes and devalues figures of authority.
>
> In the idealization phase, he strives to emulate them, he admires them, imitates them (often ludicrously), and defends them. They cannot go wrong, or be wrong. The narcissist regards them as bigger than life, infallible, perfect, whole, and brilliant. But as the narcissist's unrealistic and inflated expectations are inevitably frustrated, he begins to devalue his former idols.
>
> Now they are "human" (to the narcissist, a derogatory term). They are small, fragile, error-prone, pusillanimous, mean, dumb, and mediocre. The narcissist goes through the same cycle in his relationship with God, the quintessential authority figure.
>
> But often, even when disillusionment and iconoclastic despair have set in - the narcissist continues to pretend to love God and follow Him. The narcissist maintains this deception because his continued proximity to God confers on him authority. Priests, leaders of the congregation, preachers, evangelists, cultists, politicians, intellectuals - all derive authority from their allegedly privileged relationship with God.
>
> Religious authority allows the narcissist to indulge his sadistic urges and to exercise his misogyny freely and openly. …The narcissist whose source of authority is religious is looking for obedient and unquestioning slaves upon whom to exercise his capricious and wicked mastery. The narcissist transforms even the most

---

[103] "For Love of God – Narcissists and Religion", by Dr. Sam Vaknin, at http://samvak.tripod.com/journal45.html (no date given) (accessed June 22, 2007), first published in "Narcissistic Personality Disorder" Topic Page on Suite 101, also appearing in *Malignant Self Love – Narcissism Revisited*, Ibid.

innocuous and pure religious sentiments into a cultish ritual and a virulent hierarchy. He preys on the gullible. His flock becomes his hostages.

Religious authority also secures the narcissist's Narcissistic Supply. His coreligionists, members of his congregation, his parish, his constituency, his audience - are transformed into loyal and stable Sources of Narcissistic Supply. They obey his commands, heed his admonitions, follow his creed, admire his personality, applaud his personal traits, satisfy his needs (sometimes even his carnal desires), revere and idolize him.

Moreover, being a part of a "bigger thing" is very gratifying narcissistically. Being a particle of God, being immersed in His grandeur, experiencing His power and blessings first hand, communing with him - are all Sources of unending Narcissistic Supply. The narcissist becomes God by observing His commandments, following His instructions, loving Him, obeying Him, succumbing to Him, merging with Him, communicating with Him - or even by defying him (the bigger the narcissist's enemy - the more grandiosely important the narcissist feels).

Like everything else in the narcissist's life, he mutates God into a kind of inverted narcissist. God becomes his dominant Source of Supply. He forms a personal relationship with this overwhelming and overpowering entity - in order to overwhelm and overpower others. He becomes God vicariously, by the proxy of his relationship with Him. He idealizes God, then devalues Him, then abuses Him. This is the classic narcissistic pattern and even God himself cannot escape it.[104]

Narcissists do not directly promote themselves. They hide behind the veneer of modesty, while they elevate their god, ideology, cause or religion, which in reality is their own alter ego. They may present themselves as mere messengers, simple, humble, self-effacing heralds of this or that mighty and all-powerful deity, or all-encompassing cause, but they make it clear that they are the only ones who know the cause and are extremely intolerant and unforgiving of dissenters and recalcitrants.

Narcissists are ruthless, but not stupid. They are very much aware of the hurt they cause. They enjoy the sensation of power they get from hurting others. They enjoy being gods – deciding whom to reward and whom to punish – who should live and who should die. Pathological

---

[104] "For Love of God – Narcissists and Religion", by Dr. Sam Vaknin, Ibid.

narcissism explains everything that Muhammad was – his ruthlessness, his outlandish claims of grandiosity, his acts of generosity devised to impress those who submitted to him and to establish his superiority, and his self-assurance, as well as his manic and charismatic personality.

What Causes Narcissism?

The hallmark of a narcissist is the development of a superiority complex as a response to feeling inferior. This involves exaggerating one's own achievements and putting down anyone the narcissist perceives as a threat.

Faulty parenting is the major contributing cause of narcissistic personality disorder in a child. For example, permissive parents who give excessive praise, overindulge, spoil, fail to impose adequate discipline, and idealize the child are all factors. As a result, the narcissist generally feels unprepared for adulthood, having been raised with an unrealistic view of life. Conversely, a child who does not receive enough support and encouragement may also develop a narcissistic personality.

We know that Muhammad was given away in infancy to be raised by a stranger. Did his mother lack interest in him? Why did he not pray at her grave even when he was over sixty years old? Was he still resentful toward her?

Halima did not want to take baby Muhammad because he was a little orphan of a poor widow and the pay was not great. Did this affect the way she or her family treated him? Children can be cruel. Being an orphan in those days was a stigma, as it still is in many Islamic countries. Muhammad's childhood condition was not conducive to building a healthy self esteem.

Jon Mardi Horowitz, the author of *Stress Response Syndromes,* explains: "When the habitual narcissistic gratifications that come from being adored, given special treatment, and admiring the self are threatened, the results may be depression, hypochondria, anxiety, shame, self destructiveness, or rage directed toward any other person who can be blamed for the troubled situation. The child can learn to avoid these painful emotional states by acquiring a narcissistic mode of information processing."[105]

Muhammad, indeed, had a difficult childhood. In Sura 93 verses 3-8 (quoted at the beginning of chapter one of this book) he tenderly calls to mind his lonesome orphanhood and reassures himself that Allâh will be kind to him and will not forsake him. This shows how much the memory of his lonesome childhood pained him. The fact that Muhammad created an imaginary world to escape from reality, so vivid that it scared his foster parents, is another clue that his early childhood was anything but pleasant. Muhammad may not have remembered the details of what happened during his first years of life, but obviously he bore the psychological scars for the rest of his life. To him, the imaginary world he created was real. It was a safe refuge, a pleasant place to retreat and escape from reality. In this imaginary world, he could be loved, respected, admired, powerful, important, and even feared. He could be anything he wanted to be and compensate for the lack of attention he was getting from the world outside.

According to Vaknin, "the true cause of Narcissism is not fully understood but it does start in early childhood (before the age of five). It is believed it is caused by serious and repetitive failures on the part of the child's Primary Object (parents or other caregiver). Adult Narcissists often come from homes where one or both parents severely neglected (ignored) or abused the child... ALL children (healthy and otherwise) when they are not allowed to do something by their parents will sometimes enter into a narcissistic state where they see themselves and act as if they are all powerful. This is healthy and natural as it gives the child the confidence needed to rebound from the parental rejection with self-confidence."[106]

Neglected children internalize a feeling of inadequacy. They come to believe they are undeserving of love and attention. In reaction to that, they tend to defend their egos by puffing themselves up. They see their own weakness and they feel that if others come to see it, they will not be loved, admired and respected. So they lie and invent fantastic stories bragging about their self-importance. Their imaginary power often originates from an external source. It could be their daddy or a strong friend. This kind of narcissism in children is normal, but if they retain

---

[105] Jon Mardi Horowitz – *Stress Response Syndromes: PTSD, Grief, and Adjustment Disorder"* New Jersey:Jason Aronson Inc., Third Edition, 1997, ISBN-10: 0765700255, ISBN-13: 978-0765700254.

[106] www.faqfarm.com/Q/Can_you_be_responsible_for_your_spouse's_narcissism

these thoughts into adulthood, it develops into narcissistic personality disorder. In Muhammad, this external source of power was no one but Allâh, the most powerful, the most fearful, and the almighty. By associating himself with Allâh and presenting himself as his sole intermediary, he incarnated all of Allah's power.

After the death of his mother, when Muhammad was six years old, he was under the tutelage of his aging grandfather, who spoiled him. As various ahadith show, Abdul Muttalib was too permissive and he overindulged his orphaned grandchild. The child Muhammad would sit on a mat next to the patriarch while his uncles sat reverentially around them.

His claims that Abdul Muttalib told his uncle Abu Talib, "Let him alone for he has a great destiny, and will be the inheritor of a kingdom"[107] or telling his nurse, "Beware lest you let him fall into the hands of the Jews and Christians, for they are looking out for him, and would injure him!"[108] are obviously figments of his imagination. They were lies that he concocted and possibly believed. These are typical fantasies of narcissists, who think of themselves as so important they believe everyone is after them to harm them out of jealousy. Nonetheless, it is clear that Abdul Mutalib made Muhammad feel special. He pampered and loved his orphaned grandchild. The old man spoiled him out of pity. However, Muhammad interpreted that extra attention as the confirmation of his reveries of grandeur. The image he cast about himself in his fantasy world during his childhood was thus bolstered by his grandfather's overindulgence of him. He was reconfirmed as unique, special, and exceptional.

After the death of Abdul Muttalib, his kind-hearted uncle, Abu Talib, also treated him differently from other children. His status as an orphan, with no parents or siblings, evoked compassion. Both his grandfather and uncle overindulged and spoiled him. They failed to impose adequate discipline on him. All these extremes contributed to him developing a narcissistic personality. Psychologists J. D. Levine and Rona H. Weiss write:

> Just as we know, from the point of view of the physiologist, that a child needs to be given certain foods, that he needs to be protected against extreme temperatures, and that the atmosphere he breathes has to contain sufficient oxygen, if his body is to

---

[107] Tabaqat Vol 1 p. 107
[108] Ibid.

become strong and resilient, so do we also know, from the point of view of the depth-psychologist, that he requires an empathic environment, specifically, an environment that responds (a) to his need to have his presence confirmed by the glow of parental pleasure and (b) to his need to merge into the reassuring calmness of the powerful adult, if he is to acquire a firm and resilient self. [109]

Muhammad experienced neglect and abandonment during the first six years of his life, and excessive permissiveness after that. His circumstances were therefore ripe and conducive for him to become a narcissist.

Muhammad never spoke of his mother. If he had, it would have been recorded in a hadith. He visited her tomb after he conquered Mecca, but he refused to pray for her. What was the point of that visit? Perhaps this was his vindication, a way to prove to her that despite her neglect, he had made it. On the other hand, he remembered his grandfather, who had showered him with love and provided for him plenty of narcissistic gratifications, fondly.

Psychologists tell us that the first five years of a child's life are the years that either make him or break him. Muhammad's emotional needs during the first five years of his life were not met. He carried the painful memories of those lonesome years of abandonment and neglect into his adulthood and old age. He grew up insecure and had a fluctuating sense of self-worth, a weakness he tried to hide with overwhelming haughtiness by growing a sense of entitlement, grandiosity, lack of empathy, and an illusion of superiority.

Muhammad chose Allah as his mate. His imaginary ally was mighty and powerful. This made him infinitely strong. He was the only one with direct access to Allâh and was his only viceroy on Earth. To make sure that no one would ever usurp his position, he also claimed to be the last messenger. His power thus was absolute and eternal.

Khadijah's Influence on Muhammad

Khadijah's role in Islam has not yet been fully appreciated. Her influence on Muhammad cannot be overemphasized. Khadijah should be

---

[109] J. D. Levine and Rona H. Weiss. The Dynamics and Treatment of Alcoholism. Jason Aronson, 1994

regarded as Muhammad's partner in giving birth to Islam. Without her, perhaps, Islam would not exist.

We know that Khadijah adored her young husband. There is no report that Muhammad ever worked after marrying Khadijah. After the marriage, Khadijah's business seems to have gone down the tubes. When she died, the family became penniless.

Muhammad did not take care of the children, either. Dejected by the world, he spent most of his time alone in caves retreating to his pleasant imaginary world and contemplation. At times he would take food for several days, returning only when it was finished. Then he would head down to the city, procure more provisions and go back.

Khadijah remained at home to take care of her ten children alone. But she did not seem to complain. She was taking care of not only her children and the house but also of her young husband, who acted just like another irresponsible child. But Khadijah was happy to sacrifice. Why?

That is an important question. The answer is that Khadijah had her own personality disorder. She was what we today would call a codependent. This knowledge will help us understand why she stood by her husband and encouraged him to launch his prophetic career.

The National Mental Health Association (NMHA) defines codependency as "A learned behavior that can be passed down from one generation to another. It is an emotional and behavioral condition that affects an individual's ability to have a healthy, mutually satisfying relationship. It is also known as 'relationship addiction' because people with codependency often form or maintain relationships that are one-sided, emotionally destructive and/or abusive. The disorder was first identified about ten years ago as the result of years of studying interpersonal relationships in families of alcoholics. Codependent behavior is learned by watching and imitating other family members who display this type of behavior."[110]

Khadijah was a comely woman. She was the favorite daughter of her father Khuwaylid. In fact Khuwaylid relied on her, more than he did on his sons. She was a "daddy's girl." She had rejected the hands of the powerful men of Mecca. But when she saw the youthful but dispossessed and needy Muhammad, she fell in love with him on the spot and sent a maid to him to propose marriage.

---

[110] http://www.nmha.org/infoctr/factsheets/43.cfm

Muhammad's Personality Profile

On the surface it seems that Muhammad had such a magnetic personality that he mesmerized this powerful woman. This, however, is a superficial understanding of a complex dynamic.

Tabari writes: "Khadijah sent a message to Muhammad inviting him to take her. She called her father to her house, plied him with wine until he was drunk, anointed him with perfume, clothed him in a striped robe and slaughtered a cow. Then she sent for Muhammad and his uncles. When they came in, her father married him to her. When he recovered from his intoxication, he said, 'What is this meat, this perfume, and this garment?' She replied, 'You have married me to Muhammad bin Abdullah.' 'I have not done so,' he said. 'Would I do this when the greatest men of Mecca have asked for you and I have not agreed, why would I give you to a bum?'"[111]

The party of Muhammad replied indignantly that the alliance had been arranged by his own daughter. The old man drew his sword in anger and the relatives of Muhammad drew theirs. Blood was about to be shed when Khadijah made her love for Muhammad known and confessed to having masterminded the whole proceeding. Khuwaylid was then pacified, as he resigned to the *fait accompli* and reconciliation ensued.

Khadijah was a dainty, accomplished woman. She had rejected marriage proposal of many Quraish dignitaries. How can one explain a seemingly levelheaded and successful woman suddenly falling in love with an indigent youth 15 years her junior? This erratic behavior belies a certain personality disorder in Khadijah.

Evidence indicates that Khadijah's father was an alcoholic. Khadijah must have known her father's weakness for alcohol to devise such an audacious plan. Alcoholic people tend to lose control and get drunk. Non-alcoholic people often drink moderately and know when to stop. When Khuwaylid became drunk, the party had not yet started and the guests had not yet arrived. This tells us that he was not a social drinker but a real alcoholic. Now, why this should matter at all? Because it is another clue in support of the speculation that Khadijah was a codependent. Children of alcoholics often develop co-dependency

Khadijah's father was overly protective of his daughter and had high expectations for her. From his reaction to the marriage of his 40-year-old daughter to an ordinary man and his words saying "the greatest men of Mecca have asked for you and I have not agreed," it is clear that Khadijah

---

[111] Persian Tabari v. 3 p.832

was the apple of his eye. Khuwaylid had other children too, including a few sons, but it is clear that this daughter was his pride and joy. She was his only accomplished offspring.

Children who are adored and placed on a pedestal by their domineering and needy parents grow in their shadow. They often develop codependency personality disorder. They become obsessed with their father (or mother) and see their function as making their parents look good in the eyes of the outsiders. They are expected to be the *"wunderkind."*

Under the constant demand for better performance, the child becomes unable to develop her own independent personality. She seeks her fulfillment in satisfying the needs of her perfectionist and narcissistic parent. She does not feel loved for WHO she is, but rather for HOW she performs. The alcoholic parent unloads his own emotional baggage on his children, especially on the one with more potential. He expects her to excel in everything to make up for his own shortcomings and failures.

Codependents cannot find fulfillment and happiness in normal and emotionally healthy relationships that can happen only among equals. Only in the capacity of **caregivers** and **pleasers** can codependents find their happiness. The "perfect" match for the codependent is a needy narcissist.

Khadijah rejected her successful and mature suitors, falling in love with a poor young man who was both emotionally and financially needy. Codependents confuse love and pity. They have the tendency to "love" people they should pity and rescue.

Vaknin uses the term "self effacing" or "inverted narcissism" instead of codependency. Here is what he says about the co-dependent-narcissist relationship: "The inverted narcissist can only truly FEEL anything when he is in relationship with another narcissist. The inverted narcissist is conditioned and programmed from the very beginning to be the perfect companion to the narcissist - to feed their Ego, to be purely their extension, to seek only praise and adulation if it brings greater praise and adulation to the narcissist."[112]

The above explains why a successful and beautiful woman like Khadijah would become interested in a needy and narcissistic man like Muhammad. Although inverted narcissists tend to be successful in their businesses, their relationships are often unhealthy. Vaknin further explains: "In a primary relationship, the inverted narcissist attempts to re-create the parent-child relationship. The invert thrives on mirroring to the

---

[112] http://samvak.tripod.com/faq66.html

narcissist his own grandiosity and in so doing the invert obtains his OWN Narcissistic Supply (the dependence of the narcissist upon the invert for their Secondary Narcissistic Supply). The invert must have this form of relationship with a narcissist in order to feel complete and whole. The invert will go as far as he needs to ensure that the narcissist is happy, cared for, properly adored, as he feels is the narcissist's right. The invert glorifies his narcissist, places him on a pedestal, endures any and all narcissistic devaluation with calm equanimity, impervious to the overt slights of the narcissist.[113]

With no pun intended, the marriage of Muhammad and Khadijah was made in heaven. Muhammad was a narcissist who craved constant praise, attention and adulation. He was poor, an orphan and emotionally needy. He was an adult, but his inner child was still yearning for attention. He was in need of someone to take care of him and provide for him, someone to exploit and abuse, as only an infant can exploit and abuse his mother.

The emotional maturity of the narcissist is frozen in childhood. His infantile needs have never been satisfied. He is constantly trying to satisfy those childish needs. All babies are narcissists and that is a necessary part of their growth. But if their narcissistic needs are not satisfied in childhood, their emotional maturity will freeze at that stage. They seek the attention they missed in infancy in their relationships with their mates and others, including their children.

Muhammad's craving for love was expressed by him on many occasions. Ibn Sa'd quotes him saying, the families of Quraish are all related to me and even if they do not love me for the message I am bringing them, they should love me because of my kinship to them.[114] In the Qur'an Muhammad says: "No reward do I ask of you for this except the love of those near of kin."[115] These words are indeed desperate cries of one craving love and attention.

Khadijah, on the other hand, was an inverted narcissist who needed someone to fulfill her own fantasies as a caregiver. Not only does the codependent not mind being taken advantage of, she actually enjoys it.

Vaknin writes: "The inverted narcissist feeds on the primary narcissist and this is his narcissistic supply. So these two typologies can, in essence become a self-supporting, symbiotic system. In reality though,

---

[113] http://www.toddlertime.com/sam/66.htm
[114] "I do not ask of you any reward for it but love for my near relatives" Tabaqat vol.1 page.3
[115] Qur'an Sura 42: verse 23

both the narcissist and the inverted narcissist need to be well aware of the dynamics of this relationship in order to make this work as a successful long-term arrangement."[116]

Psychologist Dr. Florence W. Kaslow, explaining this symbiosis says that both parties have personality disorders (PDs) – but on opposite ends of the spectrum. "They seem to have a fatal attraction for each other in that their personality patterns are complementary and reciprocal – which is one reason why, if they get divorced, they are likely to be attracted over and over to someone similar to their former partner."[117]

The symbiotic relationship between the narcissist Muhammad and the inverted narcissist Khadijah worked to perfection. Muhammad no longer needed to be preoccupied with work after marrying the wealthy Khadijah. He spent his days wandering in the caves and wilderness of his fertile fantasies, the delightful and affable realm where he was loved, admired, respected and feared. Khadijah became so engulfed in this self-absorbed narcissist and in attending to his needs that she neglected her commerce. Her thriving business dwindled and her wealth evaporated. She must have been around fifty years old when her youngest child was born. She stayed home while her husband was away most of the time, a recluse in his mental and physical caves.

According to Vaknin, "the inverted narcissist is extinguishingly selfless, sacrificial, even unctuous in his interpersonal relationships and will avoid the assistance of others at all costs. He can only interact with others when he can be seen to be giving, supportive, and expending an unusual effort to assist."[118]

He also defines codependents as "people who depend on other people for their emotional gratification and the performance of Ego or daily functions." He says "they are needy, demanding, submissive. They fear abandonment, cling and display immature behaviours in their effort to maintain the 'relationship' with their companion or mate upon whom they depend."[119]

---

[116] http://samvak.tripod.com/faq66.html

[117] Quoted from "Mixing oil and water" by Bridget Murray, APA Online Monitor On Psychology, Vol. 35, No. 3, March 2004, (online version), Print version: page 52, online version found at http://www.apa.org/monitor/mar04/mixing.html (accessed June 22, 2007www.apa.org/monitor/mar04/mixing.html

[118] www.toddlertime.com/sam/66.htm

[119] "The Inverted Narcissist" Sam Vaknin, HealthyPlace.com Personality Disorders Community, at www.healthyplace.com/communities/Personality_Disorders/narcissism/faq66.html (date not given) (accessed June 22, 2007)

Muhammad's Personality Profile

Melody Beattie, the author of *Codependent No More* explains that codependents unconsciously pick troubled partners in order to have purpose, be needed and feel fulfilled.

Any sensible person would have interpreted Muhammad's bizarre experience as psychosis or "demon possession," as they used to call it in those days. Even Muhammad himself thought he had become a *kahin* (sorcerer) or demon-possessed. As we read in the Qur'an, the reasonable people of Mecca thought Muhammad had become a *majnoon,* which literally means possessed by jinns and is understood as insane. But such a thought was too much to bear for Khadijah, who sought her fulfillment and happiness in fulfilling the needs of her husband. She had to cling to her narcissist at any cost. As a codependent, Khadijah felt the urge to step in, be helpful, give advice and salvage her own source of narcissistic supply.

The narcissist often demands sacrifices from people around him and expects them to become his codependents. They also live above the moral code. They are too big to abide by any morality or rule.

John de Ruiter is a self-proclaimed messiah from Alberta, Canada. His followers worship him like God. "One day we were sitting around the kitchen smoking cigarettes," said Joyce, de Ruiter's estranged wife of 18 years, in an interview. "He was talking about my 'death.' He acknowledged that I had gone through a lot of dying, which was a good thing. I had let go of ninety-five percent of the life that I had to let go of. But he said I wasn't letting myself go completely. He suggested that my ultimate death would be if he took on two more wives." Joyce said she thought he was joking. He wasn't. He brought up the matter a second time, and asked Joyce if she thought his three wives could live in the same house.[120]

Fortunately Joyce was not codependent enough to agree to this much humiliation, and left her degenerate narcissist husband. A true codependent would do anything to appease his or her narcissist. The relationship of a codependent and her narcissist is that of sadomasochism.

Unfortunately for mankind, Khadijah was a real codependent, who was willing to sacrifice everything for her adored narcissist. It was she who encouraged Muhammad to pursue his prophetic ambitions and spurred him in that direction. When Muhammad no longer had epileptic seizures

---

[120] "The Gospel According to John," by Brian Hutchison, Saturday Night Magazine, May 5, 2001, at http://www.rickross.com/reference/ruiter/ruiter3.html (accessed June 22, 2007

or saw any angels, Khadijah was disappointed. Ibn Ishaq writes: "After this, Gabriel did not come to him for a while and Khadijah said, 'I think that your Lord must hate you.'"[121] This demonstrates how eager she was for her narcissist to become a prophet.

Why did Muhammad not take other wives when Khadijah was still alive? Because he was living off her money and in her house. Furthermore, the majority of the people of Mecca derided him. He was called a lunatic. No one would have married him even if he had had money of his own and Khadijah had not been an issue. In Mecca, his followers were a handful of teenagers and slaves with only a few women among them – and none was eligible for him to marry. Had Khadijah survived to see Muhammad's rise to power, most likely she would have had to put up with her husband's vagaries and the humiliation of sharing him with younger and prettier women.

After the death of Khadijah, Muhammad never found another codependent to take care of his emotional needs like she had. Instead, he sought fulfillment by becoming a sexual butterfly. Only a month after his wife's death, Muhammad convinced his loyal friend and follower, Abu Bakr, to betroth to him his six-year-old daughter, Aisha. Abu Bakr was shocked. He tried to dissuade him, saying, "But we are brothers." Muhammad reassured him they were only brothers in faith and that his marriage to that little child was not haram.[122]

He further told him that she had been shown to him twice in dreams in which he saw an angel carrying the little Aisha in a silken piece of cloth. "I said (to myself), 'If this is from Allâh, then it must happen.'"[123] Now Abu Bakr was left with the options: Leaving Muhammad, for whom he had made so many sacrifices, denouncing him, calling him a liar and going back to his people, acknowledging he had been a fool; or doing whatever Muhammad asked of him. This is often the difficult choice cultists must make. Abu Bakr even built a mosque in the backyard of his house for Muslims to pray. He would often cry when reciting Muhammad's allegedly revealed verses. Denoucing him at this stage, was not easy. Cultitsts are trapped. They have often sacrificed so much for the cult that going back is more painful than submitting. Abu Bakr pleaded

---

[121] Sira Ibn Ishaq, p. 108
[122] Sahih Bukhari 7.62.18 Narrated 'Ursa: The Prophet asked Abu Bakr for 'Aisha's hand in marriage. Abu Bakr said "But I am your brother." The Prophet said, "You are my brother in Allâh's religion and His Book, but she (Aisha) is lawful for me to marry."
[123] Sahih Bukhari, Volume 9, Book 87, Number 140

with Muhammad to wait three more years before consummating the marriage. Muhammad agreed, but meanwhile, he married Sauda just a few days later.

Muhammad created a harem with more than a score of women. He tried to compensate the loss of his sugar mommy with an abundance of younger women. He kept adding to the collection of his wives and concubines but none could meet his childish needs the way Khadijah had. He needed a mother to take care of his inner child, something his teenage wives could hardly do for a man who could be their grandfather.

Muhammad's Belief in His Own Cause

From his early youth, Muhammad attended the annual fair in Okaz, where people from everywhere met for commerce and fun. There, Christian preachers read stories of Biblical prophets to their captivated audiences. Muhammad was fascinated by those stories. Being loved and respected were the only thoughts that had occupied his young mind. "How great it would be to be a prophet, to be loved and feared by everyone," he must have thought while listening to those stories. Now, his wife was reassuring him he had become a prophet and that his fantasy had become a reality. It seemed that God had finally looked upon him mercifully, had chosen him from amongst all the people and had raised him to herald his cause and invite people to submit.

Muhammad's thoughts were grand. In fact it was these grandiose ideas and his unwavering faith in unlimited success that kindled his followers to rise and to champion his cause, to assassinate, loot and kill, even their own fathers, for his cause. Thanks to these grandiose ideas of superiority, he always felt entitled to having special privileges.

Muhammad was extremely manipulative and exploitative. He built his empire without ever having to fight a single battle personally. By promising otherworldly rewards and a paradise of infinite orgies to those who believed in him, he managed to make them wage wars on his behalf, spend their wealth for his cause, sacrifice their lives, loot to make him rich and catapult him to the acme of power.

Narcissists are masters of deception. They themselves are, inevitably, the first victims of their own deception. They unconsciously deny their intolerably poor self-images by inflating their egos with grandiosity. They turn themselves into glittering images of immense grandeur surrounded by walls of denial. The goal of this self-deception is to be impervious to external criticism and to their roiling sea of doubts. Narcissists are pathological liars, while they genuinely believe in their own lies, and are extremely offended if contradicted.

Vaknin says, "The narcissist is ever in the pursuit of excitement and drama intended to alleviate his all-pervasive boredom and melancholy. Needless to say, both the pursuit itself and its goals must conform to the grandiose vision that the narcissist has of his (False) Self. They must be commensurate with his vision of his uniqueness and entitlement."[124]

This explains Muhammad's constant warfare. The drama, the rush of adrenaline and excitement were his narcissistic supplies. However, the narcissist is the first to believe in his own malarkey.

Dr. Vaknin explains: "Granted, the narcissist's hold on reality is tenuous (narcissists sometimes fail the reality test). Admittedly, narcissists often seem to believe in their own confabulations. They are unaware of the pathological nature and origin of their self-delusions and are, thus, technically delusional (though they rarely suffer from hallucinations, disorganized speech, or disorganized or catatonic behaviour). In the strictest sense of the word, narcissists appear to be psychotic."[125]

Vaknin says however, that narcissists, while masters of self-deception or even malignant con-artistry, "are usually fully aware of the difference between true and false, real and make-believe, the invented and the extant, right and wrong. The narcissist consciously chooses to adopt one version of the events, an aggrandizing narrative, a fairy-tale existence, a 'what-if' counterfactual life. He is emotionally invested in his personal myth. The narcissist feels better as fiction than as fact – but he never loses sight of the fact that it is all just fiction. The narcissist is in full control of his faculties, cognizant of his choices, and goal-oriented. His behavior is intentional and directional. He is a manipulator, and his delusions are in the service of his stratagems. Hence his chameleon-like ability to change guises, his conduct, and his convictions on a dime...The narcissist attempts to condition his nearest and dearest to positively reinforce his delusional

---

[124] Dr. Sam Vaknin Narcissism FAQ #57
[125] "Pathological Narcissism, Psychosis, and Delusions" by Sam Vaknin, at Sam Vaknin Sites, http://samvak.tripod.com/journal91.html (accessed June 22, 2007)

Muhammad's Personality Profile

False Self."[126]   In the case of Muhammad, that role was played by Khadijah.

This is somewhat difficult to understand. On the one hand, Vaknin says the narcissist never loses sight of the fact that it is all his fiction, and on the other hand he says that the narcissist's hold on reality is tenuous and that often he believes in his confabulations. Although this presents a logical dilemma for normal people, it is no problem for the narcissist who lies and then goes on to convince himself of those lies as if they were absolute truth, and will also change his story whenever it suits him.

We tend to believe that either a person is insane or he is a liar and that the two are mutually exclusive. This is not true. Often criminals plead insanity to escape punishment. Society, including mental health professionals, believes this nonsense. This stupidity has reached the absurd. James Pacenza, a 58-year-old man who was fired for spending his time visiting adult internet chatrooms at work, sued his employer (IBM) for wrongful dismissal, claiming that he was addicted to online chat rooms and IBM should have offered him sympathy and treatment instead of firing him. He was awarded $5,000,000 compensation.[127]

The truth is that narcissists are fully aware of their actions. New York serial killer David Berkowitz, who called himself "Son of Sam," escaped capital punishment because his crimes were so senseless that everyone thought he was not responsible for his actions by reason of insanity. Actually he knew that what he was doing was wrong. That is why he tried so hard to elude the police and even taunted them. However, he was a narcissist and craved attention. So he left clues to be found. The exhilaration of reclaiming all the celebrity that surrounded the case was more impelling to him than his freedom. He simply could not pass on basking in the glory of fame. What Berkowitz did was consistent with narcissistic personality disorder. When he was caught and locked in prison, he decided to become a born-again Christian. Why did he not do this before? Did he undergo a mental surgery in prison? No! He simply decided to change tactics to gain the attention that he so intensely craved. In prison, the only way to do that was to feign becoming a holy man. The narcissist is a chameleon. He carefully monitors others to see what elicits more attention and then acts accordingly.

---

[126] ibid.
[127] http://news.bbc.co.uk/2/hi/americas/6682827.stm

People with a mental disorder are aware of their actions. They know the difference between right and wrong. What psychopath narcissists want is attention. How they get it is not important. If they can get it by becoming serial killers, they become serial killers; and if they can get it by becoming religious, that is what they become.

To a great extent, we can compare a serial killer to a smoker. Both of them know that what they do is wrong. Yet their urges are stronger than their willpower and they give in to their cravings. A smoker kills himself slowly, one cigarette at a time, and the serial killer kills others. Why does a smoker not stop when he knows that tobacco kills him? It is because he is addicted to nicotine. Likewise, narcissist psychopaths can't stop because they are addicted to the adrenaline rush and the excitement of playing God. They know what they do is wrong because they hide and play games with the police. They leave clues about themselves until they are caught because the urge to receive attention is so strong they willingly risk their freedom and lives for it.

Another proof that psychopaths know what they do is wrong is that they do not like to be on the receiving end of it. Muhammad raided villages; and after massacring unarmed civilians, he looted their belongings. Yet, he tortured to death those who killed one of his shepherds and stole his stolen camels. He raped women captured in his raids, even if they were married; yet he was intolerant of anyone looking at his own wives and he ordered them to cover themselves. Can we say he was unaware that what he was doing was wrong? Of course not! He prohibited killing and stealing, but he justified his own killing and robbing. As a narcissist, he believed himself to be a superior being, entitled to special rights and at liberty to do anything his whims dictated. Muhammad was both insane *and* a liar. This is possible only if you are a psychopathic narcissist.

Did the Meccans call Muhammad Honest?

Muslims claim that Muhammad was known to be an honest man and consequently the Meccans called him *Amin* (trusted). This claim is simply not true. *Amin* was the title of those who sold and bought merchandise on behalf of others. One is called school trustee, or city trustee because of his profession and not because he is honest. The title "*Amin*" is a label for

Muhammad's Personality Profile

every sort of profession. Here are some examples: *Amin El-Makataba* (Trustee of the library); *Amin El-Shortaa* (Police Trustee); and *Majlass El-Omnaa* (counsil of trustees.)

In fact, Abul Aas, husband of Zeinab and son-in-law of Muhammad was also known as Amin because of his business. He did not accept Islam until he was forced to, because Muhammad ordered Zeinab to leave him unless he converted.

Muhammad acted as the trustee of Khadijah once, when he took her merchandise to Damascus and sold it on her behalf. The claim that the Meccans called Muhammad *Amin* because they had found him truthful is simply false. Had this claim been true, they would not have rejected and derided him when he told them that he had received a message from God. According to Muhammad's own claim in the Quran, those who knew him best called him a liar and a madman, (Q.15:6) a charged that he tried to deny by making his Allah testify: "Therefore continue to remind, for by the grace of your Lord, you are not a soothsayer, or a madman." (Q.52:29)

More on the Policy of Divide and Rule

As stated in the previous chapter, Muhammad severed his followers' ties to their families in order to secure his absolute dominance over them. He ordered his Meccan followers, who had immigrated to Medina, not to contact their relatives back home. Despite his warnings, some of them did, probably because they needed money for their sustenance. To stop this, he dictated the following verse from his Allâh.[128]

> O you who believe! Take not my enemies and yours as friends (or protectors), - offering them (your) love, even though they have rejected the Truth that has come to you, and have (on the contrary) driven out the Prophet and yourselves (from your homes), (simply) because you believe in Allâh your Lord! If you have come out to strive in My Way and to seek My Good Pleasure, (take them not as friends), holding secret converse of love (and friendship) with them: for I know full well all that you

---

[128] The Qur'an can be tedious, and that is mainly why few Muslims have read it. However, at the risk of boring my readers, in this chapter I will have to quote several Qur'anic verses as evidence to support my portrait of Muhammad.

conceal and all that you reveal. And any of you that do this has strayed from the Straight Path.[129]

We see this urge to alienate in a later verse too:

O you who believe! Take not for protectors your fathers and your brothers if they love infidelity above Faith: if any of you do so, they do wrong. (Q. 9:23)

Why was Muhammad so keen to isolate his followers? Vaknin explains: "The narcissist is the guru at the centre of a cult. Like other gurus, he demands complete obedience from his flock: his spouse, his offspring, other family members, friends, and colleagues. He feels entitled to adulation and special treatment by his followers. He punishes the wayward and the straying lambs. He enforces discipline, adherence to his teachings, and common goals. The less accomplished he is in reality – the more stringent his mastery and the more pervasive the brainwashing."[130]

This was something Muhammad could not accomplish while his followers still lived in Mecca, where they still could, if things got tough, return to their families. Due to the need to isolate his followers, the cult leader often encloses them in compounds where it is easy to brainwash them and to exert total control over them. At first Muhammad sent the early believers to Abyssinia, but later, when he made a pact with the Arabs of Yathrib, he chose that town as his compound. He even changed the name of Yathrib and called it Medina (which is short for *Medinatul Nabi*, the Prophet's Town).

Vaknin says: "The – often involuntary – members of the narcissist's mini-cult inhabit a twilight zone of his own construction. He imposes on them a shared psychosis, replete with persecutory delusions, 'enemies,' mythical narratives, and apocalyptic scenarios if he is flouted."[131]

Note how accurate is this description about Muhammad and Muslims who up to this day have persecutory delusions and see enemies everywhere. They believe in mythical narratives such as the Angel Gabriel bringing a revelation to Muhammad and in other fairy tales like Jinns, Mi'raj (ascension of Muhammad to heaven), Doomsday, etc.

---

[129] Qur'an, sura 60, Verse 1
[130] http://samvak.tripod.com/journal79.html
[131] ibid.

Muhammad's Personality Profile

According to Vaknin, "the narcissist's deep-rooted conviction that he is being persecuted by his inferiors, detractors, or powerful ill-wishers, serves two psychodynamic purposes. It upholds the narcissist's grandiosity and it fends off intimacy."[132]

Vaknin writes: "The narcissist claims to be infallible, superior, talented, skilful, omnipotent, and omniscient. He often lies and confabulates to support these unfounded claims. Within his cult, he expects awe, admiration, adulation, and constant attention commensurate with his outlandish stories and assertions. He reinterprets reality to fit his fantasies. His thinking is dogmatic, rigid, and doctrinaire. He does not welcome free thought, pluralism, or free speech, and doesn't brook criticism and disagreement. He demands – and often gets – complete trust and the relegation to his capable hands of all decision-making. He forces the participants in his cult to be hostile to critics, the authorities, institutions, his personal enemies, or the media – if they try to uncover his actions and reveal the truth. He closely monitors and censors information from the outside, exposing his captive audience only to selective data and analyses."[133]

By elucidating the characteristics of the narcissist, Vaknin unintentionally and with astounding accuracy describes Muhammad's mind and the Muslim mindset. Muslims are narcissists to the extent that they emulate their prophet.

A Comparison between Islam and the Cult of the Narcissist

The following is a description of the cult of the narcissist. First let us see what Vaknin says about the cult of the narcissist and then I will quote episodes from Muhammad's life and leave the reader to decide whether they coincide.

> The narcissist's cult is "missionary" and "imperialistic." He is always on the lookout for new recruits – his spouse's friends, his daughter's girlfriends, his neighbors, new colleagues at work. He immediately attempts to 'convert' them to his 'creed' – to convince them how wonderful and admirable he is. In other words, he tries to render them Sources of Narcissistic Supply.

---

[132] www.suite101.com/article.cfm/6514/95897
[133] http://samvak.tripod.com/journal79.html

Often, his behavior on these 'recruiting missions' is different to his conduct within the 'cult'. In the first phases of wooing new admirers and proselytising to potential 'conscripts' – the narcissist is attentive, compassionate, empathic, flexible, self-effacing, and helpful. At home, among the "veterans" he is tyrannical, demanding, wilful, opinionated, aggressive, and exploitative.

As the leader of his congregation, the narcissist feels entitled to special amenities and benefits not accorded the "rank and file." He expects to be waited on hand and foot, to make free use of everyone's money and dispose of their assets liberally, and to be cynically exempt from the rules that he himself established (if such violation is pleasurable or gainful).

In extreme cases, the narcissist feels above the law – any kind of law. This grandiose and haughty conviction leads to criminal acts, incestuous or polygamous relationships, and recurrent friction with the authorities.

Hence the narcissist's panicky and sometimes violent reactions to "dropouts" from his cult. There's a lot going on that the narcissist wants kept under wraps. Moreover, the narcissist stabilizes his fluctuating sense of self-worth by deriving Narcissistic Supply from his victims. Abandonment threatens the narcissist's precariously balanced personality.

Add to that the narcissist's paranoid and schizoid tendencies, his lack of introspective self-awareness, and his stunted sense of humor (lack of self-deprecation) and the risks to the grudging members of his cult are clear.

The narcissist sees enemies and conspiracies everywhere. He often casts himself as the heroic victim (martyr) of dark and stupendous forces. In every deviation from his tenets he espies malevolent and ominous subversion. He, therefore, is bent on disempowering his devotees – by any and all means.

The narcissist is dangerous.[134]

Now let us see if there are similarities between this description and what we know about Muhammad and his religion.

Islam is both missionary and imperialistic. Muhammad's main objective was to conquer and dominate. He tried to force everyone to

---

[134] The Cult of Narcissist http://samvak.tripod.com/journal79.html

convert to his cult, starting with his family and relatives. He asked Abu Talib, his uncle and guardian to convert to Islam on his deathbed. When the old man declined, Muhammad walked out of the room mumbling, "I wanted to pray for him but Allâh prohibited me from doing so." However, he managed to convert Abu-Talib's children, including Ali, his own wife and some of his friends.

At first, when Muhammad was still weak and had few followers, he was courteous, attentive, compassionate, empathic, flexible, helpful and even self-effacing. There is a sharp contrast between the Qur'anic verses written during this period and those written in Medina when he became powerful and did not need to wear a mask to woo new converts. Once he had become powerful, he was demanding, tyrannical, willful, aggressive and exploitative. Then he raided villages and towns and after killing their able-bodied men and looting them, demanded survivors submit to him or face death.

The following are examples of the kind of verses Muhammad wrote in Mecca.

1. Be patient with what they say, and part from them courteously. (Q.73:10)
2. To you be your religion, and to me my religion. (Q. 109:6)
3. Therefore be patient with what they say, and celebrate (constantly) the praises of your Lord. (Q.20:103)
4. Speak well to men. (Q.2:83)
5. We well know what the infidels say: but you are not to compel them. (Q.50:45)
6. Hold to forgiveness; command what is right; but turn away from the ignorant. (Q.7:119)
7. Pardon thou, with a gracious pardoning. (Q.15:85)
8. Tell those who believe, to forgive those who do not look forward to the Days of Allâh. (Q.45:14)
9. Those who follow the Jewish (scriptures), and the Christians - any who believe in Allâh and the Last Day, and work righteousness, shall have their reward with their Lord; on them shall be no fear, nor shall they grieve. (Q.2:62)
10. And do not dispute with the followers of the Book except by what is best. (Q.29:46)

Now let us compare them to those written later in Medina when Muhammad became powerful.

1. Oh you who believe! Murder those of the disbelievers and let them find harshness in you. (Q.9:123)
2. I will instill terror into the hearts of the unbelievers: smite above their necks and smite all their finger-tips off. (Q.8:12)
3. Whoso desires another religion than Islam, it shall not be accepted of him. (Q.3:85)
4. Slay the idolaters wherever you find them. (Q.9:5)
5. Kill them wherever you find them, and drive them out from wherever they drove you out. (Q.2:191)
6. Fight them on until there is no more dissension and religion becomes that of Allâh. (Q.9:193)
7. Fight them, and Allâh will punish them by your hands, cover them with shame. (Q.9:14)
8. Make no excuses: you have rejected Faith after you had accepted it. If we pardon some of you, we will punish others amongst you, for that they are in sin. (Q.9:66)
9. You who believe! Verily, the Mushrikûn (unbelievers) are Najasun (impure). So let them not come near Al-Masjid-al-Harâm (the grand mosque at Mecca) after this year. (Q.9:28)
10. Fight those who do not believe in Allâh and the last day... and fight People of the Book, who do not accept the religion of truth (Islam) until they pay tribute by hand, being inferior. (Q.9:29)

This much should suffice as evidence that Muhammad changed drastically after he came to power. The gentle, attentive, compassionate and empathic preacher was transformed into a demanding, tyrannical, ruthless, and willful despot.

It was after the battle of Badr that the cruel and vindictive spirit of Muhammad towards his opponents first began to display itself. Muir narrates:

> The prisoners were brought up before him. As he scrutinized each, his eye fell fiercely on Nadhr, the son of Harith (Muhammad's own cousin who was a poet and critical of him). 'There was death in that glance,' whispered Nadhr, trembling, to a bystander. 'Not so,' replied the other; 'it is but your own imagination.'

Muhammad's Personality Profile

The unfortunate prisoner thought otherwise, and besought Musab (a friend of him who had converted to Islam) to intercede for him. Musab reminded him that he had denied the faith and ridiculed Muhammad. 'Ah!' said Nadhr, 'had the Quraish made you a prisoner, they would never have put you to death!' 'Even were it so,' Musab scornfully replied, '*I am not as you are; Islam has rent all bonds asunder.*' (Emphasis added) Musad, the captor, seeing that the captive, and with him the chance of a rich ransom, was about to slip from his hands, cried out, 'The prisoner is mine!' At this moment, the command to "strike off his head!" was interposed by Muhammad, who had been watching all that passed. 'And, O Lord!' he added, 'do thou of thy bounty grant unto Musab better prey than this?' Nadhr was forthwith beheaded by Ali.

Two days afterwards, about half-way to Medina, Oqba, another prisoner, was ordered out for execution. He ventured to expostulate, and demand why he should be treated more vigorously than the other captives. 'Because of your enmity to God and to his Prophet,' replied Muhammad. '*And my little girl!*' cried Oqba, in the bitterness of his soul, '*Who will take care of her?*' – 'Hellfire!' exclaimed the heartless conqueror; and on the instant his victim was hewn to the ground. 'Wretch that he was!' continued Muhammad, 'and persecutor! Unbeliever in God, in his Prophet, and in his Book! I give thanks unto the Lord that has slain you, and comforted mine eyes thereby.'[135]

There is a tender love story in all this that highlights even more the ruthlessness of Muhammad. After some of the prisoners captured in the battle of Badr were put to death because they had insulted Muhammad years earlier, when he was in Mecca, the rest were kept for ransom. Among them was Abul Aas, the above mentioned husband of Muhammad's daughter, Zeinab. The families of the prisoners procured what the bandit demanded to rescue their loved ones from death. Zeinab sent a gold necklace, which she had received from her mother Khadijah at her wedding to ransom her husband. Muhammad, upon seeing that necklace and recognizing it as once worn by Khadijah, was moved. He agreed to release Abul Aas without ransom provided that Zeinab abandon him (her husband) and join him (Muhammad) in Medina. This man was incapable of any act of kindness or of giving anything up without demanding something in exchange. Even his largesse was designed to impress the recipients and win them over to his side. Abul Aas could not bear the

---

[135] Sir William Muir: The Life of Mohamet, Vol. 3 Ch. XII Page 115-116

separation from his wife; and to be with her he converted to Islam and joined her in Medina, only to lose her to death shortly afterwards.

Muslims present Islam as a religion of peacefulness and tolerance toward outsiders, and will assume a smiling countenance to proselytize potential recruits. They are extremely helpful, humble, and charming to those whom they want to woo and in front of the media. Among themselves, however, they act very differently. They are tyrannical and demanding. Once you convert to Islam and the honeymoon period is over, Muslims will drop the smiling mask and become high-handed, aggressive and abusive. They expect the convert's questioning of Islam to end, and after conversion any possibility of going back is also considered terminated. This is consistent with the guidelines Muhammad himself laid down through his own conduct – guidelines that have been encoded in Islamic law.

Muhammad felt entitled to special benefits and treatments not accorded to others, including his followers. He not only did things that were against universally acclaimed ethical principles, even by the society in which he lived, but he also went against his own stated rules. He basically did whatever he pleased and when that shocked his followers, he brought a verse from his imaginary Allâh to justify his actions and silence any critic. With a verse from Allâh under his belt, anyone whispering a word against his indecency was denying God and, of course, the fate of those questioning Allah and his messenger was death. His words were *faslul-khitab* (the end of discussion). Examples abound. Here are a few:

The Qur'an limits believers to four wives. However, Muhammad thought that he should not be restricted by his own rules and therefore made his Allâh reveal verses 33:49-50 telling him he was exempt and could have any number of women he pleases, as wives, concubines or slaves. Then he added "This only for you, [O Muhammad] and not for the Believers (at large)...in order that there should be no difficulty for you. And Allâh is Oft-Forgiving, Most Merciful."

What difficulty? The difficulty of having to control his lustfulness, of being a decent human being, faithful to one woman! Are we to believe in a man who found it difficult to control his basest animal instincts as the best of creation? Don't actions speak louder than words? On one hand, he lived like the vilest beasts, and on the other he spoke of himself so loftily, putting words in the mouth of the Almighty to praise him. Remember that while still in Mecca, living off the wealth of his wife Muhammad did not

Muhammad's Personality Profile

dare to bring another woman to her house. All his vagaries started when he came to power. Are we to believe that as a young and virile man he did not have difficulty sleeping with an older woman and that his difficulties appeared in the last ten years of his life when he was old and beset by all sorts of ailments? Or shall we interpret this as another sign of an aging man gone wild with his newfound liberties who, like a child left unchecked in a candy store, was unable to set limits for himself?

One day Muhammad visited his wife Hafsa, daughter of Omar and upon meeting her maid Mariyah, lusted for her. Mariyah was an extremely beautiful young Coptic girl sent as a gift by Maquaqis (Patriarch) of Egypt to Muhammad. He sent Hafsa on an errand, lying that her father wanted to see her. No sooner had she left, than he took Mariyah to Hafsa's bed and had sex with her. Upon learning her father had not sent for her, Hafsa returned to discover what was going on and why Muhammad had wanted to get rid of her. She became upset and started to make a scene. (Ah, women will be always women!) To pacify her, Muhammad promised to prohibit Mariyah to himself. (Hence the name of the sura given for this incident *Tahrim*, Prohibition.) However, he still lusted after the pretty young slave girl. How could he now break his oath? Well, that is easy when you have God up your sleeve. The maker of the universe revealed the sura Tahrim and told him it is okay to break his oath and have sex with that slave girl because he was his "right hand possession." Actually the almighty God, now acting as a pimp for his favorite prophet, was even angry at Muhammad, and rebuked him for denying himself carnal pleasures and for promising to be decent just to please his wives!

> O Prophet! Why do you ban (for yourself) that which Allâh has made lawful to you, seeking to please your wives? And Allâh is Oft-Forgiving, Most Merciful. Allâh has already ordained for you (O men), the dissolution of your oaths. And Allâh is your Maula (Lord, or Master, or Protector, etc.) and He is the All-Knower, the All-Wise. (Q.66:1-5)

Ibn Sa'd writes: "Abu Bakr has narrated that the messenger of Allâh (PBUH) had sexual intercourse with Mariyah in the house of Hafsa. When the messenger came out of the house, Hafsa was sitting at the gate (behind the locked door). She told the prophet, 'O Messenger of Allâh, do you do this in my house and during my turn? The Prophet said, control yourself and let me go for I make her haram to me. Hafsa said, I do not accept, unless you swear for me. The Prophet said, by Allâh I will not touch her again."'[136]

As usual, Muslims have justified Muhammad for the breach of his oath. No matter what Muhammad did, Muslims will always justify his actions. They have submitted their intelligence to him and have stopped thinking rationally. Ibn Sa'd continues: "Qasim ibn Muhammad has said that this promise of the Prophet that had forbidden Mariyah to himself is invalid – it does not become a violation (*hormat*).[137]

The question is, if that oath was invalid, why did he make it; and if it was valid, why he did he break it? There are countless other examples of Muhammad breaking his own promises. Here he had sworn to God and not even that was an impediment to him. His god was a figment of his own imagination and he was not so stupid as to let his imagination stop him from having sex with the beautiful Mariyah. The whole idea of inventing that god was to approve whatever he desired without restrictions. A god putting restrictions on him would have defeated the whole purpose of becoming a prophet.

My copy of the Qur'an contains the following tafseer (interpretation) side by side with the Sura Tahrim:

> Also it is reported that the Prophet had divided his days among his wives. And when it was the turn of Hafsa, he sent her for an errand to the house of her father Omar Khattab. When she took this order and went, the prophet called his slave girl Mariyah the Copt who (later) bore his son Ibrahim, and who was a gift from Najashi, and had sexual intercourse with her. When Hafsa returned, she found the door locked from inside. She sat there behind the locked door until the prophet finished the business and came out of the house while sweat was dripping from his face. When Hafsa found him in that condition she rebuked him saying, you did not respect my honor; you sent me out of my house with an excuse so you could sleep with the slave girl. And in the day that was my turn you had intercourse with someone else. Then the Prophet said, be quiet for although she is my slave and halal to me, for your contentment I, at this moment, make her haram to myself. But Hafsa did not do this and when the Prophet went out of her house she knocked at the wall that separated her quarter from that of Aisha and told her everything.[138]

---

[136] Ibn Sa'd, Tabaqat Vol 8: p 195
[137] Ibid
[138] Published by Entesharat-e Elmiyyeh Eslami Tehran 1377 lunar H. Tafseer and translation into Farsi by Mohammad Kazem Mo'refi

Muhammad's Personality Profile

For Muslims oaths have no meaning. They promise something and then renege if they so choose. Bukhari reports a hadith where Muhammad says: "By Allah, and Allah willing, if I take an oath and later find something better than that, then I do what is better and expiate my oath."[139] And he advised his followers to do the same: "If you ever take an oath to do something and later on you find that something else is better, then you should expiate your oath and do what is better."[140]

Narcissists believe they are entitled to anything they desire and that their promises and obligations are not binding on them.

One day Muhammad went to see his adopted son Zeid and there he saw his wife Zeinab, in her revealing home clothing. He was aroused by her beauty and could not control his desire. When Zeid learned this, he felt obliged to divorce his wife so Muhammad could have her. The interesting thing is that a few years earlier, when Muhammad had claimed to have ascended to heaven, he said that there he had met a woman. He inquired about her, and they said she was Zeinab, the wife of Zeid. Later he told this anachronistic story to Zeid who, thinking that his marriage had been arranged in heaven, married her. However, when Muhammad saw Zeinab semi-nude, he forgot all about his own heavenly fable. Of course, no one knew better than he that the whole story of Mi'raj (ascension) was his own fabrication.

His marriage to Zeinab, his own daughter-in-law, confounded even his followers. To silence them again, his Allâh came out of his sleeve with a verse saying that Muhammad is not the father of anyone but the messenger of Allâh and the Seal of the prophets. (Q.33:40) He claimed that his marriage to Zeinab was arranged by God to show people that adoption was a bad thing and should be annulled. As you can see, just because he could not control his lust, he made his bogus deity tell people that adoption was wrong, depriving countless orphans of a second chance at life. Doesn't this alone disqualify him as a messenger of God? How can the almighty God be offended by adoption, which is perhaps one of the most humane and lofty of actions?

There is an interesting story in connection with this topic. After Muhammad annulled the institution of adoption, Abu Hudhaifa and his wife Sahla, who had an adopted son called Salim, came to Muhammad for

---

[139] Sahih Bukhari Vol.7 Book 67, No.424
[140] Sahih Bukhari Vol.9 Book 89, No.260

advice. "Messenger of Allah, Salim (the freed slave of Abu Hudhaifa) is living with us in our house," said Sahla. "He has attained (puberty) as men attain it and has acquired knowledge (of the sex problems) as men acquire." In response to her Muhammad improvised an ingenious solution. "Suckle him," he told her. "How can I suckle him as he is a grown-up man?" She asked perplexed. Muhammad smiled and said: "I already know that he is a young man." In fact Salim was old enough to have participated in the Battle of Badr. Another tradition says that Muhammad laughed.[141]

According to Muhammad, breast-feeding establishes a degree of maternal relation, even if a woman nurses a child who is not biologically hers. Inspired by these traditions, Dr. Izzat Atiya of Egypt's al-Azhar University, one of Sunni Islam's most prestigious institutions, offered a way around segregation of the sexes at work. He issued a fatwa (religious ruling) allowing women to feed a male colleague "directly from her breast" at least five times to establish a family bond and thus be allowed to be alone together at work. "Breast feeding an adult puts an end to the problem of the private meeting, and does not ban marriage," he ruled. "A woman at work can take off the veil or reveal her hair in front of someone whom she breastfed." [142]

Even though some Muslims had no problem with this fatwa, as they were told that it was based on authentic hadith, the legal ruling sparked outrage throughout Egypt and the Arab world and Dr. Atiya was forced to retract his fatwa.

Muhammad's Sacred Secretions

On June 13, 2007, MEMRI (The Middle East Media Research Institute) published the following article:[143]

> In his book *Religion and Life - Modern Everyday Fatwas,* Egyptian Mufti Dr. Ali Gum'a wrote that the companions of the Prophet Muhammad would bless themselves by drinking his urine, and described an incident of urine-drinking from a *hadith*: "Umm Ayman drank the urine of the Prophet, and the prophet told

---

[141] Sahih Muslim 8.3424, 3425, 3426, 3427, 3428

[142] http://news.bbc.co.uk/2/hi/middle_east/6681511.stm

[143] MEMRI nquiry and Analysis Series - No. 363 L. Azuri
http://memri.org/bin/articles.cgi?Page=archives&Area=ia&ID=IA36307#_edn1

Muhammad's Personality Profile

her: 'This stomach will not be dragged through the fire of Hell, because it contains something of our Lord the Messenger of Allah...' [144]

'This blessing,' Al-Gum'a added, '[can also] be done with the honorable saliva, sweat, hair, urine or blood of the Prophet. This is because anyone who knows the love of the Messenger of Allah is not repulsed [by these]; just as a mother is not repulsed by the feces of her son, this is even more so [in the case of] our Lord the Messenger of Allah, whom we love more than our fathers, sons, and wives. Anyone who was or is repulsed by the Messenger of Allah must recant his faith.' [145]

Following the ensuing uproar, Gum'a came to the defense of his fatwa, saying: 'The entire body of the Prophet, whether exposed or hidden, is pure, and there is nothing in it- including his secretions - that [can] repulse anyone. His sweat smelled better than perfume. Umm Haram would collect this sweat and distribute it to the people of Al-Madina.' [146]

Dr. Gum'a added: 'The *hadith* of Suhail bin Omar at Al-Hudaybiya says: 'Oh Lord, I was with Kisra [the ruler of Persia] and with Kaisar [the ruler of Byzantium] and I saw no instance in which the leader was glorified like the Companions of the Prophet glorified Muhammad. The second Muhammad spat, one of them would immediately hasten [to grab his saliva] and smear it upon his face.' Hence, the *ulema*, including Ibn Hajar Al-Askalani, Al-Baihaqi, Al-Daraqutni and Al-Haythami, determined that the Prophet's entire body was pure.' [147]

Egyptian Religious Endowments Minister Dr. Muhammad Hamdi Zaqzouq was extremely critical of Gum'a's statements. He said: 'Fatwas such as these do damage to Islam, serve its enemies, and push the people towards backwardness and ignorance.' [148] Writing in the government daily *Al-Ahram*, Zaqzouq explained further: 'Tragic fatwas such as [Gum'a's] have harmed Islam and the Prophet more than the Danish cartoons did, because this time the harm comes not from

---

[144] Baraka Umm Ayman was a servant of the Prophet Muhammad as well as his nursemaid.
[145] *Al-Masri Al-Yawm* (Egypt) May 20, 2007.
[146] Umm Haram bint Milhan was a cousin of the prophet on his mother's side, and one of the first to embrace Islam and emigrate to Mecca.
[147] *Al-Masri Al-Yawm* (Egypt) May 23, 2007. Dr. Gum'a made similar statements to the Egyptian weekly *Al-Liwa Al-Islami*, May 26, 2007.
[148] *Al-Masri Al-Yawm* (Egypt) May 22, 2007.

Islam's enemies but from some Muslim *ulema* who present their opinions on Islam to the public...'

'The books of the *hadith*s contain both wheat and chaff. They contain the acceptable and the unacceptable, and it is not for the good of Islam or the Muslims if we repeatedly disseminate the pollution that they contain... Those of us who speak in the name of the religion must understand that... the world has changed, circumstances have changed, and it is no longer acceptable or logical to fill the heads of the Muslim masses with the defiled sayings, sick thoughts, and groundless suppositions whose correctness is completely unproven... [149]

The Academy for Islamic Research, headed by Al-Azhar Sheikh Dr. Muhammad Sayyed Tantawi, expressed vehement objections to the fatwa issued by Gum'a, who is an academy member. According to the academy, the fatwa was not appropriate for today's circumstances...[150]

There were many other protests from Islamic scholars and the public. Attorney Nabih Al-Wahsh filed a complaint against Gum'a with the prosecutor general, claiming that Gum'a's fatwa threatened social stability and also reviled and defamed the Prophet and his companions.[151]

Al-Ahram editor Osama Saraya argued that Gum'a's fatwa was not relevant to Muslim life today, even if it did draw on religious sources: 'The books of religious law contain many questions and issues, some of which have descended into oblivion. They have nothing to do with the reality of the lives of Muslims today, and they have become theoretical, philosophical or polemic [issues]. In the past, clerics said that one does not have to reveal everything one knows. The accepted opinion is that that many issues that preoccupied the Muslim clerics in the past are no longer worthy of discussion - either because they belong to the ancient period and are too loosely linked to public life, or because they are likely to cause confusion and public pandemonium. This is a fact well-known to students of religious law..." [152]

---

[149] *Al-Ahram* (Egypt) May 29, 2007.
[150] *Al-Ahram* (Egypt), June 3, 2007.
[151] *Al-Masri Al-Yawm* (Egypt) May 30, 2007.
[152] *Al-Ahram* (Egypt) May 31, 2007.

Muhammad's Personality Profile

Gala Gaballah, columnist for the government daily *Al-Gumhouriyya,* wrote: 'Whether the story of Umm Ayman is true or not, it should not be retold by the mufti. [If asked about it], the mufti should respond: 'What use is it to you to know this? The Prophet, with his honorable past, his honorable blood and his honorable urine, is no longer among us. There is no place at all for talking about such pointless matters, which are likely to harm people and start talk that will damage Islam and the religion...'[153]

Al-Akhbar columnist Ahmad Ragab mocked Gum'a's statements, writing: '[With regard] to the fatwa of the honorable mufti... How is it possible to actually drink urine when this need is always met in a secluded place specially designated for this [purpose]? Did the Companions of the Prophet stand around and wait [there], with containers in their hands? Can any reasonable person imagine that the Prophet [actually] let them collect his urine?' [154]

There is a glimmer of hope in this. These episodes show that there is a limit to which Muslims are willing to be fooled and beyond which they will not go. Therein lies my conviction that once the naked truth about Islam is exposed and its asininity becomes manifest, a great number of Muslims will see the light and will abandon their irrational faith.

Muhammad reintroduced the pagan tradition of fasting during the month of Ramadan. However, he found it difficult to abstain from food and water from dawn to dusk, so he himself ate whenever he pleased. Ibn Sa'd writes: "The Messenger of Allâh used to say 'We the prophets are required to eat our morning food later than others and hurry in breaking our fast in the evening.'"[155]

These are just a few examples of how Muhammad did as he pleased and made his Allâh approve whatever he did. The young and perceptive Aisha noticed this and perhaps sarcastically or innocently, said to him "I feel that your Lord hastens in fulfilling your wishes and desires."[156]

In none of the wars that Muhammad waged did he put his own life in danger. He often stood behind his troops wearing two coats of chain-link mail,[157] one on top of the other. The double armoring would make him so heavy that his movements became cumbersome and he needed assistance

---

[153] *Al-Gumhouriyya* (Egypt) May 24, 2007.

[154] *Al-Akhbar* (Egypt) May 21, 2007.

[155] Tabaqat, Volume 1, page 369

[156] Sahih al-Bukhari, Volume 6, Book 60, Number 311)

[157] Flexible armor of interlinked rings.

to stand or to walk. While in that state he would shout toward the front and loudly encourage his men to be valiant and not fear death, promising them high-bosomed virgins and celestial food in the other world. Sometimes he would grab a handful of sand and throw it in the air in the direction of the enemy while cursing them.

To finance his military expeditions, the Prophet of Allâh exhorted his followers to contribute their wealth. He urged them to serve him and wait upon him. He encouraged their adulation of him and strongly frowned on dissent. The tribe of Quraish had a negotiator named Orwa, who visited Muhammad among his men in Hudaibiyyah. He later recounted that he had seen the Khusraos, the Caesar and the Najashi, but had never seen, before or since, such attention and homage lavished on any king. He told the Quraish that Muhammad's followers "rushed to save the water in which he had performed his ablutions, to catch up his spittle, or seize a hair of his if it chanced to fall."[158] This should not be interpreted or dismissed as an exaggeration of later years, as the historian Sir Willam Muir believed. Muhammad, like all other cult leaders, had created a personality cult around himself. We can see this kind of personality worship in modern cults even today. This is how the narcissist wants to be treated.

Muhammad thought himself to be above the law. He broke moral and ethical codes whenever it suited him, and then made his Allâh reveal a verse to confirm that what he had done was all right.

Arabs were simple people of the desert, but they had dignity and prided themselves on their chivalry. During the year there were a few months when they did not fight. These were known as the sacred months, when people traveled freely on pilgrimage. In one such month, Muhammad sent an expedition to Nakhlah, a place known for its palm trees, to lay siege and ambush a caravan carrying raisins, butter, wine, and other goods from Taif to Mecca. Fighting and killing at such a time of the year was a sacrilege. He sent eight men towards Nakhlah without telling them about their mission. He gave a sealed letter to the leader of the expedition instructing the men to open it only after reaching the destination. When they opened the letter, they realized Muhammad was asking them to raid a caravan during the sacred months. Two of the men conveniently lost their camels in the desert, went out to find them, and did not take part in the raid. The other six discussed the situation and finally

---

[158] Sirat Ibn Ishaq, p.823.

convinced themselves that the orders of the prophet should be obeyed even if they went against their consciences and seemed immoral and unethical. To set up the ambush, they shaved their heads and pretended to be preparing themselves for pilgrimage, and when the men of the caravan lowered their guard, they leapt upon them, killing one and taking two as hostages. The fourth person escaped. This was the first bloodshed chargeable to Islam. The first blood spilled in the history of Islam was the blood of a non-Muslim by Muslims. Muslims started the hostilities. They persecuted their detractors, not the other way around. The killing sent a shockwave through the Quraish, who realized that their opponent, in his quest for power, would not respect any law.

There are countless cases in which Muhammad broke the laws of the land and disregarded the codes of ethics, decency, and morality. Laying siege to merchant caravans or raiding villages and seizing their wealth is theft and is against the law in any society. Muhammad ambushed unarmed groups when they were least prepared to fight, killed as many of their unarmed men as he could, enslaved their women and children, and made his Allâh approve whatever he did. He also okayed having sex with women captured in war, even if the women were still married. (Q.4:24)

From incest to polygamy, from rape to pedophilia, from assassination to genocide, the Prophet of Allâh did them all and encouraged his followers to do the same. He was disdainful of authorities, and so are his followers.

The word "Islam" means "submission." The Qur'an says: "No believing man and no believing woman has a choice in their own affairs when Allâh and His Messenger have decided on an issue."(Q.33:36) The truth is that even non-believing people have no choice. They must submit or be killed. Muhammad interpreted dissent as betrayal. For narcissists, dissent is intolerable. In response they panic and feel threatened. Painful memories of being abandoned as a child rise up to shake their precariously balanced personalities. They feel deeply hurt and seek revenge.

Muhammad viewed as enemies any who were not his supporters and followers. He was paranoid and saw conspiracies everywhere. He cast himself as the heroic victim of the malicious forces of his enemies. These "enemies," of course, existed nowhere except in his fertile imagination.

One of the main factors driving Muhammad's success was that he had spies everywhere who posed as his detractors and brought news from places he wanted to ambush. So paranoid was he that he even encouraged his believers to spy on each other. Muslims do the same to this day.

Like their prophet, Muslims think they are the victims, and therefore their acts of terrorism are fully justified. They think dark stupendous forces are at work to destroy Islam and that there is a world conspiracy against Muslims led by the Jews. They are convinced Jews control the world, particularly the United States of America, who are doing their bidding and waging proxy wars against the Muslims at the order of this mysterious and omnipotent Jewish organization.

Muslims are vigilant toward each other's words and actions; each Muslim spies on others to see whether the laws of Islam are properly observed. An ambience of terror is created in all Islamic countries, where hardly anyone dares raise the slightest question of the tenets of Islam. Your own father, son or brother could report your infidelity, which, of course, would mean certain death to you.

Pathological narcissists truly believe they are special and therefore entitled to gratuitous favors from others. Muhammad found a perfect way not to thank those he made do his bidding. Instead of expressing gratitude, he told them they should be grateful for being given the privilege of serving Allâh.

> O you who believe! Do not make your charity worthless by reproach and injury, like him who spends his property to be seen of men and does not believe in Allâh and the last day. (Q. 2:263)

Muhammad tried to compensate for his craving for love with power. He yearned for love because he did not receive enough of it from his primary caregivers. A loveless childhood is the root cause of narcissism, despotism and psychopathic behavior. His grandfather's and uncle's permissiveness, and their failure to set limits, further aggravated his narcissistic trait. Muhammad cried bitterly at the tomb of his mother. Those tears were not for her, but for himself. Narcissists have no feelings for others. They are only aware, in fact too aware, of their own feelings, their own pain and their own emotional needs.

Chapter Three

Muhammad's Ecstatic Experiences

*N*ew understanding of the human mind sheds a lot of light on Muhammad's mystical experiences, which he described in striking language. To avoid being called a liar, he makes Allah describe what he saw.

And he is in the highest part of the horizon. Then he drew near, then he bowed. So he was the measure of two bows or closer still. And He revealed to His servant what He revealed. The heart was not untrue in what he saw. What! Do you then dispute with him as to what he saw? And certainly he saw him in another descent. At the farthest lote-tree; near which is the garden, the place to be resorted to. When that which covers covered the lote tree. The eye did not turn aside, nor did it exceed the limit. Certainly he saw of the greatest signs of his Lord. (Q.53:6-18)

In another passage he emphatically affirmed his visual experience:

And of a truth he saw himself on the clear horizon. (Q.81:23)

A hadith reports him recounting his experience as follows:

While I was walking I heard a voice from the sky. I looked up towards the sky, and behold! I saw the same Angel who came to me in the Cave of Hira', sitting on a chair between the sky and the earth. I was so terrified by him that I fell down on the ground. Then I went to my wife and said, 'Wrap me in garments! Wrap me in garments!' They wrapped me, and then Allâh revealed: [159]

When someone asked, "How does the divine inspiration come to you?" Muhammad replied:

Sometimes it is **like the ringing of a bell**, this form of Inspiration is the hardest of all and then this state passes ' off after I have grasped what is inspired. Sometimes the Angel comes in the form of a man and talks to me and I grasp whatever he says.' 'Aisha added: Verily I saw the Prophet being inspired divinely **on a very cold day and noticed the sweat dropping from his forehead** (as the Inspiration was over).[160]

Zayd Ibn Thabit narrated: "I used to write down the words of *wahy* (revelation) for him. When *wahy* came to him he felt burning with heat and the drops of perspiration would start rolling down on his body like pearls."[161]

Ibn Sa'd claims, "At the moment of inspiration, **anxiety** pressed upon the Prophet, and his **countenance was troubled.**"[162] He further wrote, "When the revelation descended on the Prophet, for some hours he used to become **drowsy like a sleepy person.**"[163] Bukhari says: "The commencement of divine inspiration to Allâh's Messenger was in the form of dreams that came true **like a bright light.**"[164]

A hadith recorded by Muslim reads: "A'isha, the wife of the Apostle of Allâh, reported: The first (form) with which was started the revelation to the Messenger of Allâh was the true vision in sleep. And **he did not see any vision but it came like the bright gleam of dawn.**"[165]

Tabari reports: "The Prophet said, 'I had been standing, but **fell to my knees; and crawled away, my shoulders trembling.'**"[166]

---

[159] Sahih al-Bukhari, Volume 6, Book 60, Number 448:
[160] Sahih al-Bukhari Volume 1, Book 1, Number 2
[161] Majma'uz Zawaa'id with reference to Tabraani
[162] Tabaqat Volume 1 page 184 Persian translation
[163] Ibid.
[164] Bukhari Volume 1, Book 1, Number 3:
[165] Sahih Muslim Book 001, Number 0301:
[166] Tabari VI:67

Muhammad's Ecstatic Experiences

Bukhari has also recorded a long hadith that describes the entire episode of how Muhammad received his revelations.

Narrated 'Aisha:

The commencement of the Divine Inspiration to Allâh's Apostle was in the form of good righteous (true) dreams in his sleep. He never had a dream but that it came true like bright daylight. He used to go in seclusion (the cave of) Hira' where he used to worship (Allâh Alone) continuously for many (days) nights. He used to take with him the journey food for that (stay) and then come back to (his wife) Khadijah to take his food likewise again for another period to stay, till suddenly the Truth descended upon him while he was in the cave of Hira. The angel came to him in it and asked him (the illiterate Muhammad) to read. The Prophet replied, 'I do not know how to read.' The angel caught me (forcefully) and pressed me so hard that I could not bear it anymore. He then released me and again asked me to read, and I replied, 'I do not know how to read,' whereupon he caught me again and pressed me a second time till I could not bear it anymore. He then released me and asked me again to read, but again I replied, 'I do not know how to read (or, what shall I read?)' Thereupon he caught me for the third time and pressed me and then released me and said, 'Read: In the Name of your Lord, Who has created (all that exists). Has created man from a clot. Read and Your Lord is Most Generous...up to...that which he knew not.' (Q.96:15)

Then Allâh's Apostle returned with the inspiration, his neck muscles twitching with terror till he entered upon Khadijah and said, 'Cover me! Cover me!' They covered him till his fear was over and then he said, 'O Khadijah, what is wrong with me?' Then he told her everything that had happened and said, 'I fear that something may happen to me.' Khadijah said, 'Never! But have the glad tidings, for Allâh will never disgrace you as you keep good reactions with your kith and kin, speak the truth, help the poor and the destitute, serve your guests generously and assist the deserving, calamity-afflicted ones.'

Khadijah then accompanied him to (her cousin) Waraqa bin Naufal bin Asad bin 'Abdul 'Uzza bin Qusai. Waraqa was the son of her paternal uncle, i.e., her father's brother, who during the Pre-Islamic Period became a Christian and used to write the Arabic script and used to write of the Gospels in Arabic as much as Allâh wished him to write. He was an old man and had lost his eyesight. Khadijah said to him, "O my cousin! Listen to the story of your nephew." Waraqa asked, 'O my nephew! What have you seen?' The Prophet described whatever he had seen.

Waraqa said, 'This is the same Namus (i.e., Gabriel, the Angel who keeps the secrets) whom Allâh had sent to Moses. I wish I were young and could live up to the time when your people would turn you out.' Allâh's Apostle asked, "Will they turn me out?" Waraqa replied in the affirmative and said: 'Never did a man come with something similar to what you have brought but was treated with hostility. If I should remain alive till the day when you will be turned out then I would support you strongly.' But after a few days Waraqa died and the Divine Inspiration was also paused for a while and the Prophet became so sad as we have heard that **he intended several times to throw himself from the tops of high mountains** and every time he went up the top of a mountain in order to throw himself down, Gabriel would appear before him and say, 'O Muhammad! You are indeed Allâh's Apostle in truth!' whereupon his heart would become quiet and he would calm down and would return home. And whenever the period of the coming of the inspiration used to become long, he would do as before, but when he used to reach the top of a mountain, Gabriel would appear before him and say to him what he had said before. (Ibn 'Abbas said regarding the meaning of: 'He it is that Cleaves the daybreak (from the darkness)' (6.96) that Al-Asbah. means the light of the sun during the day and the light of the moon at night). [167]

The story of Khadijah's cousin Waraqa, recognizing Muhammad as a messenger of God, based on his studies of the scriptures, is of course balderdash. This is the kind of story Muhammad would make up to bolster his claim. There is nothing in the Judaic or Christian scriptures that would point to Muhammad. Waraqa was dead, and Muhammad felt free to fabricate any lies and attribute them to him just as he made those bogus claims about his grandfather saying he would have a great destiny. It is not unlikely that Khadijah, as Muhammad's codependent, confirmed those lies. A codependent often corroborates the lies of his or her narcissist. There is a similar claim made by Muhammad pertaining to the time he went to Busra in the service of Khadijah. He claimed that as caravans entered the outskirts of Busra, he sat beneath the shade of a tree and was spotted by a Nestor monk. "Who is the man beneath that tree?" the monk reportedly inquired of Maysarah, the young servant of Khadijah who was accompanying Muhammad in this trade expedition. "A man of Quraish," the lad responded. "None other than a Prophet is sitting beneath that tree," said the monk. According to this story concocted by Muhammad, the monk noticed his rank by observing two small clouds shading him from the

---

[167] Sahih Bukhari Volume 9, Book 87, Number 111

oppressive heat of the sun. "Is there a glow, a slight redness, around his eyes that never parts with him?" asked the monk. When the young Maysarah answered in the affirmative, he said, "He most surely is the very last Prophet; congratulations to whoever believes in him."[168]

In another place he claimed that the big mole that he had between his shoulders was the sign of his prophethood. I have not yet come across any scripture confirming that a mole between the shoulders and redness around the eyes are signs of prophethood. Chronic redness of the eye is a medical condition called blepharitis caused by inflammation of the eyelids. In one kind of blepharitis, meibomian gland dysfunction (MGD) patients frequently have coexisting skin disorder known as rosacea and seborrheic dermatitis. Rosacea is also characterized by redness of the face. Ali, the son of Abu Talib, described Muhammad's face as reddish-white.[169]

Muhammad had found a credulous audience and felt free to tell them anything, knowing that they would believe, so even the symptoms of his diseases were claimed as signs of prophethood. There is no mention of Maysarah among the early believers. Had this story been true, Maysarah should have been the first to believe.

In the above hadith we can see the important role that Khadijah played in Islam. When Muhammad had his strange hallucinatory experience, he thought that he had been demon-possessed. It was Khadijah who reassured him that he had been chosen to be a prophet of God and who encouraged him to pursue his insanity.

Some of Muhammad's hallucinations were visual, some were somatic and others were auditory. Ibn Ishaq writes that "the apostle, at the time when Allâh willed to bestow His grace upon him and endow him with prophethood, would go forth for his affair and travel far afield, until he reached the glens of Mecca and the beds of its valleys, where no house was in sight, and not a stone or tree that he passed by, but would say, 'Peace unto thee, O apostle of Allâh.' And the apostle would turn to his right and left and look behind him, and he would see nothing but trees and stones."[170]

Muhammad had several other hallucinations. Narrated Abu Huraira: The Prophet once offered the prayer and said, "Satan came in front of me and tried to interrupt my prayer, but Allâh gave me an upper hand on him and I choked him. No

---

[168] Tabaqat Vol. 1. p. 119
[169] Tirmidhi Hadith, Number 1524
[170] Sira Ibn Ishaq, p. 105

doubt, I thought of tying him to one of the pillars of the mosque till you get up in the morning and see him. Then I remembered the statement of Prophet Solomon, 'My Lord! Bestow on me a kingdom such as shall not belong to any other after me.' Then Allâh made him (Satan) return with his head down (humiliated)."[171]

> Narrated Aisha:
> Magic was worked on Allâh's Apostle so that he used to think that he had sexual relations with his wives while he actually had not (Sufyan said: That is the hardest kind of magic as it has such an effect). Then one day he said, 'O 'Aisha do you know that Allâh has instructed me concerning the matter I asked Him about? Two men came to me and one of them sat near my head and the other sat near my feet. The one near my head asked the other. What is wrong with this man?' The latter replied "he is under the effect of magic.' The first one asked, 'Who has worked magic on him?' The other replied 'Labid bin Al-A'sam, a man from Bani Zuraiq who was an ally of the Jews and was a hypocrite.' The first one asked, 'What material did he use?' The other replied, 'A comb and the hair stuck to it.' The first one asked, 'Where (is that)?' The other replied. 'In a skin of pollen of a male date palm tree kept under a stone in the well of Dharwan.' So the Prophet went to that well and took out those things and said 'That was the well which was shown to me (in a dream). Its water looked like the infusion of henna leaves and its date-palm trees looked like the heads of devils.' The Prophet added, 'Then that thing was taken out.' I said (to the Prophet) 'Why do you not treat yourself with Nashra?' He said, 'Allâh has cured me; I dislike to let evil spread among my people.'[172]

In another hadith we are told:

> Revelation came to the Apostle of Allâh and he was covered with a cloth, and Ya'la said: Would that I see revelation coming to the Apostle of Allâh. He (Omar) said: Would it please you to see the Apostle of Allâh receiving the revelations? 'Omar lifted a corner of the cloth and I looked at him and he was **emitting a sound of snorting**. He (the narrator) said: I thought it was the sound of a camel.[173]

One hadith reports: "When Gabriel revealed the Divine Inspiration in Allâh's Apostle, he (Allâh's Apostle) moved his tongue and lips, and that state

---

[171] Sahih Bukhari Volume 2, Book 22, Number 301
[172] Sahih Bukhari Volume 7, Book 71, Number 660:
[173] Sahih Muslim Book 007, Number 2654:

used to be very hard for him, and that movement indicated that revelation was taking place."[174]

Here is a "laundry list" of psychological and physical effects of revelation on Muhammad's body and mind based on what is reported in various ahadith.

1. visions (hallucinations) of seeing an angel or a light and of hearing voices
2. bodily spasms and excruciating abdominal pain and discomfort
3. overwhelmed by sudden emotions of anxiety and fear
4. twitching in neck muscles
5. uncontrollable lip movement, lip smacking
6. sweating even during cold days
7. face flushed
8. countenance was troubled
9. rapid heart palpitation
10. snorting like a camel
11. drowsiness
12. suicidal thoughts

All of these are symptoms of temporal lobe epilepsy [TLE]. Another characteristic of TLE is that it happens unexpectedly with no prior warning to the patient. This too was the case in Muhammad's mystical experiences. Bukhari reports: "While Allâh's Apostle was talking about the period of pause in revelation, he said in his narration, 'Once while I was walking, all of a sudden I heard a voice from the sky. I looked up and saw to my surprise, the same Angel as had visited me in the cave of Hira'. He was sitting on a chair between the sky and the earth. I got afraid of him and came back home and said, Wrap me! Wrap me!"[175]

Suicidal Thoughts

The chroniclers tell us that Muhammad attempted to commit suicide on several occasions, only to be stopped by Gabriel every time. He at first thought that he had become a poet or a soothsayer: "I have never abhorred anyone more than a poet or a kahin. I cannot stand looking at either of them. I will never tell

---

[174] Sahih Bukhari Volume 6, Book 60, Number 451:
[175] Bukhari Volume 6, Book 60, Number 478

anyone of Quraish of my Revelation. I will climb a mountain and throw myself down and die. That will relieve me. I went to do that, but halfway up the mountain I heard a voice from the sky saying 'O Muhammad! You are the Messenger of Allâh and I am Gabriel.' I looked upwards and saw Gabriel in the form of a man putting his legs on the horizon. He said: 'O Muhammad! You are the Messenger of Allâh and I am Gabriel.' I stopped and looked at him. His sight distracted my attention from what I had intended to do. I stood in my place transfixed. I tried to shift my eyes away from him, but towards whatever region of the sky I looked, I saw him as before."[176]

The only way one can make sense of this vision is that the image that Muhammad was seeing was in his own head, moving in whichever direction he turned. The picture on the cover of the book shows Gabriel appearing in a multitude of places simultaneously. However, this is not how Muhammad described his vision. What Muhammad saw can only be defined as visual hallucination. Visual hallucinations occur in various non-psychiatric conditions including cerebral lesions, sensory deprivation, the administration of psychedelic drugs and migraine. Some hallucinations are elementary, (i.e. the patient sees light, colors or simple geometrical forms). These kinds of hallucinations often occur in occipital lobe epilepsy. Complex visual hallucination and delusions, such as those experienced by Muhammad, occur in temporal lobe seizures and other neurological disorders like Parkinson's disease and Creutzfeldt–Jakob disease. These hallucinations are usually vivid images of animals, humans or mythical creatures such as angels and jinns.[177] They can be accompanied with auditory, gustatory, olfactory and even somatosensory hallucinations. The somatosensory and kinesthetic hallucinations are mostly associated with temporal lobe seizures. This explains Muhammad's experience in the cave Hira' where he felt that Angel Gabriel had grabbed him and squeezed him so hard until he felt such an excruciating pain in his abdomen that he thought he would die.

The research scientist Scott Atran, explains: "Sudden alterations of activity in the hippocampus and amygdala can affect auditory, vestibular, gustatory, tactile, and olfactory perceptions and lead to hallucinations involving voices or music, feelings of sway or physical suspension, the tastes of elixirs, burning or caressing, the fragrance of Heaven or the stench of Hell. For example, because the middle part of the amygdala receives fibers from the

---

[176] Sira Ibn Ishaq p. 106
[177] Often mischievous form of spirits in Arab mythology, capable of appearing in human and animal forms.

olfactory tract, direct stimulation of that part of the amygdala will flood co-occurring events with strong smells. In religious rituals, incense and fragrances stimulate the amygdala so that scent can be used to focus attention and interpretation on the surrounding events. In temporal-lobe epilepsy, the sudden electrical spiking of the area infuses other aspects of the epileptic experience with an odorous aura."[178]

Muhammad described Gabriel as having 600 wings.[179] This is hard even to imagine. Buraq, the steed upon which he took his alleged night-flight to Jerusalem and then to heavens, had a human head and the wings of an eagle. Unless one decides to believe in absurdities, it is clear that Muhammad was hallucinating.

The Egyptian Muslim scholar and historian, Haykal describes the angel as seen by Muhammad while on his visit to heavens. "The first heaven was of pure silver and the stars suspended from its vault by chains of gold;" [This shows that Muhammad had no understanding of what stars are. He envisioned them something like Christmas lights hanging from the "vault of the sky." This is consistent with Ptolemy's cosmology and was commonly believed in his time.] "and in each one an angel lay awake to prevent the demons from climbing into the holy dwelling places and the spirits from listening indiscreetly to celestial secrets." [This absurdity is stated also in the Qur'an, where it says the jinns used to stand on each other's shoulders to listen to the conversation of the "Exalted Assembly," until they were shot down by stars that were fired at them like missiles. In the old days people used to think meteorites were shooting stars.[180]]

Haykal continues: "There, Muhammad greeted Adam. And in the six other heavens the Prophet met Noah, Aaron, Moses, Abraham, David, Solomon, Idris (Enoch), Yahya (John the Baptist) and Jesus. He saw the Angel of Death, Azrail, so huge that his eyes were separated by 70,000 marching days. [This is roughly ten times longer than the distance between the Moon and the Earth] He commanded 100,000 battalions and passed his time in writing in an immense book the names of those dying or being born. He saw the Angel of Tears who wept for the sins of the world; the Angel of Vengeance with brazen face, covered with warts, who presides over the elements of fire and sits on a throne of flames; and another immense angel made up half of snow and half of fire

---

[178] Scott Atran, NeuroTheology: Brain, Science, Spirituality, Religious Experience by Chapter 10 http://jeannicod.ccsd.cnrs.fr/docs/00/05/32/82/RTF/ijn_00000110_00.rtf
[179] Bukhari:Volumne 4, Book 54, Number 455
[180] Qur'an, 72:8; 37:6-10; 63:5.

surrounded by a heavenly choir continually crying: `O God, Thou hast united snow and fire, united all Thy servants in obedience to Thy Laws. In the seventh heaven where the souls of the just resided was an angel larger than the entire world, with 70,000 heads; each head had 70,000 mouths, each mouth had 70,000 tongues and each tongue spoke in 70,000 different idioms singing endlessly the praises of the Most High.'"[181]

Muhammad possessed an extraordinary imaginative power. However his thinking was warped. Such a creature cannot even be envisioned, let alone come to the realm of existence.

- Muhammad sees an angel larger than the world, which in itself is an oxymoron.
- This angel has 70,000 heads; each head has 70,000 faces. (He has 4,900,000,000 faces)
- Each face has 70,000 mouths (He has 343,000,000,000,000 mouths)
- Each mouth has 70,000 tongues (He has 24,010,000,000,000,000,000 tongues)
- Each tongue speaks 70,000 dialects (He speaks 1,680,700,000,000,000,000,000,000 different dialects. i.e. more than 1.68 septilion idioms.

Why would Allâh need to create such a monstrosity, just to praise him endlessly in that many languages? Such a creature can only be envisioned by someone suffering from severe hallucinations. Imagine someone filling his house with lots of computers and tape recorders and programming them to praise him all the time in all the languages. Wouldn't that be insane? Allâh is the personification of Muhammad's alter ego and everything he wanted to be. Allâh's psychology reflects that of Muhammad. As a narcissist, he had an insatiable craving for praise and so does his god who was a projection of his own self.

Muhammad was a loner. In spite of his marriage to an important lady, he was not an important person in his own right and was derided by his people. His hallucinatory experiences, interpreted by his wife as the sign of prophethood, were his greatest narcissistic supplies. When those experiences stopped, he felt depressed. Vaknin says: "Depression is a big component in the narcissist's

---

[181] Muhammad Husayn Haykal (1888, 1956): The Life of Muhammad, translated by Isma'il Razi A. al-Faruqi. ISBN: 0892591374 Chapter 8: From the Violation of the Boycott to al Isra'.

emotional make-up. But it mostly has to do with the absence of narcissistic supply. It mostly has to do with nostalgia to more plentiful days, full of adoration and attention and applause... Depression is a form of aggression. Transformed, this aggression is directed at the depressed person rather than at his human environment. This regime of repressed and mutated aggression is a characteristic of both narcissism and depression... However, the narcissist, even when depressed, never forgoes his narcissism: his grandiosity, sense of entitlement, haughtiness, and lack of empathy."[182]

This explains not only the cause of Muhammad's depression and his consequent thoughts of suicide but also why he never carried those thoughts to culmination. Narcissists hardly ever commit suicide. It seems strange that Muhammad, on several occasions, would attempt suicide and that each time Gabriel would come to his rescue, but then he would attempt again. Narcissists don't commit suicide, but they talk about it to garner sympathy.

"How could a narcissist who thinks of himself as a Colossus, as an immensely important person, as the center of the universe commit suicide?" writes Agatha Christie in *Dead Man's Mirror* "He is far more likely to destroy someone else - some miserable crawling ant of a human being who had dared to cause him annoyance.... Such an act may be regarded as necessary - as sanctified! But self-destruction? The destruction of such a Self?"[183]

Unlike bipolar patients who need medication to get out of their depression, all a narcissist needs is "one dose of narcissistic supply to elevate from the depth of misery to the heights of manic euphoria," says Vaknin.[184]

Temporal Lobe Epilepsy

The first to suspect that Muhammad had epilepsy was Halima, or her husband, when Muhammad was just five years old. Theophanes,[185] (752-817) a Byzantine historian, was the first recorded scholar to claim that Muhammad suffered from epilepsy. Today, we can confirm this claim.

Temporal lobe epilepsy (TLE) was defined in 1985 by the International League Against Epilepsy (ILAE) as a condition characterized by recurrent

---

[182] /www.mental-health-matters.com/articles/article.php?artID=92
[183] *Dead Man's Mirror* by Agatha Christie - in "Hercule Poirot The Complete Short Stories" - Great Britain, HarperCollins Publishers, 1999
[184] http://samvak.tripod.com/journal71.html
[185] Theophanes, 1007, Chronographia, vol. 1, p334

unprovoked seizures originating from the medial or lateral temporal lobe. The seizures associated with TLE consist of simple partial seizures without loss of awareness (with or without aura) and complex partial seizures (i.e., with loss of awareness). The individual loses awareness during a complex partial seizure because the seizure spreads to involve both temporal lobes, which in turn causes impairment of memory.[186]

Muhammad's seizures were of both kinds. Sometimes he fell and lost consciousness and at other times he did not. One hadith reports that during the construction of the Ka'ba, before he received his prophetic intimation, Muhammad fell unconscious on the ground with both his eyes towards the sky. At the time he lost his senses.[187] This is very much an epileptic seizure.

The website emedicine.com says, "90% of patients with temporal interictal epileptiform abnormalities on their EEG have a history of seizures." We know that Muhammad had seizures since his childhood. He saw two men in white opening his chest and washing his heart with white snow. American neurosurgeon and a pioneer of brain surgery, Harvey Cushing, reports of a boy with a cystic glioma in the right temporal lobe resulted in a vivid three dimensional vision of a man dressed in white.[188] The Irish-American neurologist Robert Foster Kennedy (1884-1952) was one of the first to identify vividly real hallucinations of an audio-visual nature, localized outside of the body as being temporal lobe in origin.[189]

> Talking about his youth, Muhammad said:
> I found myself among the boys of Quraish, carrying stones such as boys play with. We had all uncovered ourselves, each taking his shirt [a cloth wrap] and putting it round his neck as he carried the stones. I was going to and fro in the same way, when an unseen figure slapped me painfully saying, 'Put your shirt on' so I took it and fastened it on me, then began to carry the stones upon my neck, wearing my shirt, alone among my fellows."[190]

It seems that Muhammad's hallucinatory companions were just as violent and abusive as he was.

---

[186] www.emedicine.com/NEURO/topic365.htm
[187] Sahih Bukhari, Volume, Book 26, Number 652
[188] Cushing: Brain 1921-1922 xliv p341
[189] Kennedy: Arch Int Med 1911 viii p317.
[190] Sirat Rasoul p. 77

Muhammad's Ecstatic Experiences

The Symptoms of Temporal Lobe Seizure

A seizure originating in the temporal lobe may be preceded by an aura or warning symptom, such as abnormal sensations, epigastric sensations (a funny feeling in the stomach), hallucinations or illusions (vision, smells, tastes, or other sensory illusions), sensation of déjà vu, recalled emotions or memories, or sudden and intense emotion not related to anything occurring at the time. All these symptoms were present during Muhammad's seizures.

The epileptic experience can be partial, during which consciousness is maintained or partial complex, resulting in the loss or reduction of consciousness during the seizure or spell. Other symptoms include abnormal head movements and forced turning of the eyes. This kind of seizure happened to Muhammad during the construction of Ka'ba.

Repetitive movements and rhythmic muscle contraction affecting one side of the body, one arm, one leg, part of the face, or other isolated area are also symptoms of TLE. Other symptoms include, abdominal pain or discomfort, nausea, sweating, flushed face, rapid heart rate/pulse and changes in vision, speech, thought, awareness and personality. Of course, sensory hallucinations (visual, hearing, touch, etc.) are major symptoms.[191]

Dr. Mogens Dam, an internationally noted Danish epileptologist and author of many books on the subject, defines simple partial seizures as follows: "Simple partial seizures with mental symptoms, which can be remembered, afterwards, have from ancient times been known as 'aura'. They are often followed by a convulsion. They are often dream-like... He thinks that he is going mad."[192] Muhammad actually did think that he was going mad. It was Khadijah who persuaded him otherwise.

Dr. Dam writes: "It has long been debated as to whether persons with epilepsy have particular personality traits, which are different from other peoples. It has particularly been singled out that people with temporal lobe epilepsy are more emotionally unstable than others, perhaps with a tendency towards aggression. Some people were said to be self-centered, they could be sensitive to the point of paranoia, and took every chance remark as a personal slight. They were described as being given to brooding over things, and were particularly interested in religious, mystic, philosophical and moral issues."[193]

---

[191] www.nlm.nih.gov/medlineplus/ency/article/001399.htm
[192] www.epilepsy.dk/Handbook/Mental-complications-uk.asp
[193] Ibid.

He firther explains that people suffering from TLE are more likely to become depressed, have suicidal thoughts and hallucinate. The person gets the feeling that he is being persecuted. His emotional contact with other people, however, is always much better than in cases of true schizophrenia. Unlike schizophrenia, TLE often resolves on its own. This must have happened to Muhammad as in later years of his life there were fewer fits of seizure. However, this did not stop him from "revealing" verses for the Qur'an as situation dictated.

There is a difference in tone, language and the structure of sentences between the early Meccan verses and the later Medinan ones. The suras written during the early phase of Muhammad's prophetic career are poetic in style. They often rhyme, and they are short and striking. They are filled with exhortations to be pious and charitable, to feed the orphans and to free the slaves, and to be patient, kind and compassionate along with plenty of warnings and promises of hell for those who would not heed to his call.

Sura 91, "The Sun," is a typical sura pertaining to this period. It talks about a fable already known to Arabs, that Allâh had sent a she-camel to warn people of Samood, who in their waywardness slaughtered this animal prophetess.

I swear by the sun and its brilliance,
And the moon when it follows the sun,
And the day when it shows it,
And the night when it draws a veil over it,
And the heaven and Him Who made it,
And the earth and Him Who extended it,
And the soul and Him Who made it perfect,
Then He inspired it to understand what is right and wrong for it;
He will indeed be successful who purifies it,
And he will indeed fail who corrupts it.
Samood gave the lie (to the truth) in their inordinacy,
When the most unfortunate of them broke forth with,
So Allâh's messenger said to them (Leave alone) Allâh's she-camel, and (give) her (to) drink.
But they called him a liar and slaughtered her; therefore their Lord crushed them for their sin and leveled them (with the ground).
And He fears not its consequence.

Muhammad's Ecstatic Experiences

Sura 113, "The Dawn," is another example of the suras written in this period.

In the name of Allâh, the Beneficent, the Merciful.
Say: I seek refuge in the Lord of the dawn,
From the evil of what He has created,
And from the evil of the utterly dark night when it comes,
And from the evil of those who blow on knots,
And from the evil of the envious when he envies.

While still in Mecca, Muhammad's ambition was limited to that town alone and its surroundings. He wrote:

Thus have We sent by inspiration to you an Arabic Qur'an: that you may warn the Mother of Cities and all around her.[194]

The Mother of Cities, *Umul Qura,* is Mecca. In other verses[195] he said that he came specifically for those who had not received a revelation from God before. According to these verses, the Jews and the Christians were not his addressees. However, as time passed his ambition grew, and eventually he demanded that everyone either submit to him or die.

The language in later suras is legalistic. It is the language of a despot setting laws and ordinances for his subjects and inciting them to conquer new lands. A. S. Tritton says, "The sentences are long and unwieldly so that the hearer has to listen carefully or he will miss the rhyme altogether; the language has become prose with rhyming words at intervals. The subject matter is laws, comments on public events, statements of policy, rebukes to those who did not see eye-to-eye with the prophet, Jews especially, and references to his domestic troubles. Here imagination is weak and stock phrases are dragged in to conceal the poverty of ideas though occasionally the earlier enthusiasm bursts out."[196]

It is also important to note that Muhammad's hallucinations were not limited to seeing the Angel Gabriel. He also claimed to have seen jinns and even Satan. On one occasion, while praying in the mosque, he started moving his

---

[194] Qur'an, 42:7. The same claim is made in Qur'an, 6:92
[195] "Nay, it is the Truth from thy Lord, that thou mayest admonish a people to whom no warner has come before thee: in order that they may receive guidance."(Qur'an 32:3) and In order that thou mayest admonish a people, whose fathers had received no admonition, and who therefore remain heedless (of the Signs of Allâh). (Qura'an, 36:6)
[196] A.S. Tritton, *Islam: Belief and Practice 1951, p. 16.*

arms as if struggling with an imaginary person. He later said, "Satan came in front of me and tried to interrupt my prayer, but Allâh gave me an upper hand on him and I choked him. No doubt, I thought of tying him to one of the pillars of the mosque till you get up in the morning and see him. Then I remembered the statement of Prophet Solomon, 'My Lord! Bestow on me a kingdom such as shall not belong to any other after me.' Then Allâh made him (Satan) return with his head down (humiliated)."[197]

In several ahadith Muhammad narrated his encounters with jinns. In one story he claimed to have spent a night in their town converting many of them to Islam. In the Qur'an there are at least 30 references to jinns.

It is important to note that Muhammad was ignorant of the Bible. Solomon was a king, not a prophet, and he never made such a statement or prayer as stated by Muhammad. He did, however, ask God for wisdom rather than riches. Muhammad here reveals his own craving for kingdom and power.

Other Symptoms of TLE

People with TLE tend to demonstrate some of these five interictal traits (*between* rather than *during* seizures).

1. **Hypergraphia**: Hypergraphia is an obsessional phenomenon manifested by writing extensive notes and diaries. Even though apparently illiterate, Muhammad composed the Qur'an, asking others to write it down for him.
2. **Hyper religiosity**: Religious beliefs not only are intense, but may also be associated with elaborate theological or cosmological theories. Patients may believe that they have special divine guidance. Muhammad obviously had an unusual degree of concern with philosophy and mysticism, which led him to invent a new religion.
3. **Clingingness**: From the stories that talk about Muhammad's attachment to his uncle, when he was a boy and from other stories we can determine that Muhammad was emotionally needy and that he was very offended when rejected or abandoned.
4. **Altered interest in sex**: Muhammad's obsession with women indicates that his interest in sex was heightened even though, as we shall see later, his abilities may have diminished or entirely disappeared in his later life.

---

[197] Sahih Bukhari *Volume 2, Book 22, Number 301.*

5. **Aggressiveness**: The intense emotions are often labile, so that the patient may exhibit great warmth at one time, whereas at another time, anger and irritability may evolve into rage and aggressive behavior. Muhammad was at times friendly, particularly to his companions, but extremely short-tempered and irritable to those whom he perceived as resisting his demands. Bukhari says: "If the Prophet disliked something, the sign of aversion would appear on his face."[198]

The Heavenly Night Journey

There are various versions of the story of Muhammad's *Mi'raj*, his alleged night journey to heaven. Ibn Ishaq has wowen together these traditions stemming from stories told by his companions, particularly his wife Aisha. According to the narrative, Muhammad reported:

> While I was asleep in the hijr, Gabriel came and stirred me with his foot. I sat up, but saw nothing and lay down again. He came a second time and stirred me with his foot. I sat up, but saw nothing and lay down again. He came to me a third time, and stirred me with his foot. I sat up, and he took hold of my arm and I stood beside him. He brought me out to the door of the mosque, and there was a white animal, half mule, half donkey, with wings on its sides with which it propelled its feet, putting down each forefoot at the limit of its sight. He mounted me on it. Then he went out with me, keeping close to me. When I came up to mount him, he shied. Gabriel placed his hand on its mane and said, Are you not ashamed, O Buraq, to behave in this way? By Allâh, none more honorable before Allâh than Muhammad has ever ridden you before. The animal was so ashamed that he broke out into a sweat, and stood so that I could mount him. [199]

The narrator continues: "The apostle and Gabriel went their way, until they arrived at the temple at Jerusalem. There he found Abraham, Moses, and Jesus among a company of the prophets. The apostle acted as their imam in prayer. Then he was brought two vessels, one containing wine and the other milk. The apostle took the milk and drank it, leaving the wine. Gabriel said, 'You have been rightly guided to the way of nature, the true primeval religion, and so will your people be, Muhammad. Wine is forbidden to you.' Then the apostle returned to Mecca, and in the morning he told Quraish what had

---

[198] Bukhari, Volume 4, Book 56, Number 763.
[199] Sira: Ishaq:182

happened. Most of them said, 'By Allâh, this is a plain absurdity! A caravan takes a month to go to Syria and a month to return. How can Muhammad do the return journey in one night?'"

Ibn Sa'd says; "Upon hearing this story many who had prayed and joined Islam became renegades and left Islam." And this Qur'anic verse was allegedly revealed in response: "We made the vision which we showed you only for a test to men."[200]

Muslim chroniclers have gone out of their way to embellish this story and give it credibility. Ibn Ishaq has added that people asked for proof and Muhammad replied that he had passed the caravan of so-and-so in such-and-such a valley, and the animal he rode scared them and a camel bolted. Then Muhammad is quoted as saying, "And I showed them where it was, as I was on the way to Syria. I carried on until, in Dajanan, a mountain near Tihama, some 25 miles from Mecca. I passed by a caravan of the Banu so-and-so. I found the people asleep. They had a jar of water covered with something. I took the covering off and drank the water, replacing the cover. The proof of that is that their caravan is this moment coming down from al-Baida' by the pass of al-Tan'im, led by a dusky camel loaded with two sacks, one black and the other multihued.' Baida is a hill near Mecca, on the Medina side. Tan'im is on the high ground near Mecca. The people hurried to the pass, and the first camel they met was as he had described. They asked the men about the vessel, and they told them that they had left it full of water and covered it, and that when they woke, it was covered but empty. They asked the others too, who were in Mecca and they said that it was quite right, they had been scared, and a camel had bolted. They had heard a man calling them to it, so that they were able recover it."

These traditions were written down more than a hundred years after the death of Muhammad. There was no way to prove the authenticity of such claims after the lapse of this much time. However, what Muslims in general have missed is that at the time that Muhammad allegedly visited the Temple in Jerusalem, there was no temple in Jerusalem. Six centuries before al-Buraq took flight, the Romans had destroyed it. By 70 A.D. not one stone stood upon another. The Temple of Solomon was built around 10th century BC, according to the Bible. The Dome of the Rock was raised on the foundations of the Roman Temple of Jupiter in 691 A.D. Al-Aqsa mosque was constructed over a Roman basilica on the southern end of the Temple Mount by the Umayyads in 710 AD. It is ironic that Muhammad sees the caravan of the tribe of so-and-so on his way

---

[200] Qur'an: Sura 13, Verse 62

120

Muhammad's Ecstatic Experiences

but fails to see that the temple, in which he claims to have been praying, actually did not exist.

Another hadith says that to test the truth of what Muhammad was claiming Abu Bakr asked him to describe Jerusalem and when he did that, Abu Bakr said 'That's true. I testify that you are the apostle of Allâh'. It is not clear whether Abu Bakr had ever been in Jerusalem. This wasn't an important town for Arabs to visit. However, it is also surprising that Abu Bakr did not say anything about the temple. These are all apocryphal stories that Muslims fabricated to give credibility to this most bizarre tale narrated by their prophet.

There is another version of this story that is probably the most reliable one because it is also ratified in the Qur'an. In this version Muhammad says:

After the completion of my business in Jerusalem, a ladder was brought to me, finer than any I have ever seen. It was that to which the dying man looks when death approaches. My companion mounted it with me, until we came to one of the gates of heaven, called the Gate of the Watchers. An angel called Isma'il was in charge of it, and under his command were twelve thousand angels, each of them having twelve thousand angels under his command.

When Gabriel brought me in, Isma'il asked who I was, and when he was told that I was Muhammad, he asked if I had been given a mission, or sent for, and on being assured of this, he wished me well.

All the angels who met me when I entered the lowest heaven smiled welcomingly and wished me well, except one who said the same things, but did not smile or show that joyful expression which the others had. And when I asked Gabriel the reason, he told me that if he had ever smiled on anyone before, or would smile on anyone hereafter, he would have smiled on me. He does not smile, because he is Malik, the Keeper of Hell. I said to Gabriel, he holding the position with regard to Allâh, which he has described to you 'obeyed there, trustworthy.' (Surah 81:21) 'Will you not order him to show me hell?' And he said, 'Certainly! O Malik, show Muhammad Hell.' Thereupon he removed its covering, and the flames blazed high into the air, until I thought that they would consume everything. So I asked Gabriel to order him to send them back to their place, which he did.

I can only compare the effect of their withdrawal to the falling of a shadow, until, when the flames retreated whence they had come, Malik placed their cover on them.

Understanding Muhammad

When I entered the lowest heaven, I saw a man sitting there, with the spirits of men passing before him. To one he would speak well and rejoice in him, saying, 'A good spirit from a good body.' Of another, he would say 'Faugh' and frown, saying: 'An evil spirit from an evil body.'

In answer to my question, Gabriel told me that this was our father Adam, reviewing the spirits of his offspring. The spirit of a believer excited his pleasure, and the spirit of an infidel excited his disgust. 'Then I saw men with lips like camels. In their hands were pieces of fire, like stones, which they used to thrust into their mouths, and they would come out of their posteriors. I was told that these were those who sinfully devoured the wealth of orphans.[201] Then I saw men in the way of the family of Pharaoh, with such bellies as I have never seen, there were passing over them, camels maddened by thirst when they were cast into hell, treading them down, they being unable to move out of the way. These were the usurers.[202]

Then I saw women hanging by their breasts. These were those who had fathered bastards on their husbands.[203]

Then I was taken to the second heaven, and there were the two maternal cousins, Jesus, son of Mary, and John, son of Zakariah. Then to the third heaven, and there was a man whose face was as the moon at the full. This was my brother Joseph, son of Jacob. Then to the fourth heaven, and there as a man called Idris. 'And we have exalted him to a lofty place.' Surah 19:58 Then to the fifth heaven, and there was a man with white hair and a long beard, never have I seen a more handsome man than he. This was the beloved among his people, Aaron, son of 'Imran. Then to the sixth heaven, and there was a dark man with a hooked nose, like the Shanu'a. This was my brother Moses, son of 'Imran. Then to the seventh heaven, and there was a man sitting on a throne at the gate of the immortal mansion, Paradise. Every day, seventy

---

[201] Some years later, when Muhammad came to power, he reduced children to orphans by killing their fathers, enslaving their mothers and taking their belongings.

[202] The allusion is to Surah 40:46, 'Cast the family of Pharaoh into the worst of all punishments

[203] Sahih Bukhari *Volume 1, Book 6, Number 301* reports Muhammad saying "I have seen that the majority of the dwellers of Hell-fire were you (women)." They asked, "Why is it so, O Allâh's Apostle ?" He replied, "You curse frequently and are ungrateful to your husbands. I have not seen anyone more deficient in intelligence and religion than you. A cautious sensible man could be led astray by some of you." The women asked, "O Allâh's Apostle! What is deficient in our intelligence and religion?" He said, "Is not the evidence of two women equal to the witness of one man?" They replied in the affirmative. He said, "This is the deficiency in her intelligence. Isn't it true that a woman can neither pray nor fast during her menses?" The women replied in the affirmative. He said, "This is the deficiency in her religion."

thousand angels went in, not to come back until the resurrection day. Never have I seen a man more like myself. This was my father, Abraham. Then he took me into Paradise, and there I saw a damsel with dark red lips and asked her to whom she belonged, for she pleased me much when I saw her, and she told me 'Zeid b. Haritha.' The apostle gave Zeid the good news about her.[204]

One tradition says that when Gabriel took Muhammad up to each of the heavens and asked permission to enter, Gabriel had to inform the guards whom he had brought, and whether his guest had received a mission or had been sent for, to which the gate keepers would respond "Allâh grant him life, brother and friend!" and let them pass until they reached the seventh heaven and there Muhammad met Allâh. There the duty of fifty prayers a day was laid upon his followers. On his return he met Moses and here is what he says happened:

On my return, I passed by Moses, and what a fine friend of yours he was! He asked me how many prayers had been laid upon me, and when I told him fifty, he said, 'Prayer is a weighty matter, and your people are weak, so go back to your Lord and ask him to reduce the number for you and your community.' I did so, and He took off ten prayers. Again I passed by Moses, and he said the same again, and so it went on, until only five prayers for the whole day and night were left. Moses again gave me same advice. I replied that I had been back to my Lord and asked him to reduce the number until I was ashamed, and I would not do it again. He of you who performs them in faith and trust will have the reward of fifty prayers.[205]

There are Muslims who say this epic did not actually happen in the physical world but it was a spiritual experience. However, the claims of Muhammad about spotting the caravan of Banu so-and-so on his way and all the details about scaring a camel or drinking water from the jar of the people on the way negate that claim. The biggest proof that this experience was claimed as actually happening in the physical realm comes from the Qur'an, which says this ascension was intended to test the faith of the believers. People are willing to buy any absurdity as long as it is labeled "spiritual" but when a claim is made to have happened in the real world, they tend to be a bit more skeptical.

---

[204] Some years later in Medina Muhammad fell in love with Zayd's wife and made his lust known. Zayd felt compelled to divorce his wife so Muhammad could marry her.
[205] Bukhari *Volume 9, Book 93, Number 608:*

Understanding Muhammad

Muhammad Was Telling the Truth (sometimes)

The Russian existential writer Fyodor Dostoyevsky, actually thought that Muhammad was telling the truth. He believed that Muhammad's experiences were real, at least to him. Dostoyevsky himself suffered from temporal lobe epilepsy. He alleged, via one of his characters, that when he had a seizure the gates of Heaven would open and he could see row upon row of angels blowing on great golden trumpets. Then two great golden doors would open and he could see a golden stairway that would lead right up to the throne of God.[206]

In an article entitled "Religion and the Brain" published in *Newsweek*, on May 7, 2001, a Canadian neuropsychology researcher explained this phenomenon as follows:

When the image of a cross, or a Torah crowned in silver, triggers a sense of religious awe, it is because the brain's visual-association area, which interprets what the eyes see and connects images to emotions and memories, has learned to link those images to that feeling. Visions that arise during prayer or ritual are also generated in the association area: electrical stimulation of the temporal lobes (which nestle along the sides of the head and house the circuits responsible for language, conceptual thinking and associations) produces visions.

Temporal-lobe epilepsy—abnormal bursts of electrical activity in these regions—takes this to extremes. Although some studies have cast doubt on the connection between temporal-lobe epilepsy and religiosity, others find that the condition seems to trigger vivid, Joan of Arc-type religious visions and voices.

Although temporal-lobe epilepsy is rare, researchers suspect that focused bursts of electrical activity called "temporal-lobe transients" may yield mystical experiences. To test this idea, Michael Persinger of Laurentian University in Canada fits a helmet jury-rigged with electromagnets onto a volunteer's head. The helmet creates a weak magnetic field, no stronger than that produced by a computer monitor. The field triggers bursts of electrical activity in the temporal lobes, Persinger finds, producing sensations that volunteers describe as supernatural or spiritual: an out-of-body experience, a sense of the divine. He suspects that religious experiences are evoked by mini electrical storms in the temporal lobes, and that such storms can be triggered

---

[206] www.emedicine.com/neuro/topic658.htm

by anxiety, personal crisis, lack of oxygen, low blood sugar and simple fatigue—suggesting a reason that some people "find God" in such moments.[207]

The Origin of Muhammad's Mystical Experiences

Is it possible to tickle the temporal lobe and induce mystical experiences such as sensing a "presence," hearing sounds, seeing lights, or even ghosts?

Michael Persinger, the neuropsychologist at Canada's Laurentian University cited above, thinks so. He has been able to demonstrate that the sensation described as "having a religious experience" is merely a side effect of our bicameral brain's feverish activities. In simple words: When the right hemisphere of the brain, the seat of emotion, is stimulated in the cerebral region presumed to control notions of self, and then the left hemisphere, the seat of language, is called upon to make sense of this nonexistent entity, the mind generates a "sensed presence."[208]

Persinger's work is further described in an article entitled "The Exorcism" by Ken Hollings, who writes:

> Persinger… argues that religious experience is created within the brain. Current studies suggest that our sense of self is produced by the left temporal lobe, located in the logical and precise hemisphere of our brains, which helps maintain the boundary between individual consciousness and the outside world. Shut that lobe down, and you feel at one with the Universe – a prime form of religious experience. Stimulate the right temporal lobe, on the creative and more emotional side of our brains, and a right hemispheric sense of self is invoked, which we tend to experience as a 'separate' entity.[209]

Persinger fitted a motorcycle helmet with solenoids emitting mild electromagnetic fields around the volunteers' temples. The volunteers were made to sit blindfolded in an empty room – "the chamber of heaven and hell" as it was jokingly called. By alternating the electrical charges, 80% of the subjects that took part in this experiment sensed "presence" of a ghostly being in the room, sometimes touching or grabbing them. Some of them said that they

---

[207] Newsweek May 7, 2001, U.S. Edition; Section: SCIENCE AND TECHNOLOGY; Religion And The Brain By Sharon Begley With Anne Underwood

[208] http://web.ionsys.com/~remedy/Persinger,%20Michael.htm

[209] Ken Hollings http://www.channel4.com/science/microsites/S/science/body/exorcism.html

smelled the fragrance of paradise or the stench of hell. They heard voices, saw dark tunnels, lights and had profound religious experiences.

Ed Conroy, also reporting on Michael Persinger's experiments writes:

> The personalities of normal people who display enhanced temporal lobe activity... display enhanced: creativity, suggestibility, memory capacity and intuitive processing. Most of them experience a rich fantasy or subjective world that fosters their adaptability. Many of them are prone to bouts of physical and mental activity followed by mild depression. These people have more frequent experiences of a sense of presence during which time 'an entity is felt and sometimes seen'; exotic beliefs rather than traditional religious concepts are endorsed.[210]

Persinger has found out that different subjects label this ghostly perception with the names that are familiar to them. Religious people experience the holy personalities of their faith - Elijah, Jesus, the Virgin Mary, Mohammad, the Sky Spirit, etc. Some subjects have emerged with Freudian interpretations - describing the presence as one's grandfather, for instance.

This method has been used also to induce near-death experiences (NDEs). Hollings writes "In 1933 Montreal neurosurgeon Wilder Penfield discovered that when he electrically stimulated certain nerve cells in the temporal lobe, the patient would 'relive' previous experiences in convincing sensory detail. In his controversial 1976 publication, *The Origin of Consciousness in the Breakdown of the Bicameral Mind*, Princeton psychologist Julian Jaynes argued that the sensation commonly described as 'having a religious experience' is merely a side effect of the feverish interactivity between the right and left halves of our brain. Our ancient ancestors, he suggested, lacked a strong enough sense of individual identity to explain such exchanges as anything but voices and visions from the gods on high."[211]

What exactly happens in that moment of intense spiritual awareness? Hollings says, "Activity in the brain's amygdala, which monitors the environment for threats and registers fear, is dampened. Parietal lobe circuits, which orient you, go quiet, while circuits in the frontal and temporal lobes, which mark time and generate self-awareness, become disengaged. Using brain-imaging data collected from Tibetan Buddhists during meditation and Franciscan nuns at prayer, Dr. Andrew Newberg of the University of

---

[210] Michael Persinger in Report on Communion by Ed Conroy
http://www.futurepundit.com/archives/000721.html
[211] Ken Hollings http://www.channel4.com/science/microsites/S/science/body/exorcism.html

Muhammad's Ecstatic Experiences

Pennsylvania observed that a bundle of neurons in the superior parietal lobe, toward the top and back of the brain, had shut down. This region also helps processes information about orientation and time."[212]

Persinger has shown that "spiritual" and "supernatural" experiences are the result of the lack of proper communication and coordination between the left and right temporal lobes. The sense of a presence in the room, an out-of-body experience, bizarre distortion of body parts, and even religious feelings are all caused in the brain. Persinger calls these experiences 'temporal lobe transients', or increases and instabilities in neuronal firing patterns in the temporal lobe.

How do these experiences produce religious states? Our "sense of self," says Persinger, "is maintained by the left hemisphere temporal cortex. Under normal brain functioning this is matched by the corresponding systems in the right hemisphere temporal cortex. When these two systems become uncoordinated, such as during a seizure or a transient event, the left hemisphere interprets the uncoordinated activity as 'another self', or a 'sensed presence', thus accounting for subjects' experiences of a 'presence' in the room (which might be interpreted as angels, demons, aliens, or ghosts), or leaving their bodies (as in near-death experiences), or even 'God'. When the amygdala (deep-seated region of the brain involved with emotion) is involved in the transient events, emotional factors significantly enhance the experience which, when connected to spiritual themes, can be a powerful force for intense religious feelings."[213]

Brain Stimulation Creates Shadow Person

Swiss scientists have found that electrical stimulation of the brain can create the sensation of a "shadow person" mimicking one's bodily movements, according to a brief report in the journal *Nature* and in an article entitled "Brain stimulation creates shadow person" appearing in the on-line science journal Physorg.com:

> Olaf Blanke and colleagues at the Federal Polytechnic School of Lausanne say their discovery might help shed light on brain processes that contribute to the symptoms of schizophrenia, which can include the sensation that one's own actions are being performed by someone else.

---

[212] Ibid
[213] How We Believe, 2000, Michael Shermer p.66

Doctors evaluating a woman with no history of psychiatric problems found stimulation of an area of her brain called the left temporoparietal junction caused her to believe a person was standing behind her.

The patient reported that "person" adopted the same bodily positions as her, although she didn't recognize the effect as an illusion. At one point in the investigation, the patient was asked to lean forward and clasp her knees: this led to a sensation that the shadow figure was embracing her, which she described as unpleasant.

The finding could be a step towards understanding psychiatric affects such as feelings of paranoia, persecution and alien control, say neuroscientists.

The discovery is reported in a Brief Communication in this week's issue of the journal Nature.[214]

Could these findings explain what Muhammad heard, saw and felt during his epiphanic experiences? Muhammad came from a culture that believed in jinns, angels, ghouls and demons and these were the creatures that he saw in his hallucinations. The dispute about whether there is one God, as the Jews, the Christians and the Hanifis[215] believed, or whether there are many gods, as Muhammad's clan thought, was an ongoing debate. Muhammad sided with the more "exotic" belief of monotheism, instead of the traditional religious concept endorsed by his own people. It is also important not to undermine the influence that Khadijah exerted on him in interpreting his hallucinatory experiences.

What Muhammad experienced was real to him, but it was only mental. When he relayed his story to Khadijah, all she could think of was that her beloved husband had either become possessed by demons or had been touched by angels. So when Muhammad told her "I fear that something may happen to me", she replied, "Never! Allâh will never disgrace you."[216] Since she could not accept that Muhammad had gone mad, she was left with the only alternative that she could think of and therefore she concluded that he must have been chosen to be a prophet. If it had not been for Khadijah's unconditional support and encouragement, Muhammad might have continued thinking that he had become

---

[214] www.physorg.com/news77992285.html, published 17:31 EST, September 20, 2006, copyright 2006 by United Press International, accessed June 21, 2007
[215] a pre-Islamic monotheistic sect propagated in Arabia to which Khadijah belonged
[216] Bukhari *Volume 1, Book 1, Number 3*

possessed, and he might have to grasp the reality of his condition as most epileptics do.

Camel Kneeling Under the Power of Revelation

Muslims often exaggerate and attribute false miracles to Muhammad. This is quite normal for cultists who are fond of attributing miracles to their leaders. One hadith claims that one day when Muhammad was on a camel and a revelation descended on him, the weight of the revelation was so great that the camel could not withstand it and had to kneel down on the ground.

Kneeling down by the animal at the time that Muhammad was allegedly having a revelation could have had something to do with what Muhammad was experiencing and could be another indication that he was epileptic.

Bonnie Beaver, an expert in animal behavior at the College of Veterinary Medicine at Texas A&M University, says "Dogs and cats have been known to alert some people when a seizure is about to begin. It's common for animals to sense a seizure in their owners, and some dogs can even be trained to warn a person of an impending seizure."[217]

The ability to predict seizure is not restricted to dogs and cats alone. Animals seem to have sensory perceptions that we humans don't have or may have lost. Animals can sense when an earthquake is coming, hours before it actually happens. Many animals - especially horses and cattle - can sense a thunderstorm before it occurs.

On January 4, 2005, Mayann Mott wrote in an article for The National Geographic News:

> Before giant waves slammed into Sri Lanka and India coastlines ten days ago, wild and domestic animals seemed to know what was about to happen and fled to safety. According to eyewitness accounts, elephants screamed and ran for higher ground, dogs refused to go outdoors, flamingos abandoned their low-lying breeding areas and zoo animals rushed into their shelters and could not be enticed to come back out. The belief that wild and domestic animals possess a sixth sense—and know in advance when the earth is going to shake—has been around for centuries.[218]

---

[217] http://www.tamu.edu/univrel/aggiedaily/news/stories/04/070104-3.html
[218] National Geographic: "Did Animals Sense Tsunami Was Coming?"
http://news.nationalgeographic.com/news/2005/01/0104_050104_tsunami_animals.html

The point is that animals are known to perceive things, especially pending epilepsy in their owners that humans can't. It is not unusual for an animal to become distressed and behave erratically when his owner is about to have a fit of seizure. We know that neither Muhammad's wives nor his companions were affected or sensed anything when he was receiving "revelations." During one of his hallucinations Muhammad told Aisha, "This is Gabriel. He sends his greetings and salutations to you. Aisha replied, 'Salutations and greetings to him.' Then addressing the Prophet she said, 'You see what I don't see.'"[219] So if only a camel could feel what was happening to Muhammad, it is another clue that what he was experiencing was a seizure.

The Case of Phil K. Dick

Case studies of other epileptic sufferers can give us a better understanding of what may have happened to Muhammad. The similarities are often astounding.

The American science fiction writer Philip Kindred Dick (1928-1982), speaking of his own strange visions to Charles Platt said, "I experienced an invasion of my mind by a transcendentally rational mind, as if I had been insane all my life and suddenly I had become sane."[220] All Dick's works start with the basic assumption that there cannot be one single, objective reality. Charles Platt describes Dick's novels. "Everything is a matter of perception. The ground is liable to shift under your feet. A protagonist may find himself living out another person's dream, or he may enter a drug-induced state that actually makes better sense than the real world, or he may cross into a different universe completely."[221]

Like Muhammad, Dick was also paranoid, emotionally infantile, narcissistic, had suicidal thoughts and resentful of his parents. He imagined that plots against him were being perpetrated by the KGB or FBI, and that they were constantly laying traps for him. We sense the same kind of paranoia in the writings of Muhammad who constantly talked about the unbelievers and how they were plotting against him, opposing his religion and persecuting him and his followers. VALIS, the first of Dick's three final autobiographical novels,[222] is

---

[219] Bukhari:Volume4, Book 54, Number 440
[220] [220] Platt, Charles. (1980). *Dream Makers: The Uncommon People Who Write Science Fiction.* Berkley Publishing. ISBN 0-425-04668-0
[221] Ibid
[222] The others are *Divine Invasion* and *The Transmigration of Timothy Archer.*

a fool's search for God, who turns out to be a virus, a joke, and a mental hologram transmitted from an orbiting satellite.

The proponent of the novel is thrust into a theological quest when he receives communion in a burst of pink laser light and turns out to have a direct link with God. In this work, Dick examines his own supposed encounters with a divine presence.

VALIS is an acronym for *Vast Active Living Intelligence System*. He theorizes that VALIS is both a "reality generator" and a means of extraterrestrial communication.

Lawrence Sutin, in *Divine Invasions: A Life of Philip K. Dick* writes about one of Dick's mystical experiences that eerily resemble those of Muhammad.

> Monday night he called me and said that the night before, he'd been smoking some marijuana that a visitor had left, and felt himself entering that by-now-familiar state in which he had visions (generally not dope-related), and he said, 'I want to see God. Let me see you.' And then instantly, he told me, he was flattened by the most extreme terror he'd ever felt, and he saw the Ark of the Covenant, and a voice said, 'You wouldn't come to me through logical evidence or faith or anything else, so I must convince you this way.' The curtain of the Ark was drawn back, and he saw, apparently, a void and a triangle with an eye in it, staring straight at him. Phil said he was on his hands and knees, in absolute terror, enduring the Beatific Vision from nine o'clock Sunday evening until five o'clock Monday morning. He said he was certain he was dying, and if he could have reached the telephone he'd have called the paramedics. The Voice told him, in effect, 'You've managed to talk yourself into disbelieving everything else. I let you see, but this you'll never be able to forget or adapt or misrepresent.'[223]

Dick, who died prematurely at the age of 54, wrote millions of words. His biographer Sutin quotes one of his writings in which he explains his mystical experience:

> God manifested himself to me as the infinite void; but it was not the abyss, it was the vault of heaven, with blue sky and wisps of white clouds. He was not some foreign God but the God of my fathers. He was loving and kind and he had personality. He said, 'You suffer a little now in life; it is little compared with the great joys, the bliss that awaits you. Do you think I in my theodicy would allow you

---

[223] *Divine Invasion , A Life of Philip K. Dick* by Lawrence Sutin, p.264, published _____

to suffer greatly in proportion to your reward?' He made me aware, then of the bliss that would come; it was infinite and sweet. He said, 'I am the infinite. I will show you. Where I am, infinity is; where infinity is, there I am... They reckon ill who leave me out; When me they fly I am the wings. I am the doubter and the doubt.'[224]

Other Cases of TLE

On October 23, 2001 PBS television aired a documentary on TLE. One of the persons interviewed was a man with temporal lobe epilepsy, John Sharon. Also present at the interview were Sharon's father and V. S. Ramachandran, a neurologist with the University of California-San Diego. It is interesting to read his case and compare it to what we know about Muhammad. This could shed more light on the Prophet's state of mind and his illness.

John Sharon: The seizures involve my person and my soul and my spirit, all of it. When I get one of those feelings my whole body just tingles and I just, oh...that's that.

Narrator: John's epileptic seizures are essentially an electrical storm in his temporal lobes when a group of neurons starts firing at random, out of sync with rest of his brain.

Recently John experienced one of his worst episodes to date. He'd gone out to the desert with a girlfriend, and they'd both got very drunk, with disastrous results. John was suddenly hit by a volley of seizures, each one lasted about five minutes and involved violent convulsions that left him unconscious. Eventually, John managed to get a call through to his father who drove out to the desert to bring him home.

John Sharon: On the way home, him and I got just into some philosophical questions about everything. And I just would not shut up once I...on the way home I was going and going. It was like I was wired.

John Sharon, Sr.: It's basically an earthquake within the body, and like any earthquake there are aftershocks. And like any earthquake that does damage, things have to be rebuilt. Things have to subside. Mainly what I deal with is the aftermath, particularly with this last episode. It was very much like stepping into a Salvador Dali painting. Instantly everything was surreal. And that's, in essence, what his seizures are all about – the aftermath – where it puts his brain, where it puts his memory, where it puts his mind, his thinking ability, everything else.

---

[224] Ibid. p.269

Muhammad's Ecstatic Experiences

Narrator: When John's seizures came to an end he was exhausted but he felt omnipotent.

John Sharon: I went running down the streets screaming that I was God. And then this guy came out and I just, like, pelvic thrust at him and his wife, and I was like, "You want to f–ing bet, I ain't God?"

John Sharon Sr.: And I said, literally, 'You asshole, get back in here! What do you think you're doing? You're disturbing the neighbors. They're gonna call the cops. What is this all about?'

John Sharon: I kind of just looked at him, cool and calm, and apologized to him, and like, 'No. No one's going to call the police.' Like, I didn't say this last part, but I'm thinking to myself, 'No one's going to call the police on God!'

Narrator: John had never been religious, yet the onset of his seizures brought on overwhelming spiritual feelings.

Vilayanur S. Ramachandran is Director of the Center for Brain and Cognition and professor with the Psychology Department and the Neurosciences Program at the University of California, San Diego. He has done extensive studies on Temporal Lobe Epilepsy.

V.S. Ramachandran: It has been known for a long time that some patients with seizures originating in the temporal lobes have intense religious auras, intense experience of God visiting them. Sometimes it's a personal god, sometimes it's a more diffuse feeling of being one with the cosmos. Everything seems suffused with meaning. The patient will say, "Finally I see what it's really about, Doctor. I really understand God. I understand my place in the universe, in the cosmic scheme." Why does this happen and why does it happen so often in patients with temporal lobe seizures?

John Sharon: Oh my God. And you know what? I am so right in my own head, I know I could go out there and get people to follow me. Not like these whackos with sheets on their heads, not like those idiots...but now it's just the new generation of the prophets. And were all the prophets people who were flopping around on the ground, is that what this whole message was, the gift from the gods, this whole time?

V.S. Ramachandran: That's possible, isn't it? Yes?

John Sharon: I've never been religious, ever. People say, "No, you can't see into the future...unh unh." That's what that gift is, but you've got to pay for it by getting slammed around.

V.S. Ramachandran: Now, why do these patients have intense religious experiences when they have these seizures? And why do they become preoccupied with theological and religious matters even in between seizures?

One possibility is that the seizure activity in the temporal lobes somehow creates all kinds of odd, strange emotions in the person's mind...in the person's brain. And this welling up of bizarre emotions may be interpreted by the patient as visits from another world, or as, "God is visiting me." Maybe that's the only way he can make sense of this welter of strange emotions going on in his brain. Another possibility is that this is something to do with the way in which the temporal lobes are wired up to deal with the world emotionally. As we walk around and interact with the world, you need some way of determining what's important, what's emotionally salient and what's relevant to you versus something trivial and unimportant.

How does this come about? We think what's critical is the connection between the sensory areas in the temporal lobes and the amygdala, which is the gateway to the emotional centers in the brain. The strength of these connections is what determines how emotionally salient something is. And therefore, you could speak of a sort of emotional salience landscape, with hills and valleys corresponding to what's important and what's not important. And each of us has a slightly different emotional salience landscape. Now, consider what happens in temporal lobe epilepsy when you have repeated seizures. What might be going on is an indiscriminate strengthening of all these pathways. It's a bit like water flowing down rivulets along the cliff surface. When it rains repeatedly there's an increasing tendency for the water to make furrows along one pathway and this progressive deepening of the furrows artificially raises the emotional significance of some categories of inputs. So instead of just finding lions and tigers and mothers emotionally salient, he finds everything deeply salient. For example, a grain of sand, a piece of driftwood, seaweed, all of this becomes imbued with deep significance. Now, this tendency to ascribe cosmic significance to everything around you might be akin to what we call a mystical experience or a religious experience.

There is no specific area in the temporal lobe concerned with God. But it's possible there are parts of the temporal lobes whose activity is somehow conducive to religious belief. Now this seems unlikely, but it might be true. Now, why might we have neural machinery in the temporal lobes for belief in religion? Well belief in religion is widespread. Every tribe, every society has some form of religious worship. And maybe the reason it evolved, if it did evolve, is that it is conducive to the stability of society, and this may be easiest if you believe in some sort of supreme being. And that may be one reason why religious sentiments evolved in the brain.[225]

---

[225] www.pbs.org/wgbh/nova/transcripts/2812mind.html

Muhammad's Ecstatic Experiences

History is full of charismatic religious figures. Psychologist William James (1842 – 1910) believed the apostle Paul's new found voice of conscience on his way to Damascus may have been "a physiological nerve storm or discharging lesion like that of epilepsy." He saw lights and heard a voice asking him "Saul, Saul, why do you persecute me?"[226] He was then temporarily blinded and then converted. St. Paul talked about his visions in the following words:

> To keep me from becoming conceited because of these surpassingly great revelations, there was given me a thorn in my flesh, a messenger of Satan, to torment me. Three times I pleaded with the Lord to take it away from me. But he said to me, 'My grace is sufficient for you, for my power is made perfect in weakness.'[227]

Another famous case concerns a 16th-century nun known as Santa Teresa of Avila (1515 -1582). She experienced vivid visions, intense headaches and fainting spells, followed by "such peace, calm, and good fruits in the soul, and ... a perception of the greatness of God"[228] Biographers suggest that she may well have experienced epileptic seizures.[229]

LaPlante says that painters and writers like Vincent van Gogh, Gustave Flaubert, Lewis Carroll, Marcel Proust, Tennyson and Fyodor Dostoyevsky all had TLE. The TLE sufferers often undergo patterns of personality changes, typically including compulsive writing or drawing and hyper-religiosity.

According to LaPlante, Muhammad also suffered from TLE. More recent examples are *Joseph Smith*, the founder of Mormonism, and *Ellen White*, the founders of the Seventh Day Adventist Movement, who at the age of 9 suffered a brain injury that totally changed her personality. She also began to have powerful religious visions.

Helen Schucman, the atheist Jewish psychologist who claimed receiving messages from Jesus Christ in the form of "readings" that she called *A Course in Miracles*, was most probably a sufferer of TLE. Reportedly, Schucman spent the last two years of her life in a terrible, paranoid depression.

Syed Ali Muhammad Bab the founder of the Babi religion may also have been an epileptic sufferer. His Persian Bayan (translated into English and available online) can be defined as classical "epileptic writing."

---

[226] Acts 9:1-9.

[227] 2 Corinthians 12:7-9

[228] Theresa, Saint of Avila (1930) Interior castle. London: Thomas Baker p. 171.

[229] Sackville-West 1943, The Eagle and the Dove : a Study in Contrasts - St Teresa of Avila, St Therese of Lisieux

Other Famous People with Epilepsy

Heidi Hansen and Leif Bork Hansen who allege that *Søren Kierkegaard* wrote in his journal that he suffered from TLE and had kept it a secret all his life, quote him as saying: "Of all sufferings there is perhaps none so martyring as to become an object of pity, nothing which so tempts one to rebel against God. People usually regard such a person as stupid and shallow, but it would not be difficult to show that precisely this is the hidden secret in the lives of many of the most eminent world-historical figures."[230]

The Danish philosopher was absolutely right. Far from being stupid, the TLE sufferers are among the geniuses.

Temporal Lobe Epilepsy can well be defined as the disease of creativity. Many famous and talented people in the history suffered from TLE and arguably they owed their creativity to this disease. Between five to ten persons in every 1,000 people have TLE. Not all of them, of course, reach fame.

Steven C. Schachter, M.D., professor of neurology at Harvard Medical School and author of several books on epilepsy, has compiled a list of prominent people in history who possibly suffered from TLE. This list comprises philosophers, writers, world leaders, religious figures, painters, poets, composers, actors and other celebrities.

"Ancient people" writes Schachter, "thought epileptic seizures were caused by evil spirits or demons that had invaded a person's body. Priests attempted to cure people with epilepsy by driving the demons out of them with magic and prayers. This superstition was challenged by ancient physicians like Atreya of India and later Hippocrates of Greece, both of whom recognized a seizure as a dysfunction of the brain and not a supernatural event." He further says, "Epileptic seizures have a power and symbolism which, historically, have suggested a relationship with creativity or unusual leadership abilities. Scholars have long been fascinated by evidence that prominent prophets and other holy men, political leaders, philosophers, and many who achieved greatness in the arts and sciences, suffered from epilepsy."[231]

Aristotle, who was the first to connect epilepsy to genius, claimed that Socrates had epilepsy. Schachter notes that Dr. Jerome Engel, professor of

---

[230] www.utas.edu.au/docs/humsoc/kierkegaard/docs/Kierkepilepsy.pdf

[231] Epilepsy.com, "Famous People with Epilepsy", at www.epilepsy.com/epilepsy/famous.html , Topic Editor: Steven C. Schachter, M.D., Last Reviewed 12/15/06, accessed June 21, 2007

neurology at the University of California School of Medicine, considers the co-existence of epilepsy and genius to be a coincidence.[232]

However, Schachter continues: "Others disagree, claiming to have found an association between epilepsy and giftedness in some people. Eve LaPlante in her book *Seized,* writes that the abnormal brain activity found in temporal lobe (complex partial) epilepsy plays a role in creative thinking and the making of art. Neuropsychologist Dr. Paul Spiers maintains: 'Sometimes the same things that cause epilepsy result in giftedness. If you damage an area [of the brain] early enough in life, the corresponding area on the other side has a chance to overdevelop.'"[233]

This is an interesting theory. If Spiers is right, it is not the TLE that brings forth genius and creativity but the reaction of the brain to compensate for what it damages.

The following is a short list of some of the geniuses who Schachter believes may have had epileptic seizures.

Harriet Tubman: the black woman who led hundreds of her fellow slaves from the American South to freedom in Canada. She came to be known as the "Moses" of her people.

Saint Paul: the greatest Christian evangelist without whom Christianity would probably never have reached Europe to become a World Religion.

Joan of Arc: the young uneducated farmer's daughter in a remote village of medieval France who altered the course of history through her amazing military victories. From age thirteen Joan reported ecstatic moments in which she saw flashes of light, heard voices of saints and saw visions of angels.

Alfred Nobel: the Swedish chemist and industrialist who invented dynamite and financed the Nobel Prize.

Dante: the author of *La Divina Comedia*;

Sir Walter Scott: one of the foremost literary figures of the romantic period; the 18th century.

Jonathan Swift: English satirist, author of *Gulliver's Travels.*

Edgar Allan Poe: the nineteenth century American author.

Lord Byron, Percy Bysshe Shelley, and *Alfred Lord Tennyson:* three of the greatest English Romantic poets,

Charles Dickens: the Victorian author of such classic books as *A Christmas Carol* and *Oliver Twist.*

---

[232] Dr. Jerome Engel, *Seizures and Epilepsy:*, F. A. Davis Co., Philadelphia, 1989.
[233] www.epilepsy.com/epilepsy/famous.html

Understanding Muhammad

Lewis Carroll: the author of *Alice's Adventures in Wonderland* who may have been writing about his own temporal lobe seizures. The sensation initiating Alice's adventures- that of falling down a hole is a typical one to many people with seizures.

Fyodor Dostoyevsky, the great Russian novelist, author of such classics as *Crime and Punishment* and *The Brothers Karamazov*, who is considered by many to have brought the Western novel to the peak of its possibilities.

Muhammad probably had his first seizure at age five. Dostoyevsky had his first seizure at age nine. After a remission, which lasted up to age 25, he had seizures every few days or months, fluctuating between good and bad periods. His ecstatic auras occurring seconds before his bigger seizures were moments of transcendent happiness, which then changed to an anguished feeling of dread. His experiences were similar to those of Muhammad, whose vision of hell was dreadful, filled with doom and horrendous scenes of torture. Here are a couple of examples of what Muhammad saw:

> But those who deny for them will be cut out a garment of Fire: over their heads will be poured out boiling water. With it will be scalded what is within their bodies as well as (their) skins. In addition there will be maces of iron (to punish) them. Every time they wish to get away therefrom from anguish they will be forced back therein and (it will be said), 'Taste ye the Penalty of Burning!' (Q. 22: 19-22)

> But those, whose balance is light, will be those who have lost their souls; in Hell will they abide. The fire will burn their faces, and they will therein grin, with their lips displaced. (Q. 23: 103-104)

Dostoyevsky also saw a blinding flash of light. Then he would cry out and lose consciousness for a second or two. Sometimes the epileptic discharge generalized across his brain, producing a secondary tonic-clonic (grand mal) seizure. Afterward he could not recall events and conversations that had occurred during the seizure, and he often felt depressed, guilty and irritable for days.

Count Leo Tolstoy: The great nineteenth century Russian author of *Anna Karenina* and *War and Peace*, also may have had epilepsy.

Gustave Flaubert: is another great name in literature. This nineteenth century French literary genius wrote such masterpieces as *Madame Bovary* and *A Sentimental Education*. According to Schachter, "Flaubert's typical seizure began with a feeling of impending doom, after which he felt his sense of self

Muhammad's Ecstatic Experiences

grow insecure, as if he had been transported into another dimension. He wrote that his seizures arrived as 'a whirlpool of ideas and images in my poor brain, during which it seemed that my consciousness sank like a vessel in a storm.' He moaned, had a rush of memories, saw fiery hallucinations, foamed at the mouth, moved his right arm automatically, fell into a trance of about ten minutes, and vomited."

Dame Agatha Christie: the leading British writer of mystery novels is also reported to have had epilepsy.

Truman Capote: American author of *In Cold Blood* and *Breakfast at Tiffany's.*

George Frederick Handel: the famous baroque composer of the *Messiah.*

Niccolo Paganini: one of the greatest violinists.

Peter Tchaikovsky: The eminent Russian composer of the ballets *Sleeping Beauty* and *The Nutcracker.*

Ludwig van Beethoven: One of the greatest classical composers ever.

Schachter says, "This is just a sampling of the many, many famous people whose epilepsy has been recorded by historians." In fact the list of famous people diagnosed or suspected for having epilepsy is long. Muhammad is not among bad company. His imaginative power, his depression, his suicidal thoughts, his irritability, his interest in religion, his vision of the Doomsday and the afterlife, his visual and auditory hallucinations and many of his physical and psychological characteristics can all be explained by TLE.

However, epilepsy does not explain Muhammad's ruthlessness, his mass murders and his dogged determination. Those were the results of his pathological narcissistic disorder. It was this combination of personality and mental disorders that made him the phenomenon that he had become. Muhammad harbored thoughts of grandiosity and omnipotence. His epileptic visions reaffirmed his megalomania and gave him the confirmation that he was indeed the chosen prophet of God. As if that were not enough, he married a codependent woman who sought her own greatness in lionizing her husband.

Muhammad was convinced of his prophetic mission. It was this self-assurance that inspired those who were close to him and confirmed their faiths in him. This does not mean that all the verses of the Qur'an have been "revealed" to him during his epileptic trances. The seizures probably stopped in his later years. However, convinced of his righteousness, he kept reciting verses as situation dictated. As a narcissist, he received his confirmation from those who believed in him. It is difficult to say who was fooling whom. Muhammad was convinced of his claim – even though he freely lied, making up verses as he needed them – and yet, when people believed in him he was reconfirmed. As a result, he thought to be vested with divine authority to exact punishment on those who disagreed with him. He was the voice of God and opposition to him meant opposition to the Almighty. He felt entitled to lie. If he lied, it was for a good cause and therefore justified. When he looted and massacred innocent people, he did it with a clear conscience. The end was so august that all means to achieve it were deemed legitimate by him. He was so convinced of his hallucinations, it felt right to kill anyone who stood in his way. The following Qura'nic verses are self-explanatory.

And whoever disobeys Allâh and His Messenger and goes beyond His limits, He will cause him to enter fire to abide in it, and he shall have an abasing chastisement. (Q.4:14)

On that day will those who disbelieve and disobey the Messenger desire that the earth were leveled with them, and they shall not hide any word from Allâh. (Q.4:42)

Whoever disobeys Allâh and His Messenger surely he shall have the fire of hell to abide therein for a long time. (Q. 72:23)

Sexuality, Religious Experience and Temporal Lobe Hyper Activation

The ahadith shed a lot of light into Muhammad's sexual conduct. Does TLE affect sexuality as well? If it does and if it can explain Muhammad's sexual habits, then we have one more piece of evidence that he suffered from TLE. Neuroscientist Rhawn Joseph thinks it does. He writes:

A not uncommon characteristic of high levels of limbic system and inferior temporal lobe activity are changes in sexuality as well as a deepening of religious fervor. It is noteworthy that not just modern day evangelists, but many ancient religious leaders, including Abraham, Jacob and Muhammad, tended to be highly sexual and partook of many partners, or had sex with other men's wives, or killed other men in order to steal their wives (Muhammad, King David)... Many of the prophets and other religious figures also displayed evidence of the Kluver-Bucy syndrome, such as

Muhammad's Ecstatic Experiences

eating dung (Ezekiel),[234] as well as temporal lobe, limbic hyper activation and epilepsy, coupled with hallucinations, catalepsy, insanity, or language disorders.

Whereas Moses suffered from a severe speech impediment, Muhammad, Allâh's messenger, was apparently dyslexic and agraphic. [A cerebral disorder characterized by total or partial inability to write] Moreover, in order to receive the word of God, Muhammad would typically lose consciousness and enter into trance states (Armstrong 1994; Lings 1983). In fact, he had his first truly spiritual-religious conversion when he was torn from his sleep by the archangel Gabriel who enveloped him in a terrifying embrace so overpowering that Muhammad's breath was squeezed from his lungs. After squeezing and suffocating him repeatedly Gabriel ordered Muhammad to speak the word of God, i.e. the Qur'an. This was the first of many such episodes with the archangel Gabriel who sometimes appeared to Muhammad in a titanic kaleidoscopic panoramic form.

In accordance with the voice of 'God' or his angels, Muhammad not only spoke but he began reciting and chanting various themes of God in a random order over the course of the following 23 years; an experience he found quite painful and wrenching (Armstrong 1994; Lings 1983). In addition to his religious zest, Muhammad was reported to have the sexual prowess of forty men, and to have bedded at least 9 wives and numerous concubines including even one young girl (Lings 1983). On one occasion, after being rebuffed, he went into a trance, and then claimed 'God' had commanded that another man's wife become his wife.

He [Muhammad] was also known to fly into extreme rages and to kill (or at least order killed) infidels and merchants and those who opposed him. These behaviors when coupled with his increased sexuality, heightened religious fervor, trance states, mood swings, and possible auditory and visual hallucinations of a titanic angel, certainly point to the limbic system and inferior temporal lobe as the possible neurological foundation for these experiences. Indeed, Muhammad also suffered from horrible depressions and on one occasion sought to throw himself from a cliff – only to be stopped by the archangel Gabriel.[235]

---

[234] Muhammad prescribed camel urine for stomachache. He certainly must have drauk it himself. Camel urine is sold in Islamic countries as remedy, even today.
[235] The Limbic System And The Soul From: Zygon, the Journal of Religon and Science (in press, March, 2001) by Rhawn Joseph, Ph.D. http://brainmind.com/BrainReligion.html

Understanding Muhammad

It is a common belief that Muhammad had the sexual strength of several men. This belief is based on various ahadith. One hadith that is attributed to Salma, a maid of Muhammad who said: "One night all nine wives of the Prophet (pbuh) who were with him until his death (Muhammad had other wives whom he divorced) were in his presence. The Prophet slept with all of them. When he finished with each one, he used to ask me to bring water so he could perform ablution. I asked, oh messenger of Allâh, isn't one ablution enough? He responded this is better and cleaner."[236]

However, my research has led me to conclude that the claim of Muhammad's virility is hogwash, and that in fact in the last decade or two of his life he was actually impotent. Muhammad had an insatiable libido, which he tried to satisfy by fondling his wives and concubines, without being able to engage in complete intercourse.

Research in the University of Utrecht, in the Netherlands suggests that endogenous opioids, the so-called feel-good chemicals produced by the brain, may increase sexual appetite and diminish sexual performance.[237] In another study, researchers observed higher opioid activity during the mania phase in unmediated bipolar patients.[238] As a narcissist, Muhammad was subject to huge mood swings. Sometimes he was euphoric and full of energy while at other times he suffered from depression to the point of contemplating suicide. These findings explain why he had such a high libido yet, despite numerous young sexual partners, remained childless. This is an indication that he was unable to perform sexually.

However, there was a hole in my theory. If Muhammad was impotent in his later years, as I came to believe, how could he father Ibrahim when he was already sixty or older? Ibrahim was born to Mariyah a beautiful white Coptic slave girl with curly hairs, whom Muhammad's other wives envied and disliked. I suspected that the child could have belonged to someone else, but had no evidence to prove it. Then I found it.

I came across a story reported by Ibn Sa'd, who said there was a Coptic man who used to visit Mariyah in Medina, where rumor had circulated that he was her lover. Mariyah had been relocated to a garden to the North of Medina;

---

[236] Tabaqat Volume 8, Page 201
[237] W. R. Van Furth, I. G. Wolterink-Donselaar and J. M. van Ree. Department of Pharmacology, Rudolf Magnus Institute, University of Utrecht, The Netherlands
http://ajpregu.physiology.org/cgi/content/abstract/266/2/R606
[238]
www.ncbi.nlm.nih.gov/entrez/query.fcgi?cmd=Retrieve&db=PubMed&list_uids=6271019&dopt=A bstract

142

Muhammad's Ecstatic Experiences

apparently this was because Muhammad's other wives were at odds with her. The rumor reached Muhammad who dispatched Ali to kill that Coptic man. The man, upon seeing Ali coming towards him, immediately lifted up his garment and Ali saw that he had no genital (awrat) and spared his life.[239]

This was a convenient alibi to silence the crowd. Aisha was also accused of having an affair with Safwan, a young man from Medina, which caused some uproar. She denied the charge and later claimed that Safwan was a eunuch.

Tabari also mentions this Coptic man:

> The Messenger of God also had a eunuch called Mabur, who was presented to him by al-Muqawqis with two slave girls, one of them was called Mariyah, whom he took as a concubine, and the other [was called] Sirin, whom he gave to Hassan b. Thabit after Safwan b. al-Mu'attal had committed an offense against him. Sirin gave birth to a son called 'Abd al-Rahman b. Hassan. Al-Muqawqis had sent this eunuch with the two slave girls in order to escort them and guard them on their way [to Medina]. He presented them to the Messenger of God when they arrived. It is said that he was the one [with whom] Mariyah was accused of [wrongdoing], and that the Messenger of God sent 'Ali to kill him. When he saw 'Ali and what he intended to do with him, he uncovered himself until it became evident to 'Ali that he was completely castrated, not having anything left at all of what men [normally] have, so [Ali] refrained from killing him.[240]

The story of the Coptic man exposing his *awrat* to prove his innocence is clearly a fabrication. Why would the messenger of God want to kill an innocent man; and, further, how would this man know the reason Ali wanted to kill him?

In another tradition Mabur is said to have been extremely old. This is also an attempt to cast doubt in the mind of the reader. Why would al-Muqawiqis send an old man as a gift or even to protect two young women during the long journey?

To further cover up this affair and the embarrassment that generally accompanied such stories—particularly in patriarchal male chauvinistic societies where honor-killing is still in vogue—Muhammad reportedly claimed that when Ibrahim was born, Angel Gabriel had given him the confirmation that he was the father by saluting him "*Assalamo Alaikum ya aba Ibrahim*," (Peace to you o father of Ibrahim). This hadith may also be of a later-day forgery, fabricated to

---

[239] Tabaqat,. Volume 8, Page 224
[240] The History of Al-Tabari: The Last years of the Prophet, translated and annotated by Ismail K. Poonawala [State University of New York Press (SUNY), Albany 1990], Volume IX, p. 147

put an end to the rumors. Why the need for such confirmation? Doesn't this tell us that Muhammmad was suspicious and the story of Gabriel calling him aba Ibrahim was to stop the gossip? The trick probably worked. Muhammad himself, being a narcissist, was also a master of self-deception. He often believed anything he wanted to believe. He was reported crying for the death of Ibrahim, who died when 16 months old.

However, despite the fact that Mariyah was the only woman who bore Muhammad a son when he was past sixty, and was probably more beautiful than all his other wives, Muhammad did not marry her.

Ibn Sa'd narrates that when Ibrahim was born, Muhammad took him to Aisha and told her, "look how he looks like me." Aisha responded, "I see no resemblance in him." Muhammad said, "Don't you see his white and chubby cheeks?" Aisha then responded, "All the newborn children who drink milk have chubby cheeks."[241]

The claim that Muhammad had the sexual strength of forty men is a lie, intentionally concocted to cover up the fact that he was actually impotent. Muhammad had seven children by Khadijah, who was already forty when he married her. These children were conceived when he was between 25 to 35 years old. And yet, none of his young wives and concubines, who numbered more than twenty, bore him any child during the last ten years of his life.

"Erectile dysfunction with intact libido in men with epilepsy has been known to researchers since the 1950s," says Henri Jean Pascal Gastaut, French neurologist (1915-1995).[242] And Pritchard postulates that hyperprolactinemia resulting from CP seizures contributes to male sexual dysfunction in epilepsy.[243]

We read earlier that Muhammad imagined having sex when in reality he did not. There is also a hadith that shows he did not have intercourse with his wives but only "fondled" them. He would visit them, sometimes all of them in one night, engaging in foreplay but not in intercourse. Aisha is reported to have said, "None of you have the self-control of the Prophet for he could fondle his wives but not have intercourse"[244] Aisha was only a child. She probably did not know that her illustrious aging husband was not exercising self-control but simply could not do it. In another place she has said, "I never looked or saw the

---

[241] Tabaqat Volume I, page 125
[242] Gastaut H: So-called psychomotor and temporal epilepsy: a critical study. Epilepsia 1953; 2: 59-76.
[243] Pritchard P: Hyposexuality: a complication of complex partial epilepsy. Trans Am Neurol Assoc 1980; 105: 193-5.
[244] Sahih Bukhari *Volume 1, Book 6, Number 299.*

awrat (genitalia) of the Prophet."[245] I leave this to the imagination of the reader to decide why.

This does not mean that Muhammad did not have a lot of sexual craving. He would not miss any opportunity to solicit sex. His insatiable desire for sex only reveals that despite so many women in his harem, he was actually sex-starved. There is a hadith that says when he raided the town of Bani Jaun, a young girl called Jauniyya accompanied by her wet nurse was brought to him. The Prophet said to her, "Give me yourself as a gift." (In today's parlance: Let me have sex with you.) The girl responded, "Can a princess give herself to an ordinary man?" Muhammad then raised his hand to strike her, when she exclaimed, "I seek refuge with Allâh from you," [246] and Muhammad stoped. He apparently was overcome by momentary guilt and ordered one of his followers to give the girl two white linen dresses. It is obvious that Muhammad and his marauding gang had not brought those dresses along as gifts for their victims but those were the dresses stolen from this very girl.

Jauniyya must have been a child to have a wet nurse. The fact that she responded to a man who had the power to kill her in such an audacious way, "would a princess give herself to an ordinary man?" also makes one believe that she was only a child.

Muhammad asks this girl to "give herself to him" the word "marriage" in parenthesis is inserted by the translator. The actual word used is "habba." Which means gift and in this context it means free sex. When a women *habba* herself to a man it means she goes to bed with him for a one night stand, as we call it today. The word '*habba*' is never used for marriage.

Muhammad raises his hand to, "pat her so that she might become tranquil." Why did she need to be calmed? Obviously what Muhammad said was offensive and this girl was outraged.

Why she exclaims "I seek refuge with Allah from you?" If all Muhammad was doing was gently patting her, seeking refuge with Allah from him was not necessary. It is clear that Muhammad was not trying to "pat" her but to hit her.

When this girl exclaims in fear, "I seek refuge with Allah from you" Muhammad stops his hand in midair and does not strike her. He is then overcome by guilt and gives two of her stolen dresses back to her.

---

[245] Tabaqat Volume 1, page 368
[246] Bukhari Volume 7, Book 63, Number 182:

Understanding Muhammad

The story is clear to any sensible person who does not want to be fooled. One has to read between the lines when reading the stories of Muhammad written by his followers who did their best to portray a fiend as a holy man.

All this talk about Muhammad being impotent is speculation, you could say, but here is one hadith that leaves no doubt about the fact that Muhammad was impotent. Ibn Sa'd quotes his teacher Waqidi, who said: "The prophet of Allâh used to say that I was among those who have little strength for intercourse. Then Allâh sent me a pot with cooked meat. After I ate from it, I found strength any time I wanted to do the work."[247]

This is the confession from the mouth of the horse. Now it is up to you to decide whether to believe the fairy tale that Allâh was so concerned about his favorite prophet's sexual vagaries that he sent him a pot of meat to cure his impotence, or to conclude that our megalomaniac male chauvinist prophet—like most Arabs, who consider sexual power the symbol of their manhood and constantly boast about it—was just gasconading and trying to hide his impotence. Can't God cure people directly, through his own power? Why would he need a pot of meat? Meat of what animal has such a curing effect?

In another hadith Muhammad says, "Gabriel brought me a small pot of food. I ate from that food and gained the sexual strength of forty men."[248]

This tale, like many other stories in the hadith, is fabricated to conceal the fact that Muhammad was sexually inept. A narcissist with such a monumental ego could not possibly be seen as impotent.

Many secrets of Muhammad's life can be unveiled if one reads between the lines of his biography. Curiously, on the day that Ibrahim died, Muhammad went to the mosque and after praying delivered a sermon on, of all topics, adultery and the punishment awaiting adulterers. He exclaimed from the pulpit:

> O followers of Muhammad! By Allah! There is none who has more ghaira than Allah [read Muhammad] as He has forbidden that His slaves, male or female commit adultery (illegal sexual intercourse). O followers of Muhammad! By Allah! If you knew that which I know you would laugh little and weep much.[249]

Ghaira is one's sense of shame and his honor. One's *ghaira* is offended when something or someone that is *mahram* (sacred) to him is violated. For example, if you touch a Muslim's wife, sister or daughter, or if she flirts with

---

[247] Tabaqat Volume 8, Page 200
[248] Ibid.
[249] Bukhari, *Volume 2, Book 18, Number 154:*

you, his *ghaira* becomes injured. Consequently, he must retaliate in order to restore his honor. If he has a lot of *ghaira*, he may even kill you or kill his own female kin. Only then his honor can be restored. One who does not retaliate, is one who has no *ghaira* or sense shame.

Note that Muhammad is talking about Allah's *ghaira*. If Allah does not have a female relative how can his *ghaira* become offended? It is not hard to see that Muhammad identified himself with Allah. He was talking about his own *ghaira*. He was suspicious of Mariyah and it is for her that he is delivering this fiery and completely inappropriate sermon about the chastisement of adulterers during her child's funeral. Allah was his own alter ego. Then to add more emphasis he said:

> I have been shown the Hellfire (now) and I never saw a worse and horrible sight than the sight I have seen today.[250]

Obsessive-Compulsive Disorder (OCD)

Clinically, the sufferer of TLE is often diagnosed as having a variety of psychiatric illnesses, including schizophrenia and bipolar disorder due to the wide variety of symptoms including irritability. However, there is enough indication to suspect that Muhammad also suffered from obsessive-compulsive disorder.

According to Canadian Mental Health Association, obsessive-compulsive disorder is an anxiety disorder - one of a group of medical disorders which affects the thoughts, behavior, emotions and sensations.

> Collectively, these disorders are among the most common of mental health problems. It is estimated that 1 in 10 people suffers from an anxiety disorder sometime in their life... For people with obsessive-compulsive disorder, obsession creates a maze of persistent thoughts. Those thoughts lead them to act out rituals (compulsions), sometimes for hours a day... Worries and doubts, superstitions and rituals are common to most everyone. OCD occurs when worries become obsessions and the compulsive rituals so excessive that they dominate a person's life. It is as if the brain is a scratched vinyl record, forever skipping at the same groove and repeating one fragment of song.

---

[250] Bukhari, *Volume 1, Book 8, Number 423:*

Obsessions are persistent ideas, thoughts, impulses or images; they are intrusive and illogical. Common OCD obsessions revolve around contamination, doubts and disturbing sexual or religious thoughts... Often, a person's obsessions are accompanied by feelings of fear, disgust and doubt, or the belief that certain activities have to be done just so... People with OCD try to relieve their obsessions by performing compulsive rituals, over and over again, and often according to certain "rules."

Children with OCD appear to be more likely to have additional psychiatric problems. They may suffer from conditions such as panic disorder or social phobia, depression, learning disorders, tic disorders, disruptive behavior disorders and body dysmorphic disorder (imagined ugliness).[251]

Based on the above definition it is likely that Muhammad suffered from this anxiety disorder as well. He was obsessed with rituals, such as how to perform ablution; how many times to pray and how it should be performed. He explained in minute details how to wash one's face, nose, ears hands, etc, and in which order. All these rituals are meaningless, but to him they were significant. The only way one can understand this is that he suffered from OCD. OCD sufferers are obsessed with patterns and numbers. They may prefer odd numbers or even numbers. Mohammad was obsessed with the number three. There are many rituals that Muslims are required to do three times. There is no logical explanation for that except for the fact that it is a sunna of Muhammad.

The following are the rituals that one must perform before praying:
- Declare the intention that the act is for the purpose of worship.
- Rinse out the mouth with water three times
- Cleanse the nostrils by sniffing water in to them three times.
- Wash the whole face three times.
- Wash the right arm three times up to the far end of the elbow and then do the same with the left arm.
- Wipe the whole head or any part of it with a wet hand once.
- Wipe the inner sides of the ears with the forefingers and their outer sides with the thumbs. This should be done with wet fingers.
- Wipe around the neck with wet hands.
- Wash the two feet up to the ankles three times beginning with the right foot.

---

[251] http://www.cmha.ca/bins/content_page.asp?cid=3-94-95

Muhammad's Ecstatic Experiences

What is the meaning of washing three times? What is the point of wiping one's head, neck or feet with wet hand? Why wash the right hand first? These are pointless rituals that have nothing to do with cleanliness or spirituality.

Muhammad's obsession with rituals becomes further evident through what is known as *tayammum*. When water is not available, or for any reason it cannot be used he prescribed *tayammum*. This is performed as follows:

- Strike both hands slightly on earth or sand or stone.
- Shake the hands off and wipe the face with them once in the same way as done in the ablution.
- Strike the hands again and wipe the right arm to the elbow with the left hand and the left arm with the right hand.

These rules are absurd. The same can be said about positions for performing prayer, such as *qiyaam* (standing), *sujud* (prostrating), *ruku'* (bowing) and *jalsa* (sitting). Islam is full of rules that reveal Muhammad's obsession with patterns and numbers and betray his OCD.

Aisha narrated a story about Muhammad getting up in the middle of the night and going to the cemetery to perform prayer.

When it was my turn for Allah's Messenger (may peace be upon him) to spend the night with me, he turned his side, put on his mantle and took off his shoes and placed them near his feet, and spread the corner of his shawl on his bed and then lay down till he thought that I had gone to sleep. He took hold of his mantle slowly and put on the shoes slowly, and opened the door and went out and then closed it lightly. I covered my head, put on my veil and tightened my waist wrapper, and then went out following his steps till he reached Baqi' (cemetery). He stood there and he stood for a long time. He then lifted his hands three times, and then returned and I also returned. He hastened his steps and I also hastened my steps. He ran and I too ran. He came (to the house) and I also came (to the house). I, however, preceded him and I entered (the house), and as I lay down in the bed, he (the Holy Prophet) entered the (house), and said: Why is it, O 'A'isha, that you are out of breath? I said: There is nothing. He said: Tell me or the Subtle and the Aware would inform me. I said: Messenger of Allah, may my father and mother be ransom for you, and then I told him (the whole story). He said: Was it the darkness (of your shadow) that I saw in front of me? I said: Yes. He struck me on the chest which caused me pain, and then said: Did you think that Allah and His Apostle would deal unjustly with you? She said: Whatsoever the people conceal, Allah will know it. He said: Gabriel came to me when you saw me. He called me and he concealed it from you. I responded to his call, but I too concealed it from you (for he did not come to you), as you were not fully dressed. I thought that you had gone to sleep, and I did not like to awaken you, fearing that you may be frightened. He (Gabriel) said: Your Lord has commanded you to go to the inhabitants of Baqi' (to those lying in the graves) and beg pardon for them. I said: Messenger of Allah, how should I pray for them (How should I beg forgiveness for them)? He said: Say, Peace be upon the inhabitants of this city (graveyard) from among the Believers and the Muslims, and may Allah have mercy on those who have gone ahead of us, and those who come later on, and we shall, God willing, join you.[252]

Allah must be insane for ordering his prophet to go to the cemetery in the middle of the night to ask forgiveness from him for the dead people. Can't he forgive them without inconveniencing his prophet it in such odd hours? Ironically, Muhammad's companions misinterpreted his strange behaviors that are indication of his psychopathology as proof of his sincerity.

In a hadith Muhammad admonishes his followers to "Save your heels from the fire"[253] by wiping them with wet hand. It was not cleanliness that concerned Muhammad, but the ritual itself. He thought one can save himself from hellfire by passing wet hand over one's feet or even socks. Bukhari reports a hadith where Muhammad wiped his feet while wearing socks:

Narrated Al-Mughira bin Shu'ba: 'I was in the company of Allah's Apostle on one of the journeys and he went out to answer the call of nature (and after he finished) I poured water and he performed ablution; he washed his face, forearms and passed his wet hand over his head and over the two Khuff, (leather socks).'[254]

In another hadith Bukhari quotes Humran, (the slave of 'Othman):
I saw 'Othman bin 'Affan asking for a tumbler of water (and when it was brought) he poured water over his hands and washed them thrice and then put his right hand in the water container and rinsed his mouth, washed his nose by putting water in it and then blowing it out. Then he washed his face and forearms up to the elbows thrice, passed his wet hands over his head and washed his feet up to the ankles thrice. Then he said, "Allah's Apostle said 'If anyone Performs ablution like that of mine and offers a two-rak'at prayer during which he does not think of anything else (not

---

[252] Sahih Muslim Book 4, Number 2127
[253] Bukhari Volume 1, Book 3, Number 57
[254] Bukhari Volume 1, Book 4, Number 182

related to the present prayer) then his past sins will be forgiven.'" [Then he added] "I heard the Prophet saying, 'If a man performs ablution perfectly and then offers the compulsory congregational prayer, Allah will forgive his sins committed between that (prayer) and the (next) prayer till he offers it.[255]

This is unreasonable. Only one suffering from obsessive-compulsive disorder can think that one's sins can be forgiven by performing certain rituals. Compulsions are defined by repetitive behaviors or mental acts that the person is driven to perform according to rules that must be applied rigidly, and by behaviors or mental acts that are aimed at preventing or reducing distress or preventing some dreaded event or situation, such as hell.

Islam is full of meaningless rules and rituals. The rules of *vodoo* (ablusion), *ghosl* (bathing), obligatory prayer and the very fact that it is obligatory, hajj, fasting, etc. are all indications that Muhammad was obsessed with rules. He even said how many pebbles one must use to clean oneself after excreting. (They must be odd numbers. Three pebbles clean better than four.)

Schizophrenia

Muhammad may have also suffered from schizophrenia. The following symptoms of schizophrenia could be traced in Muhammad:

- Delusions, false personal beliefs held with conviction in spite of reason or evidence to the contrary, not explained by that person's cultural context
- Hallucinations, perceptions (can be sound, sight, touch, smell, or taste) that occur in the absence of an actual external stimulus. Auditory hallucinations, those of voice or other sounds, are the most common type of hallucinations in schizophrenia
- Disorganized thoughts and behaviors
- Disorganized speech
- Violent or Aggressive Behavior
- Restlessness
- Catatonic behavior, in which the affected person's body may be rigid and the person may be unresponsive.[256]

---

[255] Bukhari Volume 1, Book 4, Number 161:

[256] www.emedicinehealth.com/schizophrenia/article_em.htm

Muhammad's disorganized thoughts can be ascertained through the Qur'an. He was also violent and restless. In just ten years, he fought more than seventy wars, all in the form of raids. As for his catatonic behavior, a syndrome seen most frequently in schizophrenia, characterized by muscular rigidity and mental stupor, it is enough to quote Ali, who said, "When he walked he would lift his feet with vigor, as if walking up a slope. When he turned towards a person he would turn with his entire body."[257]

Bipolar Disorder:

Muhammad may have also been a manic-depressive (a more popular name for bipolar disorder). Bipolar disorder causes dramatic mood swings—from overly "high" and/or irritable to sad and hopeless, and then back again, often with periods of normal mood in between. The periods of highs and lows are called episodes of mania and depression. Extreme mood swings punctuated by periods of even-keeled behavior characterize this disorder.

The symptoms of BD are: in the manic phase irritability, inflated self-esteem, decreased need for sleep, increased energy, racing thoughts, feelings of invulnerability, poor judgment, heightened sex drive, and denial that anything is wrong, or in the depressed phase, feelings of hopelessness or worthlessness, or melancholy, fatigue, thoughts of death or suicide, and suicide attempts.

Ibn Sa'd reports a hadith that could be interpreted as a symptom of bipolar disorder. He writes: "Sometimes the Prophet used to fast so much, as if he did not want to end it, and sometimes he would not fast for so long that one thought he did not want to fast at all."[258]

Based on these findings, it is clear that Muhammad was most likely suffering from a variety of mental and personality disorders. According to Occam's razor, one should not make more assumptions than the minimum needed to explain anything. If TLE and NPD can explain the conduct and the epiphany of Muhammad, why resort to metaphysical, hocus-pocus, and unsubstantiated mystical explanations? Now we have scientific evidence that Muhammad was mentally ill, something his contemporaries already knew. Alas, they succumbed to his brute force and their voices were silenced.

---

[257] The Book of Merits (manaqib) in Sunan Imam at-Tirmidhi.
www.naqshbandi.asn.au/description.htm
[258] Tabaqat, Volume 1, Page 371

Muhammad's Ecstatic Experiences

It is ironic that over a billion people should cling to an insane man as their prophet and try to emulate him in every way. It is no wonder that the Muslim world is languishing. The actions of Muslims can only be defined as insane. It is because they have a mentally disturbed man as their role-model and guide. When sane people follow insane people they become insane too. This is perhaps, the greatest tragedy of all times. An insanity of such a colossal magnitude is a real abomination.

The Mystery of the Cave Hira

One friend, while proof reading this book made an interesting comment about the Oracles of Delphi, which may explain why Muhammad received his prophetic intimation in a cave.

The Oracle of Delphi was an ancient Greek temple site. People came from all over Europe to call on the Pythia at Mount Parnassus to have their questions about the future answered. The Pythia, a role filled by different women was the medium through which the god Apollo spoke.

Plutarch, a priest at the Temple of Apollo, attributed Pythia's prophetic powers to vapors that came from a chasm in the ground. A recent study of the area in the vicinity of the shrine is causing archaeologists to revisit the notion that intoxicating fumes loosened the lips of the Pythia. [259]

The study, reported in the August 2001 issue of *National Geology,* reveals that two faults intersect directly below the Delphic temple. The study also found evidence of hallucinogenic gases rising from a nearby spring and preserved within the temple rock.

"Plutarch made the right observation. Indeed there were gases that came through the fractures," says Jelle De Boer, a geologist at Wesleyan University in Middletown, Connecticut, and co-author of the study. One of the gases was ethylene that he found in the spring water near the site of the Delphi temple. Ethylene has a sweet smell and produces a narcotic effect described as a floating or disembodied euphoria.

Diane Harris-Cline, a classics professor at The George Washington University in Washington, D.C. believes that Ethylene is a serious contender for explaining the trance and behavior of Pythia. "Combined with social

---

[259] John Roach for National Geographic News August 14, 2001
http://news.nationalgeographic.com/news/2001/08/0814_delphioracle.html

expectations, a woman in a confined space could be induced to spout off oracles," she said. [260]

According to traditional explanations, the Pythia derived her prophecies in a small, enclosed chamber in the basement of the temple. De Boer believes that if the Pythia went to the chamber once a month, as tradition says, she could have been exposed to concentrations of the narcotic gas that were strong enough to induce a trance-like state.

Mentally ill people frequently self-medicate with alcohol and drugs. It is also likely that the cave contained euphoric gasses, which made him want to spend most of his time there.

Although Muhammad had several epileptic trances since his childhood, we must not discard the possibility that Cave Hira may have tapped hallucinogenic vapors that triggered his visions. "If ethylene in mild doses causes euphoria, this could explain why Muhammad was so keen to spend days on end in the caves," my friend remarked. "It certainly is peculiar behavior, especially for a married man with small children, to take off with several days' provision of food, just to stay in a cave! But if something in the caves made him feel euphoric, it seems a little less mysterious," she observed.

Cave Hira is no more than 3.5 meter by 1.5 meter in length and width, respectively - the size of a small bathroom. If God is omnipresent, why would Muhammad be so interested in this particular cave?

Apart from toxic gases, fungi and microbial agents present in caves and other enclosed spaces can also affect the brain. The "curse of the Pharaohs," turned out to be largely caused by a deadly fungus growing in the pyramids.

Concentration of vapors in caves fluctuates. It depends on earthquakes that keep Earth's narcotic juices flowing. The possibility that Cave Hira may have been contaminated when Muhammad used to spend days therein alone should not be discarded.

---

[260] ibid.

Chapter Four

Muhammad's Physical Ailment

hysically, Muhammad was a sick man. In his youth, he must have been handsome to Khadijah, a becoming woman herself. However in the last years of his life he acquired odd features his companions found strange. Anas narrated, "The Prophet had big hands and feet, and I have not seen anybody like him, neither before nor after him, and his palms were soft."[261]

In addition to his hands and feet, many of his facial features also grew out of proportion. Imam at-Tirmidhi,[262] in the *Book of Merits* (manaqib), has collected several ahadith that describe Muhammad's physical characteristics. A review of them may provide us with clues about his state of health and ailments. His followers have gone out of their way to describe him superlatively – praising his radiance, saying how his beauty surpassed that of the moon, or how everyone stood in awe of his moonlike beauty and awe inspiring presence, etc. These are subjective descriptions and of little scientific or factual value and I

---

[261] Bukhari Volume 7, Book 72, Number 793

[262] Abū ʿĪsā Muhammad ibn ʿĪsā ibn Mūsā ibn ad-Dahhāk as-Sulamī at-Tirmidhī (824-892) was a collector of hadith. His collection, Sunan al-Tirmidhi, is one of the six canonical hadith compilations used in Sunni Islam. The following hadiths are from his collections.

will not quote them. In the footnote I quote some of his followers' more objective description of him.[263]

The following is a list of what we can learn about Muhammad's physical traits from the hadith:

- heavy and thick fleshy hands and feet
- wide and doughlike palms
- large head
- large bones and joints
- wide chest, large upper back and shoulder-joints
- long forearms
- long thick fingers and toes

---

[263] Ali narrates: "The Prophet was neither tall nor short. He has thick-set fingers and toes. He had a large head and joints. He had a long line of thin chest-to-lower-navel hair. When he walked he would literally lean forward, as if descending from a higher place to a lower one. I never saw anyone like him before of after him. He was large of head and beard."
In another hadith the same narrator says: "He was of medium stature. His hair was slightly waved. There was roundness in his face. He was fair with redness in his complexion. His eyes were very black and his eyelashes very long. He had a large back and shoulder-joints. He had thick-set fingers and toes. When he walked he would lift his feet with vigor, as if walking up a slope. When he turned towards a person he would turn with his entire body. His neck seemed (smooth and shiny) like that of a statue molded in silver. His body was stout and muscular, of equal belly and chest (barbell like). He was wide-shouldered, big- jointed. When he disrobed his limbs emanated light (oily skin). There was hair on his arms, shoulders, and upper torso. His forearms were long, his palms wide, his fingers and toes thick-set and extended. His feet were so smooth that water rolled off them."
Hind ibn Abi Hala, has also reported: "The Prophet... had a large head. His hair was wavy. He had a rosy complexion, a wide forehead, arched dense eyebrows that did not meet in the middle. Between them there was a vein which thickened when he was angry. He had an aquiline nose touched with a light that raised it so that at first sight it seemed higher than it was. He had a thick, dense beard, expanded, not elevated cheeks, a strong mouth with a gap between his front teeth. His neck seemed smooth and shiny like that of a statue molded in silver. His body was well-proportioned, stout and muscular, of equal belly and chest. He was wide-shouldered, big- jointed. His forearms were long, his palms wide, his fingers and toes thick-set and extended. The middle of his soles rose moderately from the ground. His feet were so smooth that water rolled off them.
When he walked he lifted his feet with vigor, leaned slightly forward, and tread gently on the ground. When he turned (to look), he turned his whole body. His gaze was lowered and he looked at the ground more often than he looked at the sky. He glanced at things rather than stared."
A hadith from another companion of Muhammad, Jabir ibn Samura reports: The Prophet had a wide mouth and wide eyes.
Ibn Abbas, a cousin of Muhammad has claimed: "The Prophet's two front teeth were spaced in between."
Again Ali has said: "His hands and feet were heavy and thick [but not calloused]. He had a large head, large bones. When he walked, he leant forward as if descending a slope. He was white skinned, having a reddish tinge. His joints were large as was his upper back (Taken from Tabaqat V. Also published in livingislam.org)
Bukhari also has written that Muhammad's feet and legs were swollen. [Bukhari Volume 2, Book 21, Number 230]

Muhammad's Physical Ailments

- long, aquiline fleshy nose that looked upturned
- wide mouth and thick lips
- large eyes
- spaced teeth
- long silvery neck
- luster on his skin (looked oily)
- thick beard and hair, dense protruding eyebrows
- walked leaning forward as if ascending a slope (stiffness)
- walked briskly (restlessness)
- difficulty moving the neck and turned with full torso (catatonic behavior)
- had white skin with a reddish tinge
- sweating
- peculiar smell that he masked with excessive perfume
- snored like a camel
- suffered from head-ache (performed cupping to alleviate it)
- In later years he was impotent
- lips moved involuntarily
- was shy and prudish

These are all symptoms of acromegaly. Acromegaly is a rare endocrine syndrome characterized by mesenchymal hyperplasia (abnormal multiplication of cells that are capable of developing into connective tissues) caused by excessive secretion of pituitary gland. Its manifestation is usually extremely insidious, as it precociously develops with coetaneous alterations, (changes occurring at the same time), making the skin shiny and soft to the touch like dough. Overactive pituitary glands in children sometimes results in gigantism. The most common age at diagnosis for acromegaly is 40-45 years. If untreated, it can lead to severe illness and death that often occurs around the age of 60.

The main clinical aspect of this affliction is the elongation or intumescence of the cartilaginous tissue and acral bone ('*acro*' means extremity, while '*megaly*' refers to huge or gigantic). Fingers, hands and feet show an increase in size, as soft tissue begins to swell. A very characteristic case is acromegaloid facial appearance syndrome, featuring a prominent forehead, mandibular protrusion, enlarged nose, large ears, enlargement of the tongue, and abnormal largeness of the lips. Overgrowth of bone and cartilage often leads to arthritis. When tissue thickens, it may trap nerves, causing carpal tunnel syndrome, characterized by numbness and weakness of the hands. Enlargement of the jaw, increases the spacing between teeth .[264]

Other symptoms are a deepening of the voice due to enlarged sinuses and vocal cords, snoring due to upper airway obstruction, excessive sweating and skin odor fatigue and weakness headaches impaired vision and impotence in men. There may be enlargement of body organs, including the liver, spleen, kidneys and heart.[265]

In the description of Muhammad we read that he had a rosy complexion. However, several other ahadith say that when he raised his hands showing his armpits, or when riding a horse exposing a thigh, his companions noticed the whiteness of his skin. Hyper pigmentation occurs in roughly 40% of cases of acromegaly and almost always in photo exposed areas. It is probably due to the associated increase of melanotrophic hormone. That is why his face was reddish while the parts of his body not exposed to light were white.

Another symptom of acromegaly is the elevation of the dorsal-to-sole transition of the foot.[266] This too was reported in a hadith, as quoted above.

The ahadith say that Muhammad sweated excessively and had an unpleasant smell that he tried to camouflage with an abundance of perfume.

Haykal quotes a hadith from Sahih Muslim that says the scent that Muhammad used was so strong that its lingering smell would make people in the streets know that he had been there.

Jabir said: "Whoever pursues a road that has been trodden by the Messenger of Allâh, will certainly scent his smell and will be quite sure that the Messenger of Allâh has already passed it."[267]

Muhammad was also canny to use perfume prior to visiting his wives. In several ahadith Aisha says: "I applied perfume to the Messenger of Allâh and he then went round his wives."[268] He so exaggerated in the use of perfume that Aisha commented, "I used to perfume Allâh's Apostle with the best scent available till I saw the shine of the scent on his head and beard."[269]

---

[264] www.scielo.br/scielo.php?pid=S0365-05962004000400010&script=sci_arttext&tlng=en
[265] http://endocrine.niddk.nih.gov/pubs/acro/acro.htm
[266] www.scielo.br/scielo.php?pid=S0365-05962004000400010&script=sci_arttext&tlng=en
[267] Muhammad Husayn Haykal (1888, 1956): The Life of Muhammad, http://www.witness-pioneer.org/vil/Books/SM_tsn/ch7s12.html
[268] Sahih Muslim Book 007, Number 2700
[269] Volume 7, Book 72, Number 806

Muhammad's Physical Ailments

Muhammad is reported to have confessed, "Made beloved to me from your world are women and perfume."[270] One of his companions, Al-Hasan al-Basri, also wrote: "The Messenger of God said, "The only two things I cherish of the life of this world are women and perfume."[271] (Very down to earth!)

Another version of this tradition narrated by Aisha says, "The Prophet of God liked three things of this world: Perfume, women, and food; he had the [first] two, but missed food."[272] It is not that Muhammad could not afford food. He had the wealth of thousands of people whom he had vanquished. The fact is that excessive appetite is yet another symptom of acromegaly.[273]

This excessive preoccupation with perfume hints at the fact that Muhammad was wary of his bad odor and did his best to mask it. Another symptom of acromegaly is headache, which Muhammad tried to alleviate with cupping.[274]

> The Prophet was cupped on his head for an ailment he was suffering from while he was in a state of Ihram (dresses for hajj) at a water place called Lahl Jamal. Ibn 'Abbas further said: Allâh's Apostle was cupped on his head for unilateral headache while he was in a state of Ihram.[275]

Acromegaly causes high blood pressure and poor blood circulation in extremities. This results in cold hands and feet.

> Abu Juhaifa said: "I took his hand and put it on my head and I found that it was colder than ice and better scented than the musk perfume." [276]

Haykal also quotes the following hadith:

---

[270] Ahmad and Nasaa`i

[271] Tabaqat, Volume 1, Page 380

[272] Ibid.

[273] Several ahadith say that Muhammad often slept hungry because he could not find enough food to eat. These are exaggerations to portray Muhammad as a long-suffering and detached prophet. How could he go hungry when he had confiscated the wealth thousands of Jews of Arabia and had hundreds of slaves, is a question that only Muslim forgerers of hadith could answer. When Muhammad migrated to Medina, he was poor. However, he soon accumulated a lot of wealth through pillaging.

[274] The ancient process of drawing blood from the body by scarification and the application of a cupping glass, or by the application of a cupping glass without scarification, as for relieving internal congestion. (*Random House Unabridged Dictionary, © Random House, Inc. 2006.*)

[275] Bukhari Volume 7, Book 71, Number 602

[276] Bukhari Volume 4, Book 56, Number 753

Jabir bin Samurah — who was a little child then — said: "When he wiped my cheek, I felt it was cold and scented as if it had been taken out of a shop of a perfume workshop." [Sahih Muslim 2/256]

Some people with acromegaly may have abnormal curvature of the spine from side to side and from front to back (kyphoscoliosis). This may have been the reason why Muhammad leaned forward when walking. Additionally, abnormal enlargement of the pituitary gland, located deep within the brain, may cause headaches, fatigue, visual abnormalities, and/or hormonal imbalances.

Muhammad's body was stout and muscular, of equal belly and chest. Patients with acromegaly develop a barrel chest due to changes in vertebral and costal morphology. Vertebral bodies become enlarged and elongated, whereas the intervertebral discs thicken at the cervical and lumbar levels and become thin in the thoracic region, thus resulting in development of kyphosis, an abnormal, convex curvature of the spine, with a resultant bulge at the upper back. This is why he had a large back and shoulder joints.

The costochondral junctions may even become prominent and enlarged, thus giving a typical rosary aspect. These anatomical rearrangements alter the elastic chest mechanics and markedly impair the respiratory muscle activation, which is further aggravated by muscle weakness/wasting associated with acromegaly. The difficulty in breathing causes inadequate oxygenation of the blood or hypoxemia. The patient needs to take long breaths.

Ibn Sa'd quotes a hadith from Anas, who said: "The Messenger of God used to breathe three times when he wanted to drink something and he would say, this is better, easier and tastier. Anas then said that since I learned this, I too breathe three times when drinking." Anas thought deep breathing before drinking is a Sunnah and tried to imitate his prophet even in that, when in reality this was an indication of Muhammad's shortness of breath and a symptom of his disease. This tells us to what length Muslims would go to mindlessly emulate their prophet.

There are other ahadith that reveal Muhammad suffered from shortness of breath and that as a result he spoke slowly in order to breathe in between his words. Ibn Sa'd quotes Aisha, who said:

The Messenger of Allâh did not speak as continuous and fast as you speak. His speech was intermittent and slow so anyone who listened could understand.[277] The

---

[277] Tabaqat Volume 1 page 361

Muhammad's Physical Ailments

speech of the Prophet was not like singing, but he lengthened the words and pronounced forcefully.[278]

Acromegaly may increase metabolic rate, which results in excessive sweating (hyperhidrosis), an abnormal intolerance to heat and/or an increase in the production of oil (sebum) by the sebaceous glands in the skin, resulting in abnormally oily skin. According to hadith Muhammad used to wash frequently, perhaps to get rid of the excessive oil and his odor. Five days before he died his temperature rose so high that he fainted and suffered from pain. "Pour out on me seven Qirab (water skin pots) of various water wells so that I may go out to meet people and talk to them," he bid one of his wives.

It is not unlikely that the reason Muhammad prohibited drawing his picture was because he was conscious of his facial and bodily deformities. He preferred people pay more attention to his message rather then his looks. Now under scrutiny, his message seems to be even uglier than his looks.

---

[278] Ibid. page 362

Chapter Five

Muhammad and his Cult

e are often taken aback by the level of fanaticism of Muslims. Millions of them riot, burn churches, and kill innocent people because a newspaper has published a few cartoons of Muhammad or because the Pope has quoted a medieval emperor who said violence is not compatible with the nature of God.

People generally are biased in favor of a belief system that has so many followers. They believe that the sheer size of Islam qualifies it as a religion. But is Islam really a religion?

Some say that all religions have started as cults until, with the passage of time, they gradually gained acceptance and the status of religions. However, there are certain characteristics that distinguish cults from religions. Dr. Janja Lalich and Dr. Michael D. Langone have created a list of such traits, later published in a book co-authored by Lalich,[279] that describes cults fairly well.[280]

---

[279] Lalich, Janja and Tobias, Madeleine, Take Back Your Life: Recovering from Cults and Abusive Relationships, Bay Tree Publishing (2006), ISBN10 0972002154, ISBN 13 9780972002158.

[280] Published at ICSA (International Cultic Studies Association) website, Janja Lalich, PH.D. & Michael D. Langone, Ph.D., www.csj.org/infoserv_cult101/checklis.htm, accessed June 21, 2007.

The more a group or a doctrine has these characteristics the more it must follow that it should be defined and labeled as cult. The following characteristics make up that list, and I have compared Islam to them, point by point.

1. The group displays excessively zealous and unquestioning commitment to its leader and (whether he is alive or dead) regards his belief system, ideology, and practices as the Truth, as law.

   Muslims are extremely zealous about their faith and have an unquestioning commitment to their prophet, whose book, the Qur'an, is Truth and Law for them.

2. Questioning, doubt, and dissent are discouraged or even punished.

   Muslims are prohibited to question or doubt the basic tenets of their faith, and dissent is punishable by death.

3. Mind-altering practices (such as meditation, chanting, speaking in tongues, denunciation sessions, and debilitating work routines) are used in excess and serve to suppress doubts about the group and its leader(s).

   Five times during the day Muslims stop whatever they are doing and stand for a repetitive and ritualistic prayer and chant the Qur'an. In addition, for one whole month in the year they must fast and abstain from drinking or eating, from dawn to dusk, a practice that can be particularly taxing in summertime. The preoccupation with performing these rituals and the fear of failing them or doubting their relevance is so intense that believers will never entertain any doubts about them or any of the tenets of Islam.

4. The leadership dictates, sometimes in great detail, how members should think, act, and feel. For example, members must get permission to date, change jobs, marry— or leaders prescribe what types of clothes to wear, where to live, whether or not to have children, how to discipline children, and so forth.

   Every detail of the life of a Muslim is prescribed. He is told what is *haram* (forbidden) and what is *halal* (permitted), what food to eat, with what hand eat it and which fingers to lick, how to dress, how to shave, how to brush your teeth, what rituals to perform in order to pray, how to respond to the call of nature and why you should avoid passing wind (because it will annul your prayer). A Muslim is not allowed to date. Marriages are arranged. Corporal punishment, including torture for disobedience to the authorities, is prescribed both for children and for adults.

5. The group is elitist, claiming a special, exalted status for itself, its leader(s) and members For example, the leader is considered the Messiah, a special being, an avatar—or the group and/or the leader is on a special mission to save humanity.

Muslims claim special status for their prophet, while they vilify all other religions, including Christianity and Judaism which they claim to respect. The Isa and the Musa of the Qura'n are not the same as Jesus and Moses of the Bible. At the same time they can become extremely violent if their prophet is slighted. They regard themselves as superior to everyone else by virtue of their "superior faith." When in non-Muslim countries, they constantly lobby for concessions and preferential treatment. By doing this, they are frequently granted exceptions that would be unattainable to members of other religions— For instance in being bestowed the privilege of having a special room set aside in publicly funded schools so that the Muslim students can pray there. In Ontario, Muslims pressured to make Islamic law (Sharia) recognized and binding, so that they could bypass Canadian law. This attempt was defeated, thanks largely to the tireless opposition of ex-Muslims.

6. The group has a polarized us-versus-them mentality, which may cause conflict with the wider society.

Muslims have a very strong us-versus-them mentality. They call all non-Muslims, regardless of faith, *kafir*, an expressly derogatory term, which means one who blasphemes God. For them, the world is forever divided into Dar al Salam (House of Peace) and Dar al Harb (House of War). The non-Muslim countries are the House of War. It is the duty of every Muslim to wage jihad in the House of War, and to fight, kill and subdue non-Muslims and convert that land into the House of Peace. Peace, according to Islam, can only be attained by subduing non-Muslims and making them subordinate to Islamic rule. The idea is not so much to convert everyone to Islam, but to make Islam dominant. The non-Muslims can continue practicing their religion, but only as *dhimmis*, a term which means "protected" and is only applied to Christians and Jews. The Christians and the Jews (the people of the Book) will be protected, provided they pay the protection tax, known as the *jizyah*, and feel themselves humiliated and subdued, as stated in the Qur'an.[281] If they fail to pay the *jizyah*, they can be exiled or put to death. This is how the Mafia operates. If you own a business, you could be harassed or even killed, unless you pay them a protection fee to be left alone. As for those unbelievers who are not "protected" (i.e., the pagans, the atheists, the animists, etc.), they must either convert or be killed.

7.   The leader is not accountable to any authorities.

For Muslims, all actions of Muhammad constitute law. He cannot be held accountable for his actions. He was entitled to marry or have sex out of marriage with as many women as he wished. He could raid civilians, kill unarmed men, loot their properties and take their women and children as slaves and even rape them. He could assassinate his critics and torture them to make them reveal where they hid their treasures. He could have sex with children. He could lie and deceive his opponents. He could massacre his prisoners of war cold-bloodedly. None of that bothers his followers. At first they deny all of the above charges vehemently, accusing you of maligning their prophet, but once the evidence is presented, they suddenly change tactics and defend him, justifying the very evil deeds that they had outrageously denied. For Muslims, Muhammad's actions are not measured by what we humans know as right and wrong. Rather he *is* the standard, the measure of right and wrong. As the result, if a crime was committed by Muhammad, that crime becomes a holy deed and is emulated by his followers unquestioningly. Muslims are capable of committing the most atrocious acts of indecency and savagery with a clear conscience, because it is *sunnah* (performed by Muhammad).

8.   The group teaches or implies that its supposedly exalted ends justify whatever means it deems necessary. This may result in members' participating in behaviors or activities they would have considered reprehensible or unethical before joining the group (for example, lying to family or friends, or collecting money for bogus charities).

---

[281] Qur'an 9:29 Fight those who believe not in Allâh nor the Last Day, nor hold that forbidden which hath been forbidden by Allâh and His Messenger, nor acknowledge the religion of Truth, (even if they are) of the People of the Book, until they pay the Jizya with willing submission, and feel themselves subdued.

Muhammad and his Cult

In Islam, the ends always justify the means. For example, killing is wrong, but if it is done to promote Islam, it is good. Suicide is prohibited, but suicide bombing that will cause the death of non-Muslims is a holy act. Stealing from fellow Muslims is prohibited and the thief's hand will be chopped off, but looting non-believers was practiced by Muhammad. So stealing from non-Muslims is considered acceptable by Muslims. Sexual intercourse out of marriage is taboo, but rape of unbelieving women is okay. The goal, which is the establishment of the reign of Allâh on Earth, is regarded to be so lofty that everything else becomes secondary. In the history of Islam, we read that people murdered their own fathers or waged war against them. Such actions are praised as the sign of faith and devotion of the believer. Lying in Islam is prohibited, except when it is done to deceive non-Muslims and advance the interests of Islam.

9. The leadership induces feelings of shame and/or guilt in order to influence and/or control members. Often, this is done through peer pressure and subtle forms of persuasion.

Muslims' thoughts tend to be overridden with guilt. If a Muslim does something contrary to what is permitted, other Muslims are required to remind him or her of the Sharia law and demand compliance. In most Islamic countries, particularly in Iran and Saudi Arabia, it is the state that makes sure the individuals follow the religious law. In March 2002 Saudi Arabia's religious police stopped schoolgirls from leaving a blazing building because they were not wearing correct Islamic dress.[282] As a result, fifteen girls were burned alive.

10. Subservience to the leader or group requires members to cut ties with family and friends, and radically alter the personal goals and activities they had before joining the group.

Muslim converts are encouraged to cut their ties with family and friends if they are not Muslims. As mentioned in Chapter 2, I have received countless heart-rending stories from non-Muslim parents whose children converted to Islam, and as a result they have lost touch with them completely. Occasionally, they may receive a call or a cold visit; but the visit may be so restricted, so bereft of any love from their children and their Muslim spouses, that the outcome further saddens the already heartbroken parents. The purpose of these

---

[282] http://news.bbc.co.uk/1/hi/world/middle_east/1874471.stm

visits is usually to ask the parents to convert to Islam. The children leave, as soon as resistance is encountered.

11. The group is preoccupied with bringing in new members.

Muslims' main goal is to promote Islam. This practice of promoting Islam is called *da'wa*. It is the duty of every Muslim to make new converts, starting with their own family and friends. Expanding Islam is the main obsession of every Muslim.

12. The group is preoccupied with making money.

Raising funds for jihad is one of the main objectives of all Muslims. Today this is done through what are known as Islamic "charities". However, in Muhammad's time, and throughout the course of Islam, raising money for jihad was done principally by looting. Islam's main goal is to establish itself as the pre-eminent earthly power.

13. Members are expected to devote inordinate amounts of time to the group and group-related activities.

Muslims' main preoccupation is Islam. They are required to regularly go to the mosque, attend obligatory prayers five times a day, listen to the sermons, etc. So enwrapped do they become in their thinking about how to perform their religious duties, what to wear, what to eat, how to perform their prayers, etc. that they have very little time for thinking of anything else. In fact, they are even told what to and what not to think.

14. Members are encouraged or required to live and/or socialize only with other group members.

Muslims are taught to shun *kafirs* and are encouraged to socialize only with fellow Muslims. The Qur'an prohibits taking friends from among unbelievers (Q.3:28), calls them *najis* (filthy, impure) (Q.9:28) and orders harshness against them (Q.9:123). According to Muhammad, unbelievers are the "vilest animals" in the sight of God. (Q.8:55)

Muhammad and his Cult

15. The most loyal members ("the true believers") feel there can be no life outside the context of the group. They believe there is no other way to be, and often fear reprisals to themselves or others if they leave (or even consider leaving) the group.

The thought of leaving Islam is something so unbearable for true Muslims they can't even entertain it. Despite the fact that millions of Muslims have left Islam in recent years, hardcore Muslims remain adamant in believing that nobody ever really leaves Islam, and that such claims are all fabrications and part of the conspiracy to shake the faith of believers. Emails that I have received from Muslims share one common theme. They all warn me of hellfire in the afterlife. Between the fear of hell and fear of reprisal, Muslims are trapped in a web of terror of their own making.

Islam was not created to teach humans spirituality, nor make them enlightened. The spiritual message in Islam is secondary or virtually nonexistent. Piety in Islam means emulating Muhammad, a man who was far from pious. Rituals like prayers and fasting are mere window dressing to lure unbelievers inside, to give Islam the appearance of sacredness and spirituality. False prophets can deceive only in sheep clothing.

The Harder the Better

Muslims often ask: If Muhammad was such a liar, why would he create a religion that is so hard with so many restrictions? In fact, Islam is one of the hardest religions to practice. It is very demanding, with too many prohibitions, rituals, and obligations. Isn't difficulty in following a religion a deterrent?

A basic axiom of faith is one that also contains a paradox, which can be stated as follows: The more difficult a doctrine is to follow, the more inherently appealing it becomes. It is part of our psyche that we appreciate things for which we strive harder. On the other hand, we value less and give less importance to things we obtain easily or freely. Cults praise hardship and disdain the easy life. It is precisely their hardship that makes them attractive.

All cults are by nature difficult to follow. The followers of Warren Jeffs, the Mormon polygamist cult, known as the Fundamentalist Church of Jesus Christ of Latter Day Saints, FLDS, worked for him for free or handed over to him all their earnings. He made in excess of two million dollars per month, while his followers depended on welfare for their sustenance. Jeffs had absolute control over his followers. He prohibited them from watching TV, listening to radio or any music, except his own songs. He assigned them houses to live in and told them not to intermingle with non-believers. He chose for them their spouses, and if he was unhappy with someone he would order that person's wives to leave him, and they would obey. Cults demand total submission, and with that, great sacrifice.

Look at other cults, like the cults of Jim Jones, Shoko Asahara, the Moonies or Heaven's Gate. These were not easy cults to practice. Members were often asked to hand over their worldly possessions to the leader, to leave their jobs, friends and relatives behind in order to follow him. They were forced to live austere lives and sometimes were told to abstain from sex. Meanwhile, the cult leader had everything he desired. David Koresh told his followers that women belonged to God; and since he was the Messiah, they belonged to him. He slept with the wives and teenaged daughters of his followers, but prescribed celibacy for them. Shoko Asahara, Jim Jones and generally all cult leaders punished severely those who disobeyed them. Despite these abuses and hardships, the worst punishment for the followers was excommunication. Some cultists commit suicide after being excommunicated.

Cult leaders ostracize members who seem to be unruly. People want to belong. They will succumb if they are excommunicated and left isolated. This was how Muslims forced into conversion the non-Muslim minorities among them.

Cults demand sacrifices. Through sacrifices believers prove their faith and loyalty. The cultist is led to believe that one can gain the pleasure of God or the guru by sacrificing everything including one's life. The rationale is that the more you sacrifice for something the more you value it. No sacrifice is too great when your salvation is at stake. Muhammad offered eternal life in Paradise, a bevy of celestial houris and the sexual strength of 80 men to those who believe in him and sacrifice for his cause. As the reward is increased, the sacrifice must be proportionately bigger. To encourage his followers to do more he said:

> Not equal are those believers who sit (at home) and receive no hurt, and those who strive and fight in the cause of Allâh with their goods and their persons. Allâh has granted a grade higher to those who strive and fight with their goods and persons than to those who sit (at home). Unto all (in Faith) has Allâh promised good, but those who strive and fight has He distinguished above those who sit (at home) by a special reward. (Q. 4:95)

Muhammad and his Cult

In other words, if you believe, you will be rewarded, but your reward will not be equal to the reward of those who wage jihad, who sacrifice their wealth and very lives, in becoming martyrs for the cause.

The more dangerous a cult, the more difficult are its requirements. Some cults won't even accept you as a full member until you prove your loyalty by making huge sacrifices. Muhammad made his followers believe that these sacrifices were necessary and part of faith. Spending for the cult or handing over your wealth to its leader, are regarded as the signs of your faith and commitment.

Cult leaders are psychopath narcissists and master manipulators. They love to see people do strenuous tasks for them so they can feel the power and savor their own omnipotence. They get their narcissistic supply by observing the servitude and the sacrifices of their followers. Their befogged believers will do anything, including wage war, assassinate and give their lives to gain their approval. This servile attitude feeds the narcissist craving of the leader for domination and control. They enjoy the power and their followers mistake their intransigence with the truth of their cause.

Why are the majority of prophets men? It is because narcissism is predominantly a male disorder. Although women can also become narcissists, there are more narcissist men than women. As the result there are more male prophets, cult leaders and dictators than women.

Cults typically apply rigorous rituals. By observing these rituals meticulously, followers are led to believe they will attain salvation. They become obsessed with rituals and consider failing to observe them to be a sin. These senseless rituals must be performed, supposedly to please God or to become "enlightened." However, the true intent of the rituals is to keep the followers hooked and on their leash. The shorter the leash the more the leader can control his followers. In reality none of these rituals has anything to do with God. They are to give the narcissist maximum power over his followers.

The Islamic rituals of obligatory prayers and fasting, serve as desensitizers of thoughts and emotions. Muslims are asked to abstain from certain foods, from listening to music and from socializing with the opposite sex. If they are women they must cover themselves in layers of veiled, baggy clothing even in the scorching heat of the summer, and they must sever all ties with their non-Muslim family and friends. These are all hardships and sacrifices that make the believer think that he or she is going to gain a reward in exchange. The believer becomes obsessed with rituals and sacrifices. While he suffers, he counts his blessings and rewards in the other world and thus is filled with euphoria and bliss. Paradoxically, more pain gives the believers more joy and contentment. It is not uncommon for believers to voluntarily perform self-flagellation in order to elicit God's pleasure.

We humans tend to believe in the maxim "no pain no gain." Our primitive ancestors used to offer sacrifices to appease their gods. For greater rewards they made bigger sacrifices. This belief was so entrenched that in some cultures people sacrificed humans and even their own children.

The hardship in practicing Islam (as well as other cults) and the intense sacrifices Muslims must make to be observant and "pious" believers is in fact the main appeal of Islam. The harder a cult is to follow, the truer it appears. Those who do not sacrifice enough are filled with guilt. This guilt is often more painful than the sacrifice itself.

A Few Famous Narcissist Cult Leaders

The personality of Muhammad is an enigma to many scholars. Even those who do not accept his claim admit that he had an impressive and charismatic personality. He could mesmerize those around him to the extent that they would believe in him and became so inspired they would kill anyone at his bidding or sacrifice their own lives upon his command. How could he summon up so much determination, aspire so high, think so grandiose, and become so powerful in such a short time? What was his secret?

What drove Muhammad to such great success was his need to be loved. This is the secret behind history's great narcissists. This is what drives them so incessantly and tirelessly.

There is no shortage of people who proclaim to be messengers of God or messiahs. Likewise, there is no dearth of fools who would follow them to the extent that they would willingly kill or die in order to demonstrate their loyalty.

Respect, admiration and power are what drive the narcissists. Narcissists are con artists. They have great need for recognition. They are stubborn, manipulative and determined. They are also smart, cunning and resourceful. Some famous narcissists are: Napoleon, Hitler, Stalin, Mussolini, Pol Pot, Mao, Saddam Hussein, Idi Amin, Jim Jones, David Koresh, Shoko Asahara and Charles Manson. Narcissists are emotionally disturbed people. They only see their validation in power, and to achieve that, will stop at nothing. They lie convincingly inspire confidence and appear self-assured. All that, however, is a facade to hide their insecurity and inner fears. Let us take a closer look at a few

Muhammad and his Cult

narcissists and compare them to Muhammad. This comparison will possibly explain the behavior of Muslims and their blind devotion to Islam.

Jim Jones convinced normal decent people that he was the Messiah (of socialism of all things). He persuaded them to leave their families and follow him to his "Medina" in the middle of the jungle. He charmed the Government of Guyana to give him 300 acres of land for free. He convinced his followers that they should let him sleep with their wives. He encouraged his men to carry guns and to kill anyone who dissented. These men became so blinded by their faith in him that they shot and killed a senator and his bodyguards. Then Jim Jones persuaded, without any resistance, his followers to drink a cyanide potion and commit mass suicide. Nine hundred and eleven people willingly did what he told them to do and died. They even made their children drink the poison. We will talk more about him in the next chapter.

David Koresh gathered his followers in a compound named after himself outside of Waco, Texas. He told them he was the Son of God and they believed him. His first announcement was made to the Seventh Day Adventists Church in southern California, which read in part: "I have seven eyes and seven horns. My Name is the Word of God...Prepare to Meet Thy God."

Marc Breault, a former member of Koresh's cult wrote that Vernon (the real name of David Koresh) confided to him early in his ministry: "I'll have women begging me to make love to 'em. Just imagine; virgins without number." A couple of years later he would be attended by at least twenty young women, including two that were just 14 years old, and one who was age 12. Like Allâh, who was attentive to his apostle's sexual needs, David's god was just as concerned about his carnal needs. Starting as a preacher, he soon rose to the position of the Son of God and began demanding sex from the wives of his followers – women who he believed had married these other men without his permission and who belonged to him. "All you men are just fuckers. That's all you are," David told his followers. "You married without getting God's permission. Even worse, you married my wives. God gave them to me first. So now I'm taking them back." According to Marc Breault, everybody was shocked by these statements, but they did not react, while Koresh kept saying things like: "So Scott; how does it feel to know you're not married anymore?" According to Breault, in 1989 David "began having sex with the other men's wives... and directed the women to inform him when they had reached the fertile part of their cycle to maximize the chance of pregnancy." As per the men, he informed them that it was their job to "defend King Solomon's bed." He not only had sex with and impregnated their wives—fathering over 20 children— but began having sex with their children as well. "Children were spanked for any reason; crying during a sixteen-hour Bible study, refusing to sit on David's lap, or daring to defy the prophet's wishes…Some women thought the best way to please their Son of God lover was to be especially severe when dishing out discipline. But sometimes it wasn't easy for the adults to spank the children. They couldn't find a spot on the child's buttocks that wasn't black and blue or bleeding." The women were sometimes subjected to the same treatment. One 29-year-old woman who announced that she was hearing voices was imprisoned in one of the small cottages on their property. She was beaten, and repeatedly raped by her guards. [283]

Like Muhammad, Koresh was also a prophet of doom. His followers armed themselves. When raided, by police, they shot and killed four ATF agents and booby-trapped the compound, blowing it apart, causing their own deaths and the deaths of their families, rather than surrender. Ninety people died as the result.

This story is beyond belief. How can anyone let himself to be fooled to this extent? Albert Einstein was not joking when he said, "Two things are infinite: the universe and human stupidity; and I'm not sure about the universe."

Order of the Solar Temple: This apocalyptic cult claimed 74 victims in three bizarre mass suicide rituals. Most of the members of the sect were highly educated and well-to-do individuals, much more intelligent than Abu Bakr, Omar and Ali, and other companions of Muhammad.

The cult gave great importance to the Sun. Their fiery ritual murder-suicides were meant to take members of the sect to a new world on the star "Sirius." To assist with the trip, several of the victims, including some children, were shot in the head, asphyxiated with black plastic bags and/or poisoned.

The two known leaders of the group were Luc Jouret, a Belgian homeopathic doctor, and Joseph di Mambro, a wealthy businessman. They were Muhammad and Abu Bakr of this cult. However, they believed in their own insanity so much that along with their followers they too committed suicide. This is something Muhammad was not willing to do. Muhammad never put his life in the way of harm. He surrounded himself with bodyguards at all times and never confronted the enemy in person.

---

[283] Inside the Cult: A Member's Chilling, Exclusive Account of Madness and Depravity in David Koresh's Compound Breault & King, 1993

Muhammad and his Cult

In a letter delivered after their deaths, Jouret and di Mambro wrote that they were *"leaving this earth to find a new dimension of truth and absolution, far from the hypocrisies of this world."*[284] Cults have an infatuation with death. This sounds eerily familiar to what Muhammad used to preach, except that Muhammad was more attached to this world and its lustful pleasures and so had no intention of leaving it. He praised martyrdom, but that was for others. He did not advocate suicide. Instead, he goaded his followers to wage jihad, kill and readily die. He told them to love death more than life, to loot and to bring booty, women and slaves for "Allâh and his messenger." He was much more pragmatic than other cult leaders and therefore less sincere.

Heaven's Gate: On March 26, 1997, 39 members of the cult known as "Heaven's Gate" decided to *"shed their containers"* and get on a companion craft "hiding in the tail of the Hale-Bopp comet".

The Heaven's Gaters died in three shifts over a three-day period after celebrating their last meal on earth. As one set of cultists ingested the poison, a lethal dose of phenobarbital mixed in with pudding and/or applesauce and chased with a shot of vodka, they would lie down while other cultists would use a plastic bag on their head to speed up the death. Then the cultists would clean up after each round of killing. Before the last two killed themselves, they took out the trash leaving the rented mansion in perfect order. Wanting to be helpful even after death, all bodies had some sort of identification. Strangely, though, they also had five-dollar bills and change in their pockets and small suitcases neatly tucked under their cots and beds. Like Muslim suicide bombers who shave their bodies and some even wrap their penis in aluminum foil, supposedly to keep it intact from the blast of the bomb, in preparation for their nuptial encounter with the celestial whores, the Heaven's Gaters must have thought they would take their bodies and suitcases along on their celestial voyage.

Charles Manson: This infamous psychopath of the late sixties at one point had nearly 100 young men and women among his followers (roughly the same number of followers Muhammad had gathered in Mecca and somewhat of the same caliber), known as the "Family." He was seen as their Messiah. He had made these rebel kids believe that civilization was about to end in a racial war in which the blacks would fight the whites and would win, but since they don't know how to run the world, they would come to him for help and, he and his followers would rule the world. He was so convinced of his delusions that

---

[284] http://www-tech.mit.edu/V114/N47/swiss.47w.html

175

his followers did not question his sanity. They did everything he told them to do, including engage in prostitution, theft, and murder. This is not unlike what Muhammad urged his followers to do. He encouraged them to raid, loot and rape, and they did.

When the promised racial war did not happen in 1969, Manson thought he should kickstart it himself. He ordered his followers to enter the houses of rich people randomly, kill them and make it look as if it has been done by blacks. These young people did exactly what Manson ordered them. They were eager to please him and in fact vied with each other to obey his orders. They had came to believe Manson had special divine powers and was endowed with hidden knowledge.

The influence of Manson on his followers was such that in 1975, Lynette Fromme, one of his "girls" known as "Squeaky." attempted to assassinate President Gerald Ford and was sentenced to life in prison. "She's very bright, an intelligent, pleasant woman," Fromme's attorney said of her. "She's anything but crazy. When you talk with her, everything is fine until you mention Manson." This can be said of all cultists. They are normal, intelligent people, until you mention their cult leader. Muslims are generally affable people until the name of Muhammad is slighted. Then suddenly, blood rushes to their heads, insanity overtakes many of them and some of them become murderers and savages. Cultists are all alike. They derive their insanity from a psychopath narcissist leader.

Another of Manson's girls, Sandra Good, was convicted for sending death threats through mail in 1976 and served ten years in jail. Following her release, she moved to an area close to Corcoran prison, where Manson is held, and tended his website until 2001. That is the power of brainwashing. Sandra Good was interviewed by CBC radio about a week after Fromme's attempted assassination. She said, "People all over the world are due to be assassinated. This is just the beginning. This is just the beginning of many assassinations that are about to take place." When asked, how could she talk about the trees that she wants to protect when she does not care about men? Good responded: "Men that kill life, that kill harp seals, that kill trees, that poison oceans, rivers and life are killing all of us." [285]

Cultists justify their terrorist deeds. This is the same apologetic given by Muslims to justify Islamic terrorism. They first build a straw-man of the West accusing it of killing Muslim children and then based on that lie they justify all their heinous crimes against civilians and children. How many times have we

---

[285] http://archives.cbc.ca/IDC-1-68-368-2086/arts_entertainment/frum/

heard "respectable" and prominent Muslims appear on TV to say, "We condemn terrorism BUT (yes there is always a but) this is a reaction to what Israel, America, the West, etc. are doing to Muslims?"

Manson still receives a large amount of mail, more than any other prisoner in the United States prison system, much of it from young people who want to join the "Family." Can this possibly explain why the cult of Islam is still thriving? Evil people will always gravitate towards evil doctrines.

Like all cults, Manson's also had a cause. The cause of his cult was preservation of Air, Trees, Water, Animals (ATWA) He made his cause look so important that it justified murder. After spending more than three decades in prison, Fromme is still faithful to Manson: "Manson told me he could give me a natural world," said Fromme in an interview. "Almost forty years ago he told me that money should work as hard for people as people work for money. He was talking about air and water, land and life. I don't know how it can be done so I'm just waiting. I would work hard for and invest in a world like that because it would support not just me but the continuum of generations to come." The poor woman is still a believer. This is an eloquent testimony to the power of brainwashing. That is why Muslims are not leaving Islam; despite the fact that they know Muhammad led a despicable and shameful life. Belief is a potent drug that destroys the thinking ability of the believer. The American philosopher Elbert Hubbard said, "Genius may have its limitations, but stupidity is not thus handicapped."

In one of their killing raids, Manson, peeping through the window of the house of his victims, saw pictures of children on the wall. At first he thought this house should be spared, but then changed his mind and said, the cause is so important that children should not come in the way.

Joseph Cohen, a Jewish man who converted to Islam and who changed his name to Yusuf Khattab, in an interview available on Youtube.com said the same thing about Israeli children. He believes every Israeli is a legitimate target and should be killed. When asked about children, he said that their killing would be a blessing to them because they will die before having the chance to commit sin and therefore will go to heaven.

Joseph Kony is a mad man who claims to be a "spirit medium." He founded the Lord's Resistance Army (LRA), a guerrilla group that was until 2006 engaged in a violent campaign to establish a theocratic government in Uganda, allegedly based on the Ten Commandments. He abducted an estimated 20,000 children since 1987 and turned them into killing machines. The unfortunate children were then forcefully indoctrinated, much like Muslim children in madrassas. Savage beatings were meted out to all nonbelievers.

Like Muhammad, Kony was also a polygamist. He prayed to the God of the Christians on Sundays reciting the Rosary and quoting the Bible; but on Fridays he performed the Islamic *Al-Jummah* prayer. He celebrated Christmas, but he also fasted for 30 days during Ramadan and prohibited the consumption of pork.

Joseph Kony had convinced his young warriors that with faith and recitation of the proper prayers, the Holy Spirit would shield them in battle. He promised the fighters that a magical power will render them victorious and made them believe that bullets fired at them would turn around in mid air to hit the soldiers who were firing them. Muhammad told his followers that angels will come to their help and that twenty believers can vanquish two hundred and a hundred can vanquish a thousand of the unbelievers. (Q.8:65). Kony gave a bottle of water to his boys for protection against the Ugandan army. He told them that if they empty the bottle's contents, a river will be created that would drown the enemy soldiers. Muhammad used to throw a handful of sand in the direction of his enemy and curse them. Both Kony and Muhammad stayed safely in the rear while encouraging their followers to be courageous and not fear death. Another similarity of Kony and Muhammad is their common belief in evil spirits.

In 2005 the International Criminal Court (ICC) issued arrest warrants for Joseph Kony for crimes against humanity. The charges against him included murder, enslavement, sexual enslavement and rape, cruel treatment of civilians, intentionally directing attacks against civilian populations, pillaging, inducing rape, and forced enlisting of children into the rebel ranks. These are the very charges that Muhammad should have been indicted for.

Like Muhammad, Kony had very little tolerance for dissent. Anyone who resisted LRA indoctrination, or who attempted to escape was executed – often savagely beaten to death by those newly abducted into Kony's "Spirit Army."

Muhammad's success is due to the fact that he came in a place where there was no central government to stop him. He raided, looted and conquered unchecked, starting as a robber and making his way up to eventually become an emperor. He combined the seductiveness of a cult leader with the ruthlessness of a conqueror.

Narcissists often succeed because they have a tremendous drive and a dogged determination. They seek to satiate their feelings of loneliness and lack of love with power and domination.

Muhammad and his Cult

The Power of the Big Lie

Adolf Hitler, in his *Mein Kampf,* (1925) wrote: "The broad mass of a nation will more easily fall victim to a big lie than to a small one." If anyone should have known the power of the big lie and that the bigger the lie the more believable it sounds, it was Hitler. Another good statement is that of George Orwell, author of *Politics and the English Language.* He wrote: "Political language ... is designed to make lies sound truthful and murder respectable and to give an appearance of solidity to pure wind."[286]

Why big lies are so convincing? It's because an ordinary person generally does not dare to tell a big lie. He fears that it would not be believed and that he would be derided. And, since everyone has heard or has said a few white lies, most people generally recognize them when they hear one. The big lies are so outlandish that they often startle the listener. Most people are not equipped to process them adequately. When the lie is colossal, the average person is left to wonder how anyone can have the audacity, the impudence to say such a thing. You are left with the difficult decision between three extremes: The person, who is saying this, must be either insane, a charlatan or he must be telling the truth. Now, what if for any reason, such as your reverence for this person, his charisma, or your commitment to him, you can't bear the thought of repudiating him and accept the fact that maybe he's indeed insane, a quack? Then you force yourself to believe in whatever he tells you even if what he says makes no sense at all.

The big lie offsets the scale of our common sense. This is not unlike like loading a scale that is made to weigh *kilos* with *tons.* It stops showing the correct weight. The indicator may even stop at zero. Hence, Hitler was right. The big lie is often believed more than a small lie.

When Muhammad recounted his tale of ascending to the seventh heaven, Abu Bakr was at first taken aback. He did not know what to make of this. This sounded utterly mad. He had two choices: either to admit that his trusted friend, whom he respected so much and by following him had endured ridicules is a crackpot, or believe in his fantastical tales and whatever else he might say. There was no middle ground for him.

Ibn Ishaq says when Muhammad made his vision known, "many Muslims gave up their faith. Some people went to Abu Bakr and said, 'What do you think of your friend? He alleges that he went to Jerusalem last night and prayed there,

---

[286] Politics and the English Language 1946 http://www.resort.com/~prime8/Orwell/patee.html

and came back to Mecca!' He replied that they were lying about the apostle, but they said that he was in the mosque at that very moment, telling people about it. Abu Bakr said, 'If he says so, then it is true. And what is so surprising in that? He tells me that communication from Allâh, from heaven to earth, comes to him in an hour of a day or night, and I believe him. That is more extraordinary than that at which you boggle!'"[287]

The logic is flawless. Basically what Abu Bakr was saying is that once you give up your rational faculty and believe in an absurdity, you might as well believe in anything. Once you let yourself to be fooled, then you should be prepared to be fooled ad infinitum because there is no end to foolishness. How many people would let a 54-year-old man sleep with their nine-year-old daughter? Abu Bakr did. This requires extreme foolishness. This much foolishness is only possible through blind faith.

We must also remember that Abu Bakr, by now had spent most of his wealth for Muhammad and his cause. This man had a lot at stake. At this stage, he had no other choice but to go along with whatever Muhammad told him. Admitting he had been conned was too painful a thought to bear. How could he explain this to his wife? What could he say to the wise men of Mecca who had laughed at him and told him he is a fool? The doors of going back for Abu Bakr were shut. He had to protect his pride and that meant he could not admit to have been a fool. All he could do was to dig in deeper and blindly follow Muhammad to wherever he took him. He had to silence his conscience and believe in anything his prophet fancied. When you put your entire faith in someone and sacrifice so much for him, you give up your independence and become putty in his hand. This is what cult leaders want from their devotees. Only this kind of devotion satiates their narcissistic craving.

Hitler, Stalin and many others of history's despotic leaders were insane. Those who saw their insanity could not whisper it to others. The "superior wisdom" of the despotic leader is the invisible cloak of the emperor. Those around him pretend to see it and extol its beauty. Those who are not in the immediate circle become convinced by the conviction of others. Thus the big lie is perpetuated and no criticism of it is tolerated.

---

[287] Sira Ibn Ishaq:P 183

Muhammad and his Cult

Use of Violence

Apart from being utterly convinced, the psychopath liar is ready to use violence to defend his lies. Appealing to force in order to support a claim is a logical fallacy that has often been successfully applied by dictators. This fallacy is called *Argumentum ad baculum*. It happens when someone resorts to force, or the threat of force, to push others to accept a conclusion.

Argumentum ad baculum can be defined as "might is right." This threat can be direct like:

- Slay the idolaters wherever you find them. (Q. 9:5)
- I will instill terror into the hearts of the unbelievers: smite ye above their necks and smite all their finger-tips off them. (Q. 8:12)

Or indirect such as:

- And as for those who disbelieve and reject Our Signs, they are the people of Hell. (Q.5:10)
- For him [the disbeliever] there is disgrace in this life, and on the Day of Judgment We shall make him taste the Penalty of burning (Fire). (Q. 22:9)
- (As for) those who disbelieve in Our communications, We shall make them enter fire; so oft as their skins are thoroughly burned, We will change them for other skins, that they may taste the chastisement; surely Allâh is Mighty, Wise. (Q. 4:56)

The threat gives the big lie a dramatic sense of urgency. The impact is so intense that one can't remain indifferent. "How can one be so certain that God would punish those who disbelieve in him?" or "How can one kill so many people for the mere fact that they disbelieve in him?" You wonder and become more prone to believe than if there were no such threats. Argumentum ad baculum works. Extreme violence is extremely convincing. The North Koreans literally worship their mad leader, Kim Jung Il. This certainty comes to them through the dictator's use of extreme violence and his zero tolerance of dissent. When your life depends on believing, you will believe in anything.

When the followers of Shoko Asahara, were ordered to release sarin gas in the subways of Tokyo and murder many innocent people, they did not question the abhorrence of this order. They silenced their conscience and accepted it as the sign of the greater wisdom of their guru. They were faced with two choices: either accept that he is insane, that they have been fooled, and admit that all their sacrifices have been in vain, or convince themselves that this man's wisdom is so great that they can't fathom its depth and therefore should not question him. These people gave up everything to be with Asahara. They burned all bridges to their past. They had nothing left to fall back on and nowhere to go if they decided to leave him. Since questioning Asahara or dissenting would not have been tolerated, they had no choice but to believe that whatever he said was right. They dismissed any doubt and forced themselves to have faith.

Dr. Ikuo Hayashi was a renowned doctor who had become one of Asahara's zealous followers. He was one of five persons who were ordered to plant the toxic sarin gas in the subways of Tokyo. Hayashi was a trained physician and had taken the Hippocratic Oath to save lives. At one point, before puncturing the packages containing the deadly liquid, he looked at the woman sitting in front of him and for a moment had misgivings. He knew that he was about to cause that woman's death. But he immediately silenced his conscience convincing himself that Asahara knew best, and that it would not be right for him to question his master's wisdom.

Omeir was a 16 year old lad who accompanied Muhammad in one of his battles. Muhammad spoke so glowingly of martyrdom that this boy was kindled with zealotry. Throwing away a handful of dates, which he was eating, he exclaimed "Is it these that hold me back from Paradise? Verily, I will taste no more of them, until I meet my Lord!" With such words, he drew his sword, and casting himself upon enemy's ranks, soon obtained the fate he coveted.

Once you become a believer you dismiss the thought that your beloved prophet may be lying. Psychopaths don't have a conscience. They can lie and they are capable of killing millions of people without any compunction. They feel entitled to do so. Hitler was convinced that he was doing the work of God. Indeed, one of his most revealing statements makes this quite clear. He wrote:

Hence today I believe that I am acting in accordance with the will of the Almighty Creator: by defending myself against the Jew, I am fighting for the work of the Lord.[288]

Ayatollah Montazeri, the man who was supposed to succeed Khomeini, until he fell from grace because of his disagreements with him, in his memoir wrote that when Khomeini ordered the massacre of more than 3,000 dissident

---

[288] Adolf Hitler, Mein Kampf, Ralph Mannheim, ed., New York: Mariner Books, 1999, p. 65.

boys and girls, he objected. Khomeini said that he would respond to God for that and that Montazeri should mind his own business. Narcissist psychopaths are utterly convinced of their evil acts and are the first to believe in their own lies.

Hitler attracted the support of many Germans merely by making them feel good with his big lies. He was a spellbinding speaker. When he spoke, he became louder and louder, as he vented his rage at the perceived enemies of Germany. He aroused the patriotism of Germans. His belief, that the bigger the lie the more believable it becomes, proved true. Millions of Germans believed in his lies. They loved him and were moved to tears by his fiery speeches.

Ibn Sa'd reports a hadith that reveals more similarities between Muhammad and Hitler. He wrote:

> During the sermons, the eyes of the Prophet would turn red as he would raise his voice and spoke angrily as if he was the commander of an army warning his men 'the resurrection and I are like these two fingers (referring to his index and middle finger). He would say 'the best of guidance is the guidance of Muhammad and the worst thing is innovation and any innovation will result in perdition.[289]

In the same place Ibn Sa'd says: "During his sermons, the Prophet used to wield a stick." (Perhaps this was to symbolize his dominance!)

The art of manipulating others so brazenly is not an ability that you or I can learn and easily master. Our biggest "handicap" is our conscience. Such ability comes naturally to psychopathic narcissists who have no conscience. Narcissists like Hitler, Mao, Pol Pot, Stalin and Muhammad were bereft of conscience.

He Frowned

Islamic societies are dysfunctional, patriarchal, misogynous and dictatorial. Not only are women mistreated, children are often abused, beaten and humiliated. Consequently they grow up scarred, have low self esteem, fancy thoughts of grandiosity and often evince signs of narcissistic personality disorder.

During my youth I had an Afghani friend who had all these characteristics. One day he told me he wanted to "become a Hitler." Hitler is a

---

[289] Ibn Sa'd Tabaqat, page 362

popular figure in Islamic countries. I was annoyed with that stupid remark and after giving him a piece of my mind walked away from him. Fearing to lose my friendship the next day he came to me and said that the night before he dreamt of the Prophet scolding him and telling him that he should become a "spiritual Hitler". This ridiculous behaviour typifies the pathological thinking of a narcissist. Narcissists are master manipulators. They are always one step ahead of you. There is an interesting chapter in the Quran, called *'Abasa*, (He Frowned) that shows that Muhammad had the same pathological mindset.

Early Muslims were mostly slaves or rebellious youths in their teens with no social standing. Muhammad was aware that in order to be taken seriously he must enlist influential people in his cause. Abu Bakr's conversion is owed to Khadijah's conversion. As far as he was concerned, if an important woman like Khadijah had accepted Islam, it must be true. Once Abu Bakr converted, it became easier for Umar to convert and so on. In logic this is called *argumentum ad verecundiam* or appeal to authority. This is a fallacy that uses admiration of an important person to prove the valdity of an assertion. Muslims resort to this fallacy often, as evidence of the truth of Islam.

During the early years of his mission, Muhammad was sitting among the dignitaries of Mecca trying to convince them of his claim. One of his followers, a blind poor man named Ibn Umm Maktum, approached him with a question. Muhammad disliked his interruption and frowned. Those sitting around him noticed his contempt. They criticized him for his hypocrisy and double standard. There was no way for Muhammad to get out of this embarrassing situation by making Allah approve his snobbishness. The next day he claimed to have received a sura in which Allah rebuked him for ignoring the blind man while trying to impress the rich.

[1] He frowned and turned (his) back,

[2] Because there came to him the blind man.

[3] And what would make you know that he would purify himself,

[4] Or become reminded so that the reminder should profit him?

[5] As for him who considers himself free from need (of you),

[6] To him do you address yourself.

[7] And no blame is on you if he would not purify himself

[8] And as to him who comes to you striving hard,

[9] And he fears,

[10] From him will you divert yourself.

[11] Nay! Surely it is an admonishment.

Muhammad and his Cult

[12] So let him who pleases mind it.

[13] In honored books,

[14] Exalted, purified,

[15] In the hands of scribes. (Q. 80: 1-15)

In these verses Muhammad is taking the blame and even making Allah admonish him for his condescendence. Nonetheless, as a narcissist he had to blame his detractors even more and from verse 17 onward, he pours his venomous vituperation on those who disbelieved him.

Although this sura is another indication of Muhammad's narcissistic personality disorder, Muslims do not see it that way. They have fallen prey to his manipulations hook, line, and sinker and think that it proves his sincerity. Far from it; this should only be seen as Muhammad's attempt to repair the damage he had done to his own credibility. He had to address this situation and taking the blame was the only way to do that.

Why Did Everyone Praise Muhammad?

A question that boggles Muslims is why, if Muhammad was so evil, did his companions praise him so much? Why no one spoke opprobriously of him, even after his death?

The answer is that in a society that is based on a personality cult, speaking your mind is not always safe. Telling the truth could bring you ostracism or worse, it could cost your life. The majority of the people has sheep mentality and goes with the flow. Those who may think differently know enough to keep their mouths shut in order to keep their heads on their shoulders.

Abdullah Ibn Abi Sarh, who was one of Muhammad's scribes, had to escape from Medina and only in the safety of Mecca did he reveal there were no revelations and that Muhammad was making the Qur'an up. However, when Muhammad conquered Mecca, he immediately sought ibn Abi Sarh and ordered his execution, even though he had promised to not kill anyone should the city surrender with no fight. Ibn Abi Sarh's life was spared thanks to the intercession of Othman who happened to be his foster brother. When Othman interceded, Muhammad remained silent. His companions thought he had agreed and let Ibn Abi Sarh go. Later he complained that he had remained silent because he did not want to turn down Othman's request, but he wished that his companions read his mind and kill Ibn Abi Sarh. This is further evidence of the hypocrisy of Allâh's Prophet.

Where critics are silenced, sycophants and bootlickers will try to endear themselves by eulogizing the leader with flattery and exaggerated adulation. Saddam was hated by most of the Iraqis, and yet all you could hear about him in Iraq, while he was still in power, were his praises. The narcissist is so cut off from reality that he believes in those praises and in a sense becomes a victim of his own deception. Because Muhammad was believed to be a prophet, his reign of terror did not end with his death. Those who truly had fallen for his big lie perpetuated that terror and silenced any voice of opposition just as they do today. Once those who knew Muhammad in person were dead, later generations had no way of knowing the truth and believed in what everyone else believed and the lie passed from one generation to another. After Muhammad's death, the sycophants continued fawning over him, praising him to the skies, even attributing miracles to him, thinking that this would add to their prestige and make them look pious. There are many miracles attributed to Muhammad even though he confessed in the Qur'an that he could not perform any.[290]

Fourteen hundred years later, millions of Muslims behave in the same way they used to at the time of Muhammad in Medina. Those who dissent are afraid to talk, and if they do, are swiftly silenced, while the lackey fawners are honored for extolling the Prophet and his "virtues." How can truth triumph in such a repressive atmosphere so fraught with hypocrisy and sycophancy?

There are several stories about Muhammad ordering the assassination of those who criticized him and about Omar, as Muhammad's right hand man, who was ever ready to draw his sword and threaten to slit the throat of anyone who dared question his master's authority. Muhammad encouraged sycophantism and punished independent thinking and criticism. People trapped in such an oppressive atmosphere, eventually come to believe in the superhuman qualities of the leader and their faith in them becomes genuine and real.

Recently, a team of eye surgeons went to North Korea to help people with cataracts. Thousands of young and old lined up and after they recovered their sights, the doctors were stupefied to see that the first thing these people did was to go to the large portrait of the dictator Kim Jung Il, hanging on the wall, to prostrate themselves and thank HIM – not the doctors who helped them, but the two tyrants who kept them blind for so many years.

---

[290] The unbelievers repeatedly asked Muhammad to perform a miracle so they could believe (Qur'an 17: 90) and Muhammad kept telling them "Glory to my Lord! Am I aught but a man- a messenger?" (Qur'an 17: 93)

Muhammad and his Cult

Muhammad's mission flourished partly because he came during a time and to a place of ignorant, superstitious and largely chauvinistic people. The qualities he needed to bolster his marauding religion were already present in his early followers. Chauvinism, bigotry, haughtiness, arrogance, megalomania, stupidity, boastfulness, greed, lust for sex, disdain for life and other ignoble character traits that are the hallmarks of Islam were already present as the *materia prima* in Arabia. These attributes were later imposed on other nations who became prey to Islam. Those who already had these base attributes found in Islam a common ground to stand and a "divine" validation for their deviant, criminal penchant.

Chapter Six

When Sane People Follow Insane People

O ne way to understand Islam and the fanaticism that characterizes its followers is to compare it to other cults. Islam has roughly 1.2 billion believers. If you are not a Muslim yourself, you must know a few and may see nothing abhorrent in them. They may be like most people, working and raising their families. They are good employees, colleagues, bosses, neighbors and citizens. They are friendly, no better or worse than other people. There may be nothing particular about them that would lead one to believe they are part of a cult. However, let not appearances fool you. Islam is a cult and Muslims have a very cultic mentality.

The dictionary definition of fanaticism is excessive enthusiasm, unreasoning zeal, or wild and extravagant notions, on any subject, especially religion. People do not embrace religions to become murderers and terrorists. Is this not the antithesis of what religions are about? So what makes some become so fanatical that they would disregard commonsense, engage in despicable acts of barbarity, murder, and even readily give up their lives in the name of religion? Does the fervor of believers proove the truth of their cause?

Understanding Muhammad

Let us analyze the cult of the People's Temple and compare it to Islam. All cults share fundamentally similar characteristics. We could compare Islam to any cult and the result would be the same. Neal Osherow has studied People's Temple and in an article entitled *An Analysis of Jonestown: Making Sense of the Nonsensical,* he explains the anatomy of cults with clarity.

The members of People's Temple, stirred by their leader, Jim Jones, fed a poison-laced drink to their children, administered the potion to their infants, and drank it themselves. Their bodies were found lying together, arm in arm; over 900 perished.

How could such a tragedy occur? The answer is the insanity of one man and the credulity of many. In this chapter I will go over Osherow's analysis of People's Temple and compare it, point by point, with Islam to see the similarities and to gain a better understanding of this religion.

As long as Muslims believe that Muhammad was a prophet, whatever he did, to them is justifiable. As we shall see at the end of this chapter, the hope of recovery of those who are brainwashed in cults is slim. However, of those few whose rational faculty has not been irretrievably impaired and could be jolted back to reality, this may impel them to begin to question the tenets of their faith.

Jim Jones started his preaching in Indiana twenty years before the mass suicide, in 1965, with a handful of followers. He stressed the need for racial equality and integration. His group helped feed the poor and find them jobs. He was charismatic and persuasive. Soon his followers began to multiply; new congregations were formed and a headquarters was established in San Francisco.

Absolute Obedience

Jones was to his followers a beloved leader. They affectionately called him "Father," or simply "Dad." As time went on he gradually assumed the role of messiah. As his influence grew, he demanded more obedience and loyalty. His followers were more than eager to comply. He persuaded them that the world would be destroyed in a nuclear holocaust and if they followed him, only THEY would emerge as survivors.

Osherow writes: "Many of his harangues attacked racism and capitalism, but his most vehement anger focused on the 'enemies' of the People's Temple - its detractors and especially its defectors."[291]

---

[291] Osherow, Neal. "Making Sense of the Nonsensical: An Analysis of Jonestown." In *Readings about the Social Animal*, 7th edition, ed. Elliot Aronson. New York: W. H. Freeman. Available

When Sane People Follow Insane People

The above picture is similarly descriptive of Islam. At first, Muhammad was only a "warner," calling people to believe in God and fear the Day of Judgment. As his influence grew and the number of his followers increased, he became more demanding, asking them to leave their homes, emigrate from their homes, and threatened them with divine chastisement if they did not obey him.

Many of Muhammad's harangues attacked polytheism (*shirk*), but his most vehement anger was directed at the "enemies" of Islam, his detractors and especially the defectors.

Jim Jones took his people to a jungle in Guyana and separated them from their families. Cut off from all external influences and completely under his control he could easily brainwash and indoctrinate them. This was exactly the reason why Muhammad wanted his followers to go to Medina. He turned his more loyal followers against those who did not want to leave. The following verse expresses his sentiment.

> As to those who believed but came not into exile, you owe no duty of protection to them until they come into exile; but if they seek your aid in religion, it is your duty to help them. And (remember) Allâh sees all that you do. (Q.8:72)

This verse says Muslims should not give protection to other Muslims who did not emigrate. In other words, they should kill them, until they leave and comply. The last part of this verse is particularly telling. He is warning his followers that Allâh is watching them and that he knows, not only what they do, but is also aware of their thoughts.

Muhammad's Allâh has an uncanny resemblance to George Orwell's enigmatic dictator of Oceania, the fictional character *"Big Brother,"* in his novel, *Nineteen Eighty-Four*.

In his fictional society everybody is under complete surveillance by the authorities, mainly by telescreens. People are constantly reminded of this by the phrase "Big Brother is watching you," which is the core "truth" of the propaganda system in this state.

In the novel, it is not clear if the Big Brother actually exists as a person, or is an image crafted by the state. However, since Inner Party torturer O'Brien points out that Big Brother can never die, the apparent implication is that Big Brother is the personification of the party. Nobody has ever seen him. He is a face on the hoardings, a voice on the telescreen.... Big Brother is the guise in

---

online. [URL=http://www.academicarmageddon.co.uk/library/OSHER.htm] All Osherow's quotes in this chapter are taken from this source.

which the Party chooses to exhibit itself to the world. His function is to act as a focusing point for love, fear, and reverence, emotions which are more easily felt towards an individual than towards an organization. The loyal citizens of Oceania do not fear Big Brother, but in fact love and revere him. They feel he protects them from the evils out there.[292]

The above is also true of Allâh, an invisible and yet ever-present being, who is loved and simultaneously feared by Muslims and who watches their every move and monitors their thoughts.

Death as the Proof of Faith

Osherow continues: "But when in 1978 the concerned relatives of People's Temple persuaded the Congressman Leo Ryan to investigate the cult, he and the journalists that accompanied him heard most residents praise the settlement, expressing their joy at being there and their desire to stay. Two families, however, slipped messages to Ryan that they wanted to leave with him. But when the visiting party and these defectors tried to board planes, they were ambushed and fired at until five of them including Ryan, were murdered. Then Jim Jones gathered his followers and told them to drink from the poison-laced beverage and '*die with dignity*'".

Excerpts from a tape, recorded as the final ritual was being enacted, reveal the believers, with few exceptions, voluntarily drank the poison and fed it to their children. The talks and assurances of Jim Jones are eerily recognizable to those who are familiar with the Qur'an. A woman protests but the crowd silences her and everyone expresses their readiness to die.

The following is the text of the tape recording. It is truly shocking but at the same time, it reveals the core of fanaticism.

Jim Jones: I've tried my best to give you a good life. In spite of all I've tried, a handful of people, with their lies, have made our life impossible. If we can't live in peace then let's die in peace. (Applause) … We have been so terribly betrayed… What's going to happen here in the matter of a few minutes is that one of the people on that plane is going to shoot the pilot - I know that. I didn't plan it, but I know its going to happen … So my opinion is that you used to in ancient Greece, and step

---

[292] Wikipedia.com

When Sane People Follow Insane People

over quietly, because we are not committing suicide-it's a revolutionary act ...We can't go back

First Woman: I feel like that as there's life; there's hope.

Jones: Well, someday everybody dies.

Crowd: That's right, that's right!

Jones: What those people gone and done, and what they get through will make our lives worse than hell... But to me, death is not a fearful thing. It's living that's cursed. Not worth living like this.

First Woman: But I'm afraid to die.

Jones: I don't think you are. I don't think you are.

First Woman: I think there were too few who left for 1,200 people to give them their lives for those people who left... I look at all the babies and I think they deserve to live.

Jones: But don't they deserve much more? They deserve peace. The best testimony we can give is to leave this goddam world. (Applause)

First Man: It's over, sister... We've made a beautiful day. (Applause)

Second Man: If you tell us we have to give our lives now, we're ready. (Applause) [Baltimore Sun, 1979]

Above the cries of babies wailing, the tape continues, with Jones insisting upon the need for suicide and urging the people to complete the act:

Jones: Please get some medication. Simple! It's simple There's no convulsions with it... Don't be afraid to die. You'll see people land out here. They'll torture our people...

Second Woman: There's nothing to worry about. Everybody keep calm and try to keep your children calm... They're not crying from pain; it's just a little bitter tasting...

Third Woman: This is nothing to cry about. This is something we could all rejoice about. (Applause)

Jones: Please, for God's sake, let's get on with it... This is a revolutionary suicide. This is not a self-destructive suicide. (Voices praising, "Dad." Applause)

Third Man: Dad has brought us this far. My vote is to go with Dad...

Jones: We must die with dignity. Hurry, hurry, hurry! We must hurry... Stop this hysterics. Death is a million times more preferable to spending more days in this life... If you knew what was ahead, you'd be glad to be stepping over tonight...

Fourth Woman: It's been a pleasure walking with all of you in this revolutionary struggle... No other way I would rather go than to give my life for socialism, Communism, and I thank Dad very much.

Jones: Take our life from us... We didn't commit suicide. We committed an act of revolutionary suicide protesting against the conditions of an inhuman world.[293]

The release of this tape shocked the world. Yet absolute devotion and mindless obedience, characteristic of cults, is what Islam is all about. Islam means submission. Believers must relinquish their will and disregard everything, including their family and their own life to prove their loyalty to Allâh and his messenger. In the Qur'an we read: "...then seek for death, if you are sincere."(Q.2:94) In another place Muhammad challenges the Jews to desire death in order to prove that they are truthful.

Say: "O ye that stand on Judaism! If ye think that ye are friends to Allâh, to the exclusion of (other) men, then express your desire for Death, if ye are truthful."(Q. 62:6)

It is clear that according to the twisted mind of the narcissists such as Jim Jones and Muhammad, the ultimate test of devotion was to ask their followers to die. The Palestinian televisions often show the mothers of suicide bombers proudly speak of the sacrifice of their children and express their hope that their other children would follow suit.

Punishment and Coercion

Osherow explains: "If you hold a gun at someone's head, you can get that person to do just about anything. The Temple lived in constant fear of severe punishment, brutal beatings coupled with public humiliation for committing trivial or even accidental offenses. Jim Jones used the threat of severe punishment to impose the strict discipline and absolute devotion that he demanded, and he also took measures to eliminate those factors that might encourage resistance or rebellion among his followers."

Muslims live constantly under the threat of severe punishment. I have received thousands of emails from angry Muslims with the sole message that I

---

[293] Newsweek, 1978, 1979

will go to hell for criticizing Islam. They are not challenging my arguments; they are not disputing what my logic, but only threatening me with what frightens them most, the hell. It is enough to read a few verses from the Qur'an to see where this fear comes from. Muslims are raised with such a dread of hell and punishment for unbelief that the thought of questioning the authority of Muhammad sends shivers down their spine.

The fear is not limited to psychological intimidation. Physical punishment is also an integral part of Islamic upbringing. In Islamic *madrassas*, (religious schools) children are beaten as the norm for misdemeanors, and in some cases are chained. The beating is not limited to children; even adults are corporally punished, flogged publicly, humiliated, maimed, or stoned to death for breaching Islamic laws.

There are many laws that ban any form of independence or rebellion. Critics, freethinkers, reformers and apostates must be killed. Even asking questions is not permitted! This is the only way to maintain the illusion of Islam, with its compulsory blind faith, which can only be enforced through ignorance and fear.

Osherow says: "But the power of an authority need not be so explicitly threatening in order to induce compliance with its demands, as demonstrated by social psychological research. In Milgram's experiments,[294] a surprisingly high proportion of subjects obeyed the instructions of an experimenter to administer what they thought were very strong electric shocks to another person."

Elimination of Dissention

According to Osherow, this absolute obedience will be noticeably reduced if there is a small minority of dissenters. "Research showed," he writes, "that the presence of a 'disobedient' partner greatly reduced the extent to which most subjects in the Milgram situation[295] obeyed the instructions to shock the person designated the 'learner.' Similarly, by including just one confederate who expressed an opinion different from the majority's, Asch[296] showed that the

---

[294] Milgram, S. Behavioural study of obedience. *Journal of Abnormal and Social Psychology*, 1963, 67, 371-378.
[295] Milgram S. Liberating effects of group pressure. *Journal of personality and Social Psychology*, 1965, 1, 127-134.
[296] Asch, S. Opinions and social pressure. *Scientific American*, 1955, 193.

subject would also agree far less, even when the 'other dissenters' judgment was also incorrect and differed from the subjects."

Both Muhammad and Jim Jones could not tolerate dissent. They demanded exclusive and absolute allegiance and made the thought of questioning and criticizing them an unthinkable option. Muhammad forgave those who fought against him if they accepted Islam and his hegemony, as he did with his cousin, Abu Sofian and even put him in charge of Mecca after conquering it, but he did not forgive those who dissented and deserted him. Many people were murdered on his orders, for the simple reason that they had disagreed with him or mocked him.

That is why he was so afraid of dissent and why his followers do not tolerate it to this day. That is also why I am so confident that once the voices of the Muslim apostates are heard, many other Muslims will take courage and the criticism of Islam will become unstoppable.

Jeanne Mills, who spent six years as a high-ranking member before becoming one of the few who left the People's Temple, wrote: "There was an unwritten but perfectly understood law in the church that was very important: No one is to criticize Father, wife, or his children."[297]

Isn't this true about Muhammad, his family and his companions? Dr. Yunis Sheikh, a college professor in Pakistan commented that the parents of Muhammad were not Muslims. This sounds logical because they died when Muhammad was only a child and we have hadith that say Muhammad thought they would go to hell. Yet, his comment angered his students, who thought he had insulted the parents of their prophet and complained to the clerics who took Dr. Sheikh to a court, accused him of blasphemy and condemned him to death. He was released after a few years when many from around the world protested.

In September 2006, Mohammed Taha Mohammed Ahmed, the editor-in-chief of the Sudanese independent daily, Al-Wifaq, was kidnapped by a group of Muslim zealots who put him through a mock trial before slitting his throat in a style used to slaughter camels, then decapitated him. He was accused of blasphemy after his paper republished an article from the internet that questioned the parentage of Muhammad. All that poor Mohammad Taha did was to take small excerpts from the book and write his own rebuttal. [298]

If you live in an Islamic country, you could be put to death for criticizing Islam, Muhammad or his companions. If you live in a non-Muslim country, you could be assassinated even if you are not a Muslim. Dutch filmmaker, Theo Van

---

[297] Mills, J. *Six years with God.* New York: A & W Publishers, 1979.
[298] http://www.news24.com/News24/Africa/News/0,,2-11-1447_2034654,00.html

When Sane People Follow Insane People

Gogh, learned that lesson too late when he rolled in his own blood after he was shot and stabbed by a Muslim for assisting the Muslim dissident Ayan Hisi Ali in making a movie on women in Islam.

In July 1991 Ettore Caprioli, the Italian translator of *The Satanic Verses*, was grievously injured, and Hitoshi Igarishi – professor of literature and an admirer of Islamic civilization, who had translated the book into Japanese – was assassinated in Tokyo. William Nygaard, the Norwegian translator, was later knifed.

The idea is to instill so much terror that no one dares to speak against Islam. Deborah Blakey, another long-time member of the cult of People's Temple who managed to defect, testified: "Any disagreement with Jim Jones's dictates came to be regarded as 'treason.'... Although I felt terrible about what was happening, I was afraid to say anything because I knew that anyone with a differing opinion gained the wrath of Jones and other members."[299]

Inconsistencies

Many early Muslims, just as some members of the People's Temple, realized that the stated aim of their belief and the practices of their respective leaders were inconsistent. Jim Jones slept with many women in his congregation and he was not coy about it. Muhammad also did a lot of things that must have raised eyebrows, even among the Arabs with such a lax morality.

In one hadith Aisha narrates: "I used to look down upon those ladies who had given themselves to Allâh's Apostle and I used to say, 'Can a princess give herself (to a man)?' But when Allâh revealed: 'You (O Muhammad) can postpone (the turn of) whom you will of them (your wives), and you may receive any of them whom you will; and there is no blame on you if you invite one whose turn you have set aside,' (Q.33:51) I said (to the Prophet), 'I feel that your Lord hastens in fulfilling your wishes and desires.'"[300]

Obviously Aisha was not only a pretty girl but also a witty one. Indeed we see on many occasions Muhammad's god coming to his help and licensing him to do whatever he pleases.

Muhammad broke several social norms such as marrying Zeinab, his own daughter-in-law, and having sex with Mariyah, one of his wives' maids in her absence. He was 51 years old when he married the 6 year old Aisha and slept

---

[299] Blakey, D. Affidavit: San Francisco. June 15, 1978.
[300] Sahih Al-Bukhari, Volume 6, Book 60, Number 311

with her when she was only eight years nine months old and still playing with dolls. He claimed to have had his best 'revelations' while under the blanket with this little girl. In the height of his power, he saw another toddler girl and told her parents that when she grows up, he would like to marry her. Fortunately for the toddler, Muhammad died shortly after that. He took teenage girls as his personal reward from Allâh during his raids and after ravaging their tribes and killing their families, he added them to his harem as his sex slaves.

Of course, many early believers must have wondered why, if Muhammad was a messenger of God, his actions were so ungodly. We cannot assume that all those Arabs were completely bereft of any conscience and did not know what Muhammad was doing was wrong. However, if they had any doubts, they were unable to express them. The believers feared ostracism and punishment. Those who disagreed were quickly silenced.

On one occasion, the Meccan companions of Muhammad, the immigrants, got into fight with the Medinan men while they were out of town raiding. Abdullah ibn Ubayy, the man who had saved the Banu Nadir from being massacred by Muhammad, was enraged. He said, "Have they [the immigrants] actually done this? They dispute our priority, they outnumber us in our own country, and nothing so fits us and the vagabonds of Quraish as the ancient saying 'Feed a dog and it will devour you.' By Allâh, when we return to Medina, the stronger will drive out the weaker." Then he went to his people who were there and said, "This is what you have done to yourselves. You have let them occupy your country, and you have divided your property among them. Had you but kept your property from them they would have gone elsewhere." When this news reached Muhammad he decided to kill Ibn Ubayy. Upon hearing this, Ibn Ubayy's son who had converted to Islam came to Muhammad and told him, "I have heard that you want to kill 'Abdullah b. Ubayy for what you have heard about him. If you must do it, then order me to do it and I will bring you his head, for al-Khazraj know that they have no man more dutiful to his father than I. I am afraid that if you order someone else to kill him, my soul will not permit me to see his slayer walking among men and I shall kill him, thus killing a believer for an unbeliever, and so I should go to hell."[301]

Abdullah ibn Ubayy was a great man among his own people, and the Medinans respected their old chief. This was now a tough situation. Ordering a son to murder his own father, a father like ibn Ubbay, could have unpleasant consequences. What if the son was testing the veracity of the rumor to turn against Muhammad and rise in defense of his father? Muhammad wisely

---

[301] Ibn Ishaq. Sira

decided to let go of his macabre design. Ibn Ubayy's son's gesture, however, is praised by Muslim historians and commentators and is regarded as an example of true faith. This was the level of control Muhammad exerted on his followers. He made people to spy on each other and created an atmosphere of fear in which every dissent was nipped in the bud.

One interesting note is that after Abdullah ibn Ubayy died, his son begged Muhammad to say his father's funeral prayer. Because of ibn Ubayy's stature, Muhammad felt it is expedient to oblige. As he got up to pray for the deceased, Omar, who remembered Muhammad's reluctance in praying at the grave of his own mother caught hold of his garment and said: "Allâh's Messenger, are you going to conduct prayer for this man, whereas Allâh has forbidden you to offer prayer for unbelievers?" He replied: "Allâh has given me an option as He has said: Ask pardon for them, or ask not pardon for them; if you ask pardon for them seventy times, God will not pardon them. (Q.9:80) and I am going to make an addition to the seventy." It is ironical that Muhammad should call ibn Ubayy a "hypocrite" when that title best suits Muhammad himself.

The following hadith is one example of the anger that Muhammad expressed to those who dared question his virtues. This happened when he was distributing all the booty confiscated during the war of Hunain among the chiefs of Mecca to "soften their hearts" and "sweeten Islam in their mouths," as he told his followers, leaving nothing to others who also helped him in this battle. A man said: "O Allâh's Apostle! Do Justice." The Prophet said, "Woe to you! Who could do justice if I did not? I would be a desperate loser if I did not do justice." Omar said, "O Allâh's Apostle! Allow me to chop his head off."[302]

This man was from Banu Tamim. His tribe had not become Muslim. They had joined Muhammad in this expedition for the loot alone. Now that Muhammad was victorious, he did not have to answer to anyone or keep his promises. This man was not familiar with Muhammad and his character. This experience must have been sobering for him and all those who were present. The lesson learned was that one is not allowed to question Muhammad's decisions even though they are unjust. Anyone who questioned him met his wrath and could face death. Only sycophantism met his approval. It is natural that in such an oppressive climate truth is always the casualty. Is there a lesson in this for the leftists who have joined the Muslims in their onslaught against the Judeo-Christian values? It certainly is, but are they heeding?

Osherow continues: "Conditions in the People's Temple became so oppressive, the discrepancy between Jim Jones's stated aims and his practices so

---

[302] Sahih Bukhari Volume 4, Book 56, Number 807

pronounced, that it is almost inconceivable that members failed to entertain questions about the church. But these doubts were not reinforced. There were no allies to support one's disobedience of the leader's commands and no fellow dissenters to encourage the expression of disagreement with the majority. Public disobedience or dissent was quickly punished. Questioning Jones's word, even in the company of family or friends was dangerous. Informers and 'counselors' were quick to report indiscretions, even the relatives."

Like Jones, Muhammad relied on sycophant informers, which as Osherow says: "This not only stifled dissent; it also diminished the solidarity and loyalty that individuals felt toward their families and friends."

In Islam, Muslims are asked to keep a watch on each other and warn one another if one of them deviates from the "right path." This is called *Amr bil ma'roof* (injunction of right) and *Nahi min al munkar* (forbiddance of wrong). The right and wrong, however, are not what commonsense and the Golden Rule dictate, they are what the Prophet allowed or forbade. In other words, everyone is a "Big Brother" and vigilante to others and is required to correct the conduct of his fellow believers and report them to authorities in grave cases. In Iran, after the Islamic revolution, children were encouraged to report any un-Islamic activity by their parents. Several youths were reported by their own fathers to the authorities and were executed. The informers then were lauded and glorified to encourage others to do the same.

Osherow says: "While Jones preached that a spirit of brotherhood should pervade his church, he made it clear that each member's personal dedication should be directed to "Father."

In Islam the believers are supposed to be brothers to each other but their first loyalty is to Muhammad, or as he adroitly put it, to "Allâh and his messenger." The moment one leaves Islam, those very people who professed to be brothers will not hesitate to slit one's throat.

The similarities of Muhammad and Jim Jones are astounding. One wonders whether the latter was a copycat of the former. The truth is that this is the natural expression of the psychopathic mind of all narcissists. All totalitarian polities, from Nazism to fascism, from communism to Islam, are cultic and share the same characteristics that George Orwell described in his novel *Nineteen Eighty Four*.

When Sane People Follow Insane People

Destruction of Family Ties

Jim Jones believed: "Families are part of the enemy system," because they hurt one's total dedication to the "Cause."[303] The "Cause" was of course none but himself. Thus, a person called before the membership to be punished could expect his or her family to be among the first and most forceful critics.[304]

Muhammad split families by stating that the believers must pay their allegiance first to Allâh and his Messenger and disobey their parents if they come between them and Islam. The following verse from the Qur'an makes this point clear:

> Now We have enjoined on man goodness towards his parents; yet (even so) should they endeavor to make you commit Shirk (disbelief) with Me of something which you have no knowledge of, obey them not.[305]

"Why didn't more people leave?" Osherow asks. "Once inside the People's Temple, leaving was discouraged; defectors were hated," he explains. "Nothing upset Jim Jones so much; people who left became the targets of his most vitriolic attacks and were blamed for any problems that occurred. One member recalled that after several teen-age members left the Temple, 'We hated those eight with such a passion because we knew any day they were going to try bombing us. I mean Jim Jones had us totally convinced of this.'"[306]

Muslims are also brought up with the same mentality. A Muslim can't hate anyone more than the apostates. In Islam, apostates, freethinkers and critics are threatened and killed. Muslim dissenters are accused of blasphemy and lynched or executed.

Osherow writes: "Defecting became quite a risky enterprise, and, for most members, the potential benefits were very uncertain. Escape was not a viable option. Resistance was too costly. With no other alternatives apparent, compliance became the most reasonable course of action. The power that Jim Jones wielded kept the membership of the People's Temple in line, and the difficulty of defecting helped to keep them in." The Qur'an makes it clear that apostasy is not accepted.

---

[303] Mills, J. *Six years with God.* New York: A & W Publishers, 1979.
[304] Cahill, T. In the valley of the shadow of death. *Rolling Stone.* January 25, 1979.
[305] Qur'an, Sura 29, Verse 8
[306] Winfrey, C. Why 900 died in Guyana. *New York Times Magazine,* February 25, 1979.

If you renounced the faith, you would surely do evil in the land, and violate the ties of blood. Such are those on whom God has laid His curse, leaving them deaf and sightless.... Those who return to unbelief after God's guidance has been revealed to them are seduced by Satan and inspired by him.... (Q. 47:23-28)

Here Muhammad is promising divine chastisement for the apostates. He also prescribed punishment in this world. Bukhari has reported the following hadith:

Allâh's Apostle said, "The blood of a Muslim who confesses that none has the right to be worshipped but Allâh and that I am His Apostle, cannot be shed except in three cases: In Qisas for murder, a married person who commits illegal sexual intercourse and the one who reverts from Islam (apostate) and leaves the Muslims. [307]

Another hadith tells us that some apostates were brought to Ali and he burned them. When the news of this event reached Ibn 'Abbas, he said, "If I had been in his place, I would not have burnt them, as Allâh's Apostle forbade it, saying, 'Do not punish anybody with Allâh's punishment (fire).' I would have killed them according to the statement of Allâh's Apostle, 'Whoever changed his Islamic religion, then kill him.'" [308]

The Power of Persuasion

What attracted people to join Jones' church in the first place? Let us analyze this question and compare it to what attracts new converts to Islam.

Osherow credits Jones's charismatic personality to his oratory power, aided by his genius in manipulating people who were most vulnerable. With promises and carefully honing his presentation to appeal to each specific audience he would easily win their hearts and imagination. In the words of Cicero "Nothing is so unbelievable that oratory cannot make it acceptable."

Muhammad was fully aware of the power of oratory. He believed that "in eloquence there is magic"[309] and used to say: "Some eloquent speech has the influence of magic (e.g., some people refuse to do something and then a good

---

[307] Sahih Bukhari Volume 9, Book 83, Number 17
[308] Sahih Bukhari Volume 9, Book 84, Number 57
[309] Sunnan Abu Dawud; Book 41, Number 4994

eloquent speaker addresses them and then they agree to do that very thing after his speech)."[310]

Elsewhere he bragged, "I have been given the keys of eloquent speech and given victory with terror.[311] He used both the power of oratory and persuasion, and terror and intimidation to his advantage.

Osherow writes: "The bulk of the People's Temple membership was comprised of society's needy and neglected: the urban poor, the black, the elderly and a sprinkling of addicts and ex-convicts."[312]

Compare that to the early followers of Muhammad in Mecca. They were mostly the poor, the disfranchised slaves, the rebellious youths, and a few disaffected women. He preached to the slaves that they should escape the yoke of their masters and emigrate; he told the youths to disobey their parents and follow him; he spoke of social equality and the brotherhood of all the believers; he promised everyone great rewards in the afterlife and wealth in this world, wealth that was later secured through looting.

The three historians, Tabari, Ibn Sa'd and Ibn Ishaq agree that only a few converted to Islam out of faith. The majority converted out of fear or for the greed of a share in the loot. Nonetheless, and irrespective of their original reasons, they served Muhammad's goal of conquest.

Claims of Grandiosity

Cult leaders have megalomaniac personalities. Both Jim Jones and Muhammad had hyper-inflated egos. To attract new members, Jones held public services in various cities. Leaflets distributed read:

Pastor Jim Jones... Incredible! Miraculous! Amazing!
The Most Unique Prophetic Healing Service You've Ever Witnessed! Behold the Word Made Incarnate In Your Midst![313]

Muhammad made many lofty claims about himself, too. His sockpuppet Allâh often praised with words such as:

---

[310] Sahih Bukhari Volume 7, Book 62, Number 76
[311] Sahih Bukhari Volume 9, Book 87, Number 127
[312] Winfrey, C. Why 900 died in Guyana. *New York Times Magazine*, February 25, 1979.
[313] Suicide Cult: The Inside Story of the Peoples Temple Sect and the Massacre in Guyana (201P) by Marshall Kilduff and Ron Javers (1978)

- We sent you not, but as a Mercy for all creatures. (Q.21:107)
- And surely you [Muhammad] have sublime morals. (Q.68:4)
- Indeed in the Messenger of Allâh you have a good example to follow. (Q.33:21)
- Verily this is the word of a most honorable Messenger. (Q.81:19)
- But no, by the Lord, they can have no (real) faith, until they make you judge in all disputes between them, and find in their souls no resistance against your decisions, but accept them with the fullest conviction. (Q. 4:65)

The last verse makes it clear that Muhammad was seeking absolute obedience and frowned at any criticism or disagreement.

Osherow writes: "Members learned to attribute the apparent discrepancies between Jones's lofty pronouncements and the rigors of life in the People's Temple to their personal inadequacies rather than blaming them on any fault of Jones. As ex-member Neva Sly was quoted: 'We always blamed ourselves for things that didn't seem right.'[314] A unique and distorted language developed within the church, in which 'The Cause' became anything that Jim Jones said.[315] Ultimately, through the clever use of oratory, deception, and language, Jones could speak of death as 'stepping over,' thereby camouflaging a hopeless act of self-destruction as a noble and brave act of 'revolutionary suicide,' and the members accepted his words."

This is so typical in Islam, where the believers volunteer to take the blame for anything that goes wrong and attribute everything that goes right to Allâh. Also we can see the incredible similarity between the followers of Muhammad and those of Jim Jones in their approach to death.

The origin of the statement "we love to die as much as you love to live," with which Osama Bin Laden began his infamous letter to America is to be found in the Battle of Qadisiyya in the year 636, when the commander of the Muslim forces, Khalid ibn Al-Walid, sent an emissary with a message from Caliph Abu Bakr to the Persian commander, Khosrau. The message stated: "You [Khosrau and his people] should convert to Islam, and then you will be safe, for if you don't, you should know that I have come to you with an army of men that love death, as you love life." This account is recited in today's Muslim sermons, newspapers, and textbooks.

---

[314] Winfrey, C. Why 900 died in Guyana. *New York Times Magazine,* February 25, 1979.
[315] Mills, J. *Six years with God.* New York: A & W Publishers, 1979

When Sane People Follow Insane People

Claim to Secret Knowledge

One way the cult leaders try to impress their followers is by performing miracles and claiming to have the knowledge of the unknown. Jim Jones performed many miracles that were all staged. Among them was his ability to reveal something about the new members or the guests that no one except they themselves could have known. To perform this "miracle" he would send one of his confidants beforehand to search the belongings of the guest, go through his private letters or eavesdrop on their conversations and inform him of their findings. Then he would surprise them with his "secret knowledge" about them.

Muhammad did the same. He had spies everywhere and after being tipped off, he would claim "Gabriel informed me...."

In chapter two we discussed the scandal of Muhammad's sexual affair with Mariyah, Hafsa's reaction to it and Muhammad's oath to prohibit Mariyah to himself that he later broke thanks to Allâh's intervention. Relevant to our discussion is the verse that follows. This verse talks about Muhammad ordering Hafsa not to reveal the secret of his sexual affair with Mariyah to anyone, but Hafsa, unable to keep her mouth shut, divulged the secret to Aisha. Muhammad became outraged when he found out that his secret is out. Now it does not take much intelligence to know that if the secret is out, Hafsa must have done it. However, Muhammad claimed that it was Allâh who had informed him that Hafsa had disobeyed him.

> And when the prophet secretly communicated a piece of information to one of his wives-- but when she informed (others) of it, and Allâh made him to know it, he made known part of it and avoided part; so when he informed her of it, she said: Who informed you of this? He said: The Knowing, the one Aware, informed me. (Q.66:3)

The whole story is ludicrous. The maker of the Universe first takes the role of a pimp, helping his prophet to have sex with the woman he lusts for and then, he gossips, informing him about what his wives said behind his back. There is no point in discussing the silliness of this story. The point that is worth making is that Muhammad claimed to have received information from God, when the fact that Hafsa had divulged his secret was quite obvious. Anyone with the wits of a six-year-old child could have known this.

These are all ways for the cult leader to manipulate people and claim secret knowledge. The amazing thing is that the followers often become willing collaborators of the leader's scams.

Performing Miracles

Osherow reports the following story, written by Jeannie Mills, in which Jim Jones performs the miracle of multiplying the food:

> There were more people than usual at the Sunday service, and for some reason the church members hadn't brought enough food to feed everyone. It became apparent that the last fifty people in line weren't going to get any meat. Jim announced, 'Even though there isn't enough food to feed this multitude, I am blessing the food that we have and multiplying it just as Jesus did in Biblical times.'

> Sure enough, a few minutes after he made this startling announcement, Eva Pugh came out of the kitchen beaming, carrying two platters filled with fried chicken. A big cheer came from the people assembled in the room, especially from the people who were at the end of the line.

> The "blessed chicken" was extraordinarily delicious, and several of the people mentioned that Jim had produced the best-tasting chicken they had ever eaten.

> One of the men, Chuck Beikman, jokingly mentioned to a few people standing near him that he had seen Eva drive up a few moments earlier with buckets from the Kentucky Fried Chicken stand. He smiled as he said, "The person that blessed this chicken was Colonel Sanders."

> During the evening meeting Jim mentioned the fact that Chuck had made fun of his gift. "He lied to some of the members here, telling them that the chicken had come from a local shop," Jim stormed. "But the Spirit of Justice has prevailed. Because of his lie Chuck is in the men's room right now, wishing that he was dead. He is vomiting and has diarrhea so bad he can't talk!"

> An hour later a pale and shaken Chuck Beikman walked out of the men's room and up to the front, being supported by one of the guards. Jim asked him, "Do you have anything you'd like to say?"

When Sane People Follow Insane People

Chuck looked up weakly and answered, "Jim, I apologize for what I said. Please forgive me."

As we looked at Chuck, we vowed in our hearts that we would never question any of Jims "miracles," at least not out loud. Years later, we learned that Jim had put a mild poison in a piece of cake and given it to Chuck. [316]

Now, to perform this "miracle" Jones had to rely on the collaboration of Eva. The question is why would this woman knowingly participate in such a scam? There are similar miracles attributed to Muhammad.

In one hadith, someone claimed that he saw Muhammad putting his hand in a pot and water gushed out from it, so that the entire army performed ablution from one pot.

> I saw Allâh's Apostle when the 'Asr (evening) prayer was due and the people searched for water to perform ablution but they could not find it. Later on (a pot full of) water for ablution was brought to Allâh's Apostle. He put his hand in that pot and ordered the people to perform ablution from it. I saw the water springing out from underneath his fingers till all of them performed the ablution (it was one of the miracles of the Prophet). [317]

In another hadith we are told that Muhammad multiplied the bread; [318] or that he struck a huge solid rock with his spade and the rock became like sand. [319] Or, he blessed a meal that was barely enough for four or five and with it fed an army. [320]

There are tens of "miracles" that Muslims have attributed to Muhammad. Most of these so-called miracles were claimed by Muhammad himself. These were miracles that no one but he could verify and yet no Muslim doubts them. One such miracle is his claim to have visited the town of the jinns. In another place he said that a group of jinns in Medina had embraced Islam. [321] In one fantastic story he claimed to have struggled with a big demon and subdued him.

---

[316] Mills, J. *Six years with God.* New York: A & W Publishers, 1979
[317] Sahih Bukhari Volume 1, Book 4, Number 170
[318] Sahih Bukhari Volume 5, Book 59, Number 428
[319] Sahih Bukhari Volume 5, Book 59, Number 427
[320] Sahih Bukhari, Volume 7, Book 65, Number 293
[321] Shih Muslim Book 026, Number 5559

Last night a big demon (afreet) from the Jinns came to me and wanted to interrupt my prayers (or said something similar) but Allâh enabled me to overpower him. I wanted to fasten him to one of the pillars of the mosque so that all of you could see him in the morning..."[322]

These stories were for the consumption of gullible believers. Ibn Sa'd quotes a story narrated by Abu Rafi, one of the believers, who said that one day Muhammad visited him and he killed a lamb for dinner. Muhammad liked shoulders so he served him one. Then he asked for another one and when he finished, he asked for another. (Remember, he had an insatiable appetite.) Abu Rafi said, "I gave you both shoulders. How many shoulders does a lamb have?" to which Muhammad responded, "If you had not said this, you would have been able to give me as many shoulders as I had asked for."[323]

Despite such outlandish claims, when challenged by the skeptics, Muhammad repeatedly denied being able to perform miracles. He admitted that although all other prophets were given the power to perform miracles, his only miracle was the Qur'an.

The Prophet said, There was no prophet among the prophets but was given miracles because of which people had security or had belief, but what I was given was the Divine Inspiration which Allâh revealed to me. [324]

The question is why would believers go out of their way to falsely attribute miracles to their prophet? That is a question they ought to answer. My hunch is that once believers become convinced of the truth of their belief, they justify everything including lies. People with strong faith, who are usually decent and ethical, willingly lie, participate in frauds, abuse others and even kill, if necessary, to support their belief. The "cause" to them is so important that it overshadows every other consideration. When people become so convinced of the truth of a cause that they are willing to die for it, then lying, and even killing for it become a synch. The end justifies the means. Pascal, the French philosopher and mathematician wrote: "Men never do evil so completely and cheerfully, as when they do it from religious conviction." History is witness to the truth of Pascal's words. Much crime has been committed in the name of religion. Faith blinds and absolute faith blinds absolutely.

---

[322] Sahih Bukhari Volume 1, Book 8, Number 450
[323] Tabaqat, Volume 1, Page 375
[324] Sahih Bukhari Volume 9, Book 92, Number 379

When Sane People Follow Insane People

Imam Ghazzali's[325] authority in Islam is indisputable. He said: "When it is possible to achieve such an aim by lying but not by telling the truth, it is permissible to lie if attaining the goal is permissible" [326]

Osherow quotes Kasindorf, "Jim Jones skillfully manipulated the impression his church would convey to newcomers. He carefully managed its public image. He used the letter-writing and political clout of hundreds of members to praise and impress the politicians and press that supported the People's Temple, as well as to criticize and intimidate its opponents."[327]

If any newspaper writes something that Muslims find insulting, all of them flood the offices of the editor to voice their complaints. They will continue with their harassment until an apology is issued publicly and the edition is withdrawn. How can we forget the riots and killing of innocent people when the Danish newspaper, Jyllands-Posten, published a few cartoons of Muhammad, or when Pope Benedict XVI quoted a Byzantine emperor who asked "Show me just what Mohammed brought that was new?"[328]

On November 10th, 2003, the Muslim Public Affair Committee, MPAC, CAIR's counterpart in UK, published an angry letter condemning the publisher Amber Books of blasphemy. The furor was over a book called The History of Punishment that Amber Books had printed.

The book was not about Islam. It offered a view of punishment in various cultures and civilizations. It also included chapters on ancient methods of punishment, such as Biblical punishments, Roman punishments and Sharia Law. It contained many pictures, including one of Muhammad. Muslims were up in arms. The publisher received thousands of angry and threatening letters until it was cowed to withdraw the book from circulation and issue a public apology to Muslims.

In another case CAIR managed to pressure Paramount Pictures to alter the Tom Clancy novel "*The Sum of All Fears*" to exchange the Muslim terrorists in the original script to neo-Nazis. The director, Phil Alden Robinson was forced to write an apology to CAIR, telling them he had no intention of promoting negative images of Muslims, and added: "I wish you the best in your continuing efforts to combat discrimination."

---

[325] Abu Hamid Muhammad al-Ghazzâlî (1058-1111) known as Algazel is one of the most celebrated scholars in the history of Islamic thought. Born in Iran, he was an Islamic theologian, philosopher, and mystic. He contributed significantly to the development of a systematic view of Sufism and its integration and acceptance in mainstream Islam.

[326] Ahmad Ibn Naqib al-Misri, *The Reliance of the Traveler*, translated by Nuh Ha Mim Keller, Amana publications, 1997, section r8.2, page 745

[327] Kasindorf, J. Jim Jones: The seduction of San Francisco. New West, December 18, 1978.

[328] Speech of Pope Benedict XVI in münchen, altötting and regensburg (september 9-14, 2006)

When in 2002, the evangelists Pat Robertson and Jerry Falwell went on the air expressing their views about Islam, Muslims across the world rioted. The Iranian Mullahs threatened to retaliate and several Christians were killed, including some school kids in Pakistan. Bonnie Penner Witherall, a 31 year-old Christian nurse, was also shot dead in Sidon, Lebanon.

Distrust of Outsiders and Self -Blame

Osherow writes: "Jones inculcated a distrust of any contradictory messages, labeling them the product of enemies. By destroying the credibility of their sources, he inoculated the membership against being persuaded by outside criticism."

This is also typical of Muslims, who accuse their critics of being Zionists and/or paid agents of "the enemies of Islam." If anyone criticizes Islam, Muslims go after them personally, and instead of countering their arguments, they attack him *ad hominem*. They vilify their critics and try to discredit them, but will never offer a counter-argument to answer the charges.

"In Jonestown," writes Osherow, "any contradictory thoughts that might arise within members were to be discredited. Instead of seeing them as having any basis in reality, members interpreted them as indications of their own shortcomings or lack of faith." This is so typical of Muslims who although they realize that their lives are a living hell and their countries are in shambles, blame themselves and their lack of adherence to "true Islam" for their miseries, when in reality it is Islam that is the source of most of their pains.

Self- Justification

Tolstoy said, "Both salvation and punishment for man lie in the fact that if he lives wrongly he can befog himself so as not to see the misery of his position."[329]

Jim Jones created an atmosphere of total domination and control. Osherow says: "Analyzing Jonestown in terms of obedience and the power of the situation can help to explain why the people acted as they did. Once the People's Temple had moved to Jonestown, there was little the members could

---

[329] The Kreutzer Sonata

do other than follow Jim Jones's dictates. They were comforted by an authority of absolute power. They were left with few options, being surrounded by armed guards and by the jungle, having given their passports and various documents and confessions to Jones, and believing that conditions in the outside world were even more threatening. The members' poor diet, heavy workload, lack of sleep, and constant exposure to Jones's diatribes exacerbated the coerciveness of their predicament; tremendous pressures encouraged them to obey."

We know that Muhammad was not pleased with those who deserted him. As we can see, there is little difference between Muhammad's way of thinking and Jones's. However, it would be a mistake to assume that cult believers stay only because they are coerced. Psychological coercion is much more powerful and long lasting. The victims become willing, even grateful, participants in their own abuse and enslavement.

Osherow writes: "By the time of the final ritual, opposition or escape had become almost impossible for most of the members. Yet even then, it is doubtful that many wanted to resist or leave. Most had come to believe in Jones. One woman's body was found with a message scribbled on her arm during the final hours: 'Jim Jones is the only one.'[330] They seemed to have accepted the necessity, and even the 'beauty'of dying. Just before the ritual began, a guard approached Charles Garry, one of the Temples hired attorneys, and exclaimed, 'It's a great moment... we all die.'"[331]

A survivor of Jonestown, who happened to be away at the dentist, was interviewed a year following the deaths: "If I had been there, I would have been the first one to stand in that line and take that poison and I would have been proud to take it. The thing I'm sad about is this: that I missed the ending."[332]

What is it that drives normal people to these extremes? It is difficult to explain or even understand that once believers accept a cult leader as a divine being, they become willing participants and the extensions of his psychopathic mind. Could this explain the zealotry, the fanaticism and the absolute devotion of the early Muslims towards Muhammad? Did those early believers see in Muhammad what the followers of Jim Jones saw in him? The following hadith reveals this zealotry very clearly.

---

[330] Cahill T. In the valley of the shadow of death. *Rolling Stone*. January 25, 1979.

[331] Lifton, R. J. Appeal of the death trip. *New York Times Magazine,* January 7, 1979.

[332] Gallagher, N. Jonestown: The survivors' story. *New York Times Magazine,* November 18, 1979.

Allâh's Apostle came to us at noon and water for ablution was brought to him. After he had performed ablution, the remaining water was taken by the people and they started smearing their bodies with it (as a blessed thing).[333]

In another place we read:

Ali was suffering from eye-trouble, so the Prophet applied saliva to his eyes and invoked Allâh to cure him. He at once got cured as if he had no ailment.[334]

These are all lies concocted by believers. Muhammad was unable to cure his own ailments and was constantly in physical pain. How could he heal another person with his saliva?

Isolationism

Osherow describes isolationism as "the aspect of Jonestown that is perhaps the most troubling." He says, "To the end, the vast majority of the People's Temple members believed in Jim Jones. External forces, in the form of power or persuasion, can exact compliance. But one must examine a different set of processes to account for the members internalizing those beliefs. Although Jones's statements were often inconsistent and his methods cruel, most members maintained their faith in his leadership."

The Qur'an contains many inconsistencies, contradictions and errors. It is a confused book, poorly written, full of absurdities and absurd statements. It is an editor's nightmare. None of that bothers Muslims, who insist that it is a miracle, simply because Muhammad said so.

One good explanation as to why people continue to believe in absurdities is provided by Osherow in his account of People's Temple. He asserts: "Once they were isolated at Jonestown, there was little opportunity or motivation to think otherwise; resistance or escape was out of the question. In such a situation, the individual is motivated to rationalize his or her predicament; a person confronted with the inevitable tends to regard it more positively. For example, social psychological research has shown that when children believe that they will be served more of a vegetable they dislike, they will convince themselves

---

[333] Bukhari Volume 1, Book 4, Number 187
[334] Bukhari Volume 4, Book 52, Number 253

that it is not so noxious,[335] and when a person thinks that she will be interacting with someone, she tends to judge a description of that individual more favorably."[336]

Cult leaders often barricade their followers in order reduce their contact with the outside world. Jim Jones built his own town in the jungles of Guyana calling it after himself, "Jonestown." Muhammad went to *Yathrib*, a city originally founded by the Jews and after convincing its Arab inhabitants to follow him, renamed the city after himself to *Medinat ul-Nabi* (Prophet's town).

In Medina, Muhammad started killing or publicly humiliating anyone who questioned his authority. *Medinat ul Nabi* became very much like Jonestown. Muhammad was the absolute authority and any dissent was severely punished. Once a person entered Medina and became one of the believers, going back was virtually impossible.

One of the few who left Muhammad was Abdullah ibn Sa'd Abi Sarh. When Muhammad conquered Mecca, he gave amnesty to all but ten of its inhabitants. These were people who had criticized or had ridiculed him. Among them was Abi Sarh.

Abi Sarh used to write down the verses of the Qur'an that Muhammad dictated in Medina. He was more educated than Muhammad and he often would correct the Prophet's compositions and suggested better ways of writing and Muhammad would agree. This made him realize that the Qur'an is not revealed and that Muhammad was making it up. He escaped and returned to Mecca. He told everyone about his finding. When Muhammad conquered Mecca, despite giving assurances of amnesty to the Meccans for their surrender and their forced conversion to Islam, he ordered the beheading of Abi Sarh. Abi Sarh was spared thanks to Othman's intercession and Muhammad's inability to communicate properly his wishes through signals. When Othman pleaded with Muhammad to not kill Abi Sarh, who was his foster brother, Muhammad remained silent. His companions assumed that he is agreeing with Othman and Abi Sarh walked away in the company of Othman. When they left, Muhammad complained, saying that he did not wish to turn down the request of his supporter and friend, Othman, but he had hoped that they [his companions] would see the displeasure in his face and kill the man. This story also reveals the hypocrisy of the

---

[335] Brehm, J. Increasing cognitive dissonance by a *fait-accompli*. *Journal of Abnormal and Social Psychology*, 1959, 58, 379-382.

[336] Darley, J. and Bersceild, E. Increased liking as a result of the anticipation of personal contact. *Human Relations*, 1967, 20, 29-40.

messenger of Allâh who while trying to please Othman, wanted others to kill Abi Sarh, so Othman would not blame him.

Ibn Ishaq explains: "The reason he ordered him to be killed was that he had been a Muslim and used to write down revelation for Muhammad; then he apostatized and returned to Quraish [Mecca]..." He was to be killed for apostasy but was saved through Othman's intercession.[337]

The atmosphere in Medina was very tense. Islam and Jihad had become the focus of the lives of its citizens. Muhammad had ordered them to go to the mosque, pray five times per day and their men were often out raiding, plundering, pillaging caravans, destroying villages, killing men and raping women.

There is a hadith reported by both Imams Bukhari and Muslim which shows the level of coercion that Muhammad exerted to make people comply with his commands. He is reported to have said:

> I thought that I should order the prayer to be commenced and command a person to lead people in prayer, and I should then go along with some persons having a fagot of fuel with them to the people who have not attended the prayer (in congregation) and would burn their houses with fire.[338]

In this hadith Muhammad threatens to burn with fire, those who refrained from attending the congregational prayer in the mosque.

Life in Medina had completely changed. Prior to the arrival of Muhammad, the people of Yathrib were farmers, artisans and tradesmen. The bulk of the industry was in the hands of the Jews, who were hardworking, literate and prosperous. The Arabs were illiterate, lazy and indolent. They had few skills and worked for the Jews. When the Jews were exterminated, the city changed drastically. There were no more businesses where the Arabs could work and earn their livelihood. The economy of the township had collapsed altogether. The citizens relied entirely on booty and spoils of war Muhammad provided for their sustenance. For them, there was no going back. They had become dependant on Muhammad and the spoils of his wars. Even those who did not believe in him, like Abdullah ibn Ubbay and his followers, used to take part in his raids. This is not because they wanted to support Islam but because these spoils become the only source of income for the inhabitants of Medina. If they did not participate in Muhammad's raids they would have gone hungry.

---

[337] Sirat, p. 550
[338] Muslim Book 004, Number 1370; and Bukhari Volume 1, Book 11, Number 626

When Sane People Follow Insane People

Like the members of People's Temple, Muslims were confronted with an inevitable situation, which in turn led them to accept their condition more favorably. Those few who dared to speak against the new leader were either killed or ostracized.

The Arab population of Medina was the poorest. They were ignorant, impoverished and superstitious people. For them, even owning one camel and one robe was considered wealth. They worked as journeymen for the Jews. Several ahadith tell of these Arabs, whose first wealth, or as the Qur'an delicately terms it, the "bounty of Allâh," was acquired through looting. There was also plenty of sexual booty. Women captured in wars provided an added incentive for the believers, particularly the immigrants who were mostly single.

Once the Jews were killed and banished the impoverished Arabs of Medina had no alternative but to enlist in Muhammad's army and wage war for him, if they wanted to eat. The main incentive for these early believers to sally forth in jihad was wealth and sex.

Gradual Absorption

The life of a believer is an arduous life of constant inner battle and mindless religious rituals to be performed without question. He or she submits to this life gradually. Osherow writes: "A member's involvement in the Temple did not begin at Jonestown, it started much earlier, closer to home, and less dramatically. At first, the potential member would attend meetings voluntarily and might put in a few hours each week working for the church. Though the established members would urge the recruit to join, he or she felt free to choose whether to stay or leave. Upon deciding to join, a member expended more effort and became more committed to the Peoples Temple. In small increments, Jones increased the demands made on the member, and only after a long time did he escalate the oppressiveness of his rule and the desperation of his message. Little by little, the individual's alternatives became more limited. Step by step, the person was motivated to rationalize his or her commitment and to justify his or her behavior."

Those who convert to Islam report similar experiences. Their absorption is gradual. As they become more involved, the bar of expectations is raised gradually. Women are told that it is not mandatory for them to cover their hair, but it would be meritorious if they do so. Then the new believers are asked to refrain from certain foods, eat halal food, perform the prayers, fast, give zakat and slowly they are introduced to the virtues and rewards of jihad. This task is performed by every Muslim. Because the newcomers are eager to belong and be accepted, they will do whatever it is asked from them and even try to out perform the born Muslims and as the proverb goes, become "more catholic than the Pope."

The indoctrination is so gradual that the new converts feel they are doing these changes voluntarily. They finally end up doing things that they thought objectionable, even ridiculous before. An ex-Muslim American woman wrote to me that when she first saw a group of Muslim women all covered in black veil she laughed and felt sorry for them. Eventually she converted to Islam and started wearing the strictest form of veils where even the face is covered by a veil, called *neqab*. I came to know this lady online because she had created an Internet site actively promoting Islam while maligning me, warning other Muslims not to read my articles. Obviously she was not practicing what she was preaching and could not resist reading what I wrote. Eventually the truth dawned on her and she left Islam, utterly disquieted. She explained to me how gradually she had been sucked into Islam to the extent that at one point she had asked her non-Muslim husband to convert to Islam and take another wife.

I have met Muslim women (virtually) who had become so brainwashed that they defended Muhammad's claim that women are deficient in intelligence and naturally inferior to men. Paradoxically, at the same time, they were convinced that Islam liberates women. Faith is indeed a mind-numbing narcotic.

Those who convert to Islam, perhaps because they find the doctrine of monotheism attractive or simply want to be part of a large "brotherhood," in a short time will start disliking the Jews and then their own country. Soon they will find themselves hating their own non-Muslim parents and distancing themselves from their unbelieving friends. Eventually they may volunteer to fulfill their ultimate religious obligation as a Muslim, become a jihadi, a terrorist and joyfully seek the ultimate sacrifice of martyrdom.

One Canadian who converted to Islam, or as Muslims like to think, "reverted" to his natural religion, after apostatizing wrote of his experience as a Muslim:

An unadulterated Islam was difficult for the kuffaar (unbelievers) to digest so deviants evidently had a higher success rate in their propagation of Islam (da'wah) as they modified principles "to suit the nafs" (carnal self) of recipients. The moderate and sanitized version of Islam that initially brought me to conversion had to be reassessed. Through the local masjid (mosque), always available was a handshake and anticipated hug. This was a comfort unavailable at home, especially from a mother always unsatisfied with my performance and father unconcerned with my progress. Encouraged by my Muslim brothers, I desired to excel in my religion; possibly get married, master the Arabic language and be a mujaahid (partaker in jihaad) and shaheed (martyr).

Reverts to Islam, ever so gullible and naive, were easily susceptible to the prevalent dysfunctional behaviors and propaganda infecting most Muslim societies. By striving not to conform to the kuffaar, we duly had to be ignorant by circumnavigating anything unislamic. One revert declared that Osama bin Laden was better than "a million George Bushes,' and 'a thousand Tony Blairs' simply because he's a Muslim. Arrogantly speaking, we Muslims were 'the best of peoples ever raised up for mankind.' (3:110) So when an atrocity occurred that was obviously committed by Muslims in the name of Allah, my fellow brothers and sisters were complacent. We obsequiously forsook the human rights violations in Muslim countries, even when the victims were Muslims. The conspiracy theories widespread in my Muslim society were outright delusion. Not even the moderate Muslims, who neglected salaat and committed zinaa (illegal sex; fornication, adultery, etc.), could accept the Muslim identities of the 9/11 pilots. As my Afghani classmate remarked, 'It was the Jews!' When the opportunity arose for self-criticism, inevitably, we instead blamed the Jews, our favorite scapegoat. Homogenizing oneself into the Islamic ummah was ostensibly clinched if one supported the latest Arab-Muslim agenda, grew an outstanding beard, expressed hatred for the Jews, uttered the word 'bid'ah' (denouncing the modernists) occasionally, and repudiated the modern state of Israel. We proudly acknowledged the jihaad, yet acted stupid if questioned by a kaafir and responded to their accusations with, for example, 'How do you know it was done by Muslims? Where is the evidence?' Although they were not blind to the videotaped confessions by boasting Muslim terrorists, they chose to be. Not all Muslims were terrorists, although it was unequivocally but agonizingly true that most terrorists were Muslims. If some Americans or Jews died, there was sympathetic joy and I observed this particular behavior genially absorbed by one Muslimah just five years old. Reverts hopelessly adopted a rigid interpretation of Islam taught by immigrants from oppressive theocracies that incarcerated ijtihaad (free discussion) to keep freethinking and dissent criminal and their rule immutable.[339]

---

[339] www.faithfreedom.org/Testimonials/Abdulquddus.htm

Understanding Muhammad

Jeanne Mills, who managed to defect two years before the Temple relocated in Guyana, begins her account, *Six Years with God* (1979), as follows: "Every time I tell someone about the six years we spent as members of the People's Temple, I am faced with an unanswerable question: If the church was so bad, why did you and your family stay in for so long?" Osherow says, "Several classic studies from social psychological research investigating processes of self-justification and the theory of cognitive dissonance[340] can point to explanations for such seemingly irrational behavior."

John Walker Lindh, known as the "American Taliban," the young man who went to Afghanistan to serve in Al Qaeda and fight against his own country, did not become a terrorist overnight. John's interest in Islam began when he was just a 12-year-old. His mother took him to see Spike Lee's film, *Malcolm X*. Time magazine quotes her saying, "He was moved by a scene showing people of all nations bowing down to God."[341]

No one cared or knew enough to warn this young man of the dangers of Islam. On the contrary, he received approval and blessings from his parents to pursue his heart's desire, as they too were ignorant of Islam. Time Magazine, in its September 29, 2002 edition wrote, "John's parents were pleased to see that their son had found something that moved him. And at a time when other parents they knew were coping with their kids' experimentation with drugs, booze and fast driving, it all seemed fairly innocent. Marilyn (John's mother) would drop young John off at the mosque for Friday prayers. At the end of the evening, a fellow believer would drive John home."

The tolerant American society also did not see anything wrong or alarming about a young American converting to Islam. He would stroll with his awkward Islamic outfit up and down the streets, and the good American folks did not get especially worked up. "It was just another kid experimenting with his life, with his spiritual side, certainly nothing to fear or loathe," wrote Time Magazine.

Instead of investigating the truth about Islam, John's father allowed himself to be fooled by what he defined as the "Islamic custom of hospitality for fellow believers," which in itself is a warning sign of the cultic nature of Islam. Cultists are exceptionally "loving" and friendly towards those whom they want

---

[340] *See Aronson*, E. *The social animal* (3rd ed.) San Francisco: W. H. Freeman and Company, 1980. AND Aronson, E. The theory of cognitive dissonance: A current perspective. In L. Berkowitz (ed.), *Advances in experimental social psychology*. Vol. 4, New York: Academic Press, 1969.

[341] By Timothy Roche, Brian Bennett, Anne Berryman, Hilary Hylton, Siobhan Morrissey And Amany Radwan The Making of John Walker Lindh.
http://www.time.com/time/magazine/article/0,9171,1003414-5,00.html

to woo to their faith. Instead of warning his son of the dangers of Islam, he tried to "appreciate" his faith. One day he told his son, "I don't think you've really converted to Islam as much as you've found it within yourself; you sort of found your inner Muslim."

Unbeknownst to his parents and the rest of the gullible Americans, this young impressionable teenager was gradually becoming brainwashed and indoctrinated into hating his own country. Time magazine quoted, a language teacher in Yemen who said, "Lindh came from the U.S. already hating America." The magazine writes: "Lindh's correspondence from Yemen evinces an ambivalence toward the U.S. In a letter to his mother dated Sept. 23, 1998, he refers to the bombing of the U.S. embassies in Africa the previous month, saying the attacks 'seem far more likely to have been carried out by the American government than by any Muslims.'

Non-Muslims are gradually becoming familiar with the Islamic tactic of committing the crime and blaming the victim. Well known is the fantastic story of 4000 Jews not showing up for work on the fateful morning of 9/11/2001, made up by some Muslims and the conspiracy theory that they have invented to blame the CIA and the Mossad for what Bin Laden has so boastfully claimed as his victory. So this innocent boy was gradually led to believe that Islam is THE only real religion for all mankind, and he tried to learn it and practice it with sincerity and eagerness. He began studying and memorizing the Qur'an and in his notebook he wrote a passage that reads, "We shall make jihad as long as we live."[342] By becoming a Muslim, John Walker Lindh had entered in Muhammad's narcissistic bubble universe. He was already showing the signs of irrational and narcissistic Islamic thinking. He perfectly knew who was responsible for 9/11 tragedy. On the one hand he denied that it was the work of Muslims and on the other hand he was vowing to make jihad as long as he lives.

John alienated himself from the rest of his countrymen. According to the Qur'an, Muslims are not supposed to make friends with unbelievers. (Q.9:23) They are asked to fight those who do not believe in Allâh (Q.9:29) and murder them. (Q.9:123) A Muslim is not allowed to accept another religion. (Q.3:85)

It is no wonder that when John wrote back to his mother after the U.S. presidential election in 2000, he referred to George W. Bush as "your new President" and added, "I'm glad he's not mine." Of course not! A Muslim cannot accept the rule of unbelievers. He must disobey them, fight against them and endeavor to kill them. (Q.25:52)

---

[342] Ibid.

Understanding Muhammad

John Walker Lindh is one victim of the sickness of the Western society called political correctness. Wasn't it Ronald Reagan who called the Islamic terrorists in Afghanistan "freedom fighters?" John went on to become a freedom fighter. What is wrong with that? Didn't President George W. Bush and Tony Blair repeatedly announce, "Islam is a religion of peace?" Why jail a follower of the religion of peace who has simply followed the instructions of his religion of peace? The West is guilty – guilty of complicity, of appeasement and of self deception.

As required summer reading for first-year students, Prof. Michael Sells of the University of North Carolina compiled a book called *Approaching the Qur'an* where only the "nice" teachings of the Qur'an pertaining to the early Meccan verses were handpicked and the violent, bloody verses that call for killing, looting and raping unbelievers, those that churn the stomach of any sane person that were written later in Medina were deliberately left out. This is nothing but playing the game of deception. The same deception is found in the books of Karen Armstrong and John Esposito in their definition of Islam. Young Americans are being lied to. A false image of Islam is being portrayed for their consumption by some western academicians, God knows for what reason. And when these kids believe in these lies they are fed, trust others judgments, and go on to practice Islam, we brand them as terrorists, jail them, and prosecute them. Isn't this hypocrisy? These children are not guilty. They are the products of our sick ethos called political correctness.

How many newspapers, television or radio stations have the guts to call a spade a spade when it comes to Islam? Which one of our politicians has the mettle to stand in front of a camera and tell the nation that Islam is not a religion of peace? Watch your kids. If anyone dares to tell the truth, he is immediately branded as a racist and a hate-monger, and his head will roll. Meanwhile, Islamic propagandists are given freedom to twist the truth and promote their lies, knowing they will never be challenged on anything they say.

CAIR, Council of American-Islamic Relations, (or better said "Conning Americans with Islamic Ruse") furnishes thousands of libraries across the country with Islamic books, hoping to find more John Walker Lindhs. Mosques are being built in every city and town throughout the country to instill the hatred of America amongst the American kids. The situation is worse in Europe, Australia, Canada and other non-Muslim countries. According to a "secret report" divulged by Sean Rayment, Security Correspondent of the Sunday Telegraph on February 25, 2007, the Security Services in the UK believe that there are more than 2,000 Muslims plotting to engage in terrorist activities in that country. There is not a single day that someone is not killed by the hands of Muslim terrorists somewhere in the world. What will it take for the world to wake up and realize that Islam is not a religion but a dangerous cult? When are we going to pay attention to the Qur'an and the history of Islam to understand that terrorists are not "extremists" but practicing Muslims following the real, original teachings of their "holy" book and the examples set by their beloved prophet?

Once people convert to Islam, they enter an underworld of illusions, ignorance and fear, where fantasy takes the form of reality and evil is perceived as divine. Their values disintegrate and they act in ways they would have considered unbecoming and unacceptable prior to their Islamic indoctrination. The more they act in this depraved way, the more hardened they become, to the extent that returning to the real, world becomes almost impossible. Islam unfolds like a creeping paralysis, slowly corrupting minds and spirits, until it produces the best of all Muslims, the jihadi, commonly known as terrorists, the most beloved ones of Allâh and his prophet.

Osherow gives a thorough psychological explanation of this phenomenon: "According to dissonance theory, when a person commits an act or holds a cognition that is psychologically inconsistent with his or her self-concept, the inconsistency arouses an unpleasant state of tension. The individual tries to reduce this 'dissonance,' usually by altering his or her attitudes to bring them more into line with the previously discrepant action or belief. A number of occurrences in the People's Temple can be illuminated by viewing them in light of this process. The horrifying events of Jonestown were not due merely to the threat of force, nor did they erupt instantaneously. That is, it was not the case that something 'snapped' in people's minds, suddenly causing them to behave in bizarre ways. Rather, as the theory of cognitive dissonance spells out, people seek to justify their choices and commitments. Just as a towering waterfall can begin as a trickle, so too can the impetus for doing extreme or calamitous actions be provided by the consequences of agreeing to do seemingly trivial ones. In the People's Temple, the process started with the effects of undergoing a severe initiation to join the church, was reinforced by the tendency to justify ones commitments, and was strengthened by the need to rationalize ones behavior."

New converts to Islam often face more hardship, which they interpret as "test of God" and a "cleansing process." It starts by abstaining from drinking alcohol and eating pork. Watching what to eat and making sure the food is halal is a restriction on the freedom of the believers. Males gradually stop mixing with females as they struggle to suppress their sexual urges. This is an extremely arduous task that occupies their minds constantly and makes them live in a constant state of guilt. Sexual thoughts cannot be easily suppressed. As the result many of these people become completely obsessed with sex. Their entire mental energy is used to battle their inner "demon". The more guilt they feel about sex, the more they despise women whom they blame for tempting them.

Then they have the duty of performing the obligatory prayers five times per day, in a language most of them don't understand. If a prayer is missed, they are made to feel guilty and must say compensatory prayers. Adhering to these prayers and keeping count of them is another form of mental slavery. The Qur'an must be read and memorized. Understanding it is not necessary. What matters most is its right pronunciation. To question or criticize it could mean death.

Then there is a whole list of things that are "unclean" that believers must avoid, such as dog, pig, urine and kafirs (non-Muslims). Believers must be aware of these unclean things and wash each time they come in contact with them. If the believer is a woman, she has more restrictions. She has to cover herself with a veil and wear baggy clothes, even on scorching hot summer days. Going shopping, wrapped in Islamic hijab on a hot day is nothing short of torture. All these ordeals increase the faith of believers and they value Islam even more. They think the more they suffer the more rewards they will receive in the afterlife. Women must always obey the men of their family and always be docile and respectful. They will be intimidated, insulted, battered, raped or even killed, with very little, if any hope of legal or social protection. Islam is precious to its believers, precisely because practicing it is so difficult.

The psychology of this phenomenon is explained by Osherow: "Consider the prospective member's initial visit to the People's Temple, for example. When a person undergoes a severe initiation in order to gain entrance into a group, he or she is apt to judge that group as being more attractive, in order to justify expending the effort or enduring the pain. Aronson and Mills[343] demonstrated that students who suffered a greater embarrassment as a prerequisite for being allowed to participate in a discussion group rated its conversation (which actually was quite boring) to be significantly more interesting than did those students who experienced little or no embarrassment in order to be admitted. Not only is there a tendency to justify undergoing the experience by raising ones estimation of the goal in some circumstances.

---

[343] Aronson, E., AND Mills, J. The effects of severity of initiation on liking for a group. *Journal of Abnormal and Social Psychology*. 1959, 59, 177-18 1.

When Sane People Follow Insane People

Choosing to experience a hardship can go so far as to affect a person's perception of the discomfort or pain he or she felt. Zimbardo[344] and his colleagues showed that when subjects volunteered for a procedure that involved their being given electric shocks, those thinking that they had more choice in the matter reported feeling less pain from the shocks. More specifically, those who experienced greater dissonance, having little external justification to account for their choosing to endure the pain, described it as being less intense. This extended beyond their impressions and verbal reports; their performance on a task was hindered less, and they even recorded somewhat lower readings on a physiological instrument measuring galvanic skin responses. Thus the dissonance-reducing process can be double-edged: Under proper guidance, a person who voluntarily experiences a severe initiation not only comes to regard its ends more positively, but may also begin to see the means as less aversive: "We began to appreciate the long meetings, because we were told that spiritual growth comes from self-sacrifice." (Mills, 1979)

This explains why Muslims are even grateful for the tortures they undergo voluntarily and consider them to be a blessing. All these hardships are seen as little sacrifices for achieving a bigger reward. The bigger the sacrifice, the greater will be the reward. An extreme form of this devotion can be seen during the month of Ashura, when the Shiite Muslims beat themselves on the chest and lacerate their backs with a bundle of chains, and even cut their foreheads with machetes to bleed profusely. Thus, covered in their own blood, they march in processions that bring to mind Dante's description of hell. Apart from five times per day obligatory prayers, one month fasting and abstaining from water, during daylight hours, and other taxing rituals, the believer is required to give one fifth of his income to the mosque as *Khoms*, (tithes) and in addition he is encouraged to make donations in the form of *zakat* (alms).

Muhammad instructed his followers to wage jihad and plunder the wealth of non-believers. This might have concerned some of his followers, still mildly in touch with their humanity. Is the wealth earned though plundering pure? They must have wondered. Muhammad's response was that it would become pure if they paid one fifth of the spoils to him. He put the following verse in the mouth of his sock puppet god, ordering him to:

Take alms from their wealth in order to purify them and sanctify them with it.[345]

---

[344] Zimbardo, P. *The cognitive control of motivation.* Glenview, Ill.: Scott Foreman, 1969.
[345] Qur'an, Sura 9, Verse 103

Understanding Muhammad

As stated earlier, Medina after the banishment and genocide of the Jews was no longer an industrious and productive town. Its entire wealth came from the pillaging and plundering of other Arab tribes. The Muslims depended solely on looting from their continuous raids orchestrated by Muhammad. *Khoms* was instituted by the Prophet to "purify" ill-gotten gains and of course to fill the coffers of the holy Prophet and supply his bed with new flesh. Even today, Muslims who earn their living through honorable professions are required to pay khoms and zakat. There are constant reminders to believers to "spend of your substance in the cause of Allâh"(Q.2:195) and exhortations to "fight for the Faith, with their property and their persons." (Q.8:72)

Muhammad offered an orgiastic paradise filled with all sorts of carnal delights to anyone who believed in him and made jihad for him. All one has to do is stop reasoning and believe in whatever he said and this would guarantee him access to paradise and eternal sex. Once someone becomes involved in Islam or any cult for that matter, he is gradually asked to give whatever he can from his money and time. Soon he finds that he is so involved that it becomes difficult and indeed, dangerous to walk away. The pain of acknowledging that one has been duped is so intense that he'd rather not face the truth and continue to defend his faith.

Osherow explains: "Once involved, a member found ever-increasing portions of his or her time and energy devoted to the People's Temple. The services and meetings occupied weekends and several evenings each week. Working on Temple projects and writing the required letters to politicians and the press took much of one's 'spare' time. Expected monetary contributions changed from 'voluntary' donations (though they were recorded) to the required contribution of a quarter of one's income. Eventually, a member was supposed to sign over all personal property, savings, social security checks, and the like to the Peoples Temple. Before entering the meeting room for each service, a member stopped at a table and wrote self-incriminating letters or signed blank documents that were turned over to the church. If anyone objected, the refusal was interpreted as denoting a 'lack of faith' in Jones. Each new demand had two repercussions: In practical terms, it enmeshed the person further into the People's Temple web and made leaving more difficult; on an attitudinal level, it set the aforementioned processes of self-justification into motion. As Mills (1979) describes: 'We had to face painful reality. Our life savings were gone. Jim had demanded that we sell the life insurance policy and turn the equity over to the church, so that was gone. Our property had all been taken from us. Our dream of going to an overseas mission was gone. We thought that we had alienated our parents when we told them we were leaving the country. Even the children whom we had left in the care of Carol and Bill were openly hostile toward us. Jim had accomplished all this in such a short time! All we had left now was Jim and the Cause, so we decided to buckle under and give our energies to these two.'"

The same could be said of early Muslims. Those who followed Muhammad to Medina as refugees had nothing to fall back on. They had no jobs and no homes. Muhammad had asked the Ansar [Helpers, the believers native to Medina] to accommodate the immigrants and share whatever they had with them. This, of course, was not an easy life for either party. A great number of the immigrants used to live in the Mosque.

There is a curious story of an Ansar offering his wife to one of the refugees:

> Abdur Rahman bin Auf said, When we came to Medina as emigrants, Allâh's Apostle established a bond of brotherhood between me and Sa'd bin Ar-Rabi'. Sa'd bin Ar-Rabi' said (to me), 'I am the richest among the Ansar, so I will give you half of my wealth and you may look at my two wives and whichever of the two you may choose I will divorce her, and when she has completed the prescribed period (before marriage) you may marry her.' A few days later, 'Abdur Rahman came having traces of yellow (scent) on his body. Allâh's Apostle asked him whether he had got married. He replied in the affirmative. The Prophet said, 'Whom have you married?' He replied, 'A woman from the Ansar.[346]

Muslims quote this story to show how Muhammad had fostered brotherhood among believers, but it also shows that believers were so overcome with zealotry that they disregarded their own privacy and even the sanctity of their marriage. Their freedom and their independence were all but gone. In most cases they relinquished their independence willingly. Those who could see the problem did not dare to talk about it. The immigrants could not go back. Dissenting was considered to be the worst of crimes. The Helpers could not talk. Anyone could be an informer. They could be assassinated the next day and there were no dearth of zealot believers who would happily kill an uppity fellow believer, just as today, most Muslims will delightfully kill anyone who whispers a word of dissent. Those who could see the problem had no other option but to buckle under and play along. In one hadith we read:

---

[346] Sahih Bukhari *Volume 3, Book 34, Number 264*

A blind man had a slave-woman who used to abuse the Prophet and disparage him. …So he took a dagger, placed it on her belly, pressed it, and killed her. A child who came between her legs was smeared with the blood that was there. When the morning came, the Prophet was informed about it. He assembled the people called on the man to explain why he committed such horrendous murder. The man stood up while trembling and said: 'I am her master; she used to abuse you and disparage you. I have two sons like pearls from her, and she was my companion. Last night she began to abuse and disparage you. So I took a dagger, put it on her belly and pressed it till I killed her.' Thereupon the Prophet said: 'Oh be witness, no retaliation is payable for her blood.' [347]

A man commits double murder and all he had to say in his defense was that she insulted the Prophet and Muhammad set him free.

In such an atmosphere of terror, how could anyone disagree with Muhammad? What if this man lied to avoid a deserved punishment? The message that Muhammad wanted to send was clear: If anyone insults me, he should be put to death and the killer will not be charged. One can only imagine how many murderers have walked away with this alibi.

Section 295-C of Pakistan's Penal Code says: "Whoever by words, either spoken or written, or by visible representation, or by any imputation, innuendo, or insinuation, directly or indirectly defiles the sacred name of the Holy Prophet Muhammad shall be punished with death and shall also be liable to a fine."

Muhammad was not coy about his wishes. A hadith reports him say: "None of you will have faith till he loves me more than his father, his children and all mankind."[348] He was a narcissist and all he wanted was to be loved and feared. Both were the same to him. Muhammad was so desperate for attention and respect that when a group of Arabs came to visit him and did not pay him the reverence that he thought he was entitled to, he made his deity say:

O ye who believe! Raise not your voices above the voice of the Prophet, nor speak aloud to him in talk, as ye may speak aloud to one another, lest your deeds become vain and ye perceive not. Those that lower their voices in the presence of Allâh's Messenger, their hearts has Allâh tested for piety: for them is Forgiveness and a great Reward. Those who shout out to thee from without the inner apartments - most of them lack understanding.[349]

---

[347] Sunan Abu-Dawud Book 38, Number 4348
[348] Sahih Bukhari Volume 1 Number 14
[349] Qur'an, Sura 49, Verses 2-4

When Sane People Follow Insane People

Demanding the Ultimate Sacrifice

Osherow says: "Ultimately, Jim Jones and the Cause would require the members to give their lives."

The cult leader becomes so obsessed with obedience that he demands his followers prove their loyalty and love for him by sacrificing everything, including their lives. The cause is a pretext. The Qur'an offers great rewards for martyrs and encourages Muslims to sacrifice their lives for Muhammad's cause.

> Think not of those who are slain in Allâh's way as dead. Nay, they live, finding their sustenance from their Lord. They rejoice in the Bounty provided by Allâh...the (Martyrs) glory in the fact that on them is no fear, nor have they (cause to) grieve. They rejoice in the Grace and the Bounty from Allâh, and in the fact that Allâh suffers not the reward of the Faithful to be lost (in the least). [350]

There are also ahadith that talk about the rewards that a martyr would receive.

> The Prophet said, "Paradise has one hundred grades which Allâh has reserved for the Mujahidin (Muslim fighters) who fight in His Cause."[351]

> The Prophet said, "Nobody who enters Paradise likes to go back to the world even if he got everything on the earth, except a Mujahid who wishes to return to the world so that he may be martyred ten times because of the dignity he receives (from Allâh).[352]

> Our Prophet told us about the message of our Lord that 'Whoever amongst us is killed as a martyr will go to Paradise' Omar asked the Prophet, 'Is it not true that our men who are killed will go to Paradise and theirs (i.e. those of the Pagan's) will go to the (Hell) fire?' The Prophet said, 'Yes.' [353]

Osherow wonders: "What could cause people to kill their children and themselves? From a detached perspective, the image seems unbelievable. In fact, at first glance, so does the idea of so many individuals committing so much

---

[350] Qur'an, Sura 3, Verse 169
[351] Bukhari Volume 4, Book 52, Number 48
[352] Bukhari Volume 4, Book 52, Number 72
[353] Bukhari Volume 4, Book 52, Number 72

of their time, giving all of their money, and even sacrificing the control of their children to the People's Temple. Jones took advantage of rationalization processes that allow people to justify their commitments by raising their estimations of the goal and minimizing its costs."

As we can see this too was masterfully exploited by Muhammad. He convinced his followers that his was the most important cause and that they were created for the sole purpose of believing in him and worshiping the god that spoke only through him. *"I have only created Jinns and men that they may worship me"*(Q.51:56). According to a hadith *qudsi*, (believed absolutely to be true) the purpose of life is to know Allâh and to worship him and of course that is possible only through his messenger Muhammad. He gave promises of great rewards to those who sacrifice everything for him and threatened with eternal tortures those who doubt his unsubstantiated claim. In such state of mind, his befogged followers became ready to give up everything for him. They were ready to wage war even against their own fathers and brothers, kill or be killed. Like the followers of other cults, Muslims rationalize and justify all sorts of crimes, including kidnapping innocent people and beheading them, bombing civilians and massacring them by the thousands. The estimation of their cause is so elevated that everything else fades in comparison.

Overwhelming the Believers

The evolution from being a moderate Muslim to becoming a terrorist is gradual and often imperceptible. New converts are of course all moderate. They are first taught the "beauties of Islam." They are told that Islam is an easy religion, a religion of peace, of equality and worship of a single God. They are led to believe that Islam is accepting of other religions, especially Judaism and Christianity that are also monotheistic, and only disagrees with the believers of these religions in that they have corrupted their faith. They are then led to believe that Islam is the only religion that has not been contaminated. Because of that it is the only religion accepted by God. Those who do not believe in Islam reject the truth (deny God) and are doomed sinners. Eventually they are told that the *Isa* and *Musa* of the Qur'an are not the same as Jesus and Moses of the Bible. New convert, gradually come to think of people of other faiths as the enemies of Allâh and will start to hate them actively. Then they are taught that only Muslims are brothers to each other and that everyone else is out there trying to "get them".

When Sane People Follow Insane People

As you become more brainwashed, gradually you develop a sense of victimhood. You lose your own identity. You become an anonymous part of the amorphous *ummah*, a 'slave of Allâh..' You start seeing the world differently. The feeling of "us" versus "them" becomes stronger every day. "They" are the evil ones, the detractors and the enemies of God. They are the oppressors and the wrongdoers. Everyone who is not a Muslim, especially your brand of Islam, is part of "them." "Us" are the oppressed ones, the wronged ones and the victims. "Us" are the true believers, the ones that do Allâh's will and his work. Then you start believing that you have the true faith and the true religion that tells you to fight, to kill these enemies that oppress you and be harsh with them. You are told that Allâh will make you victorious, and will give you an eternity of sensual delights.

A "moderate Muslim" can become an extremist and a terrorist overnight. As long as Muslims believe in Islam, each and every one of them is a potential terrorist. Islam orders its followers to kill non-believers in the name of its god. This holy obligation is unique to Islam. Indeed, Allâh says that he loves the Mujahidin (Muslim fighters) most. They are the best of Muslims. They will inherit the most luscious and erotic eternity in paradise. The "moderate Muslims" are the hypocrites and weak in their religion. Gradual indoctrination is the modus operandi in all cults, where the core truth and the real agenda of the cult is concealed and is spoon-fed to the believers slowly. Hardcore members of cults say one thing to the outside world and another among themselves.

Osherow writes: "Much as he gradually increased his demands, Jones carefully orchestrated the members' exposure to the concept of a 'final ritual.' He utilized the leverage provided by their previous commitments to push them closer to its enactment. Gaining a 'foot in the door' by getting a person to agree to a moderate request makes it more probable that he or she will agree to do a much larger deed later, as social psychologists and sales people have found.[354] Doing the initial task makes something that might have seemed unreasonable at first appear less extreme in comparison, and it also motivates a person to make his or her behavior appear more consistent by consenting to the larger requests as well."

Osherow then explains how Jones prepared his followers to gradually commit mass suicide. "He started by undermining the member's belief that death was to be fought and feared and Jones directed several 'fake' suicide drills. These became tests of faith, of the member's willingness to follow Jones

---

[354] Freeman, J., AND Fraser, S. Compliance without pressure: The foot-in-the-door technique. *Journal of Personality and Social Psychology*, 1966, 4, 195-202.

even to death. Jones would ask people if they were ready to die and on occasion would have the membership 'decide' its own fate by voting whether to carry out his wishes. An ex-member recounted that one time, after a while Jones smiled and said, 'Well, it was a good lesson. I see you're not dead.' He made it sound like we needed the 30 minutes to do very strong, introspective type of thinking. We all felt strongly dedicated, proud of ourselves. Jones taught that it was a privilege to die for what you believe in, which is exactly what I would have been doing."[355]

Muhammad did not advocate suicide. Instead, he greatly praised martyrdom. The prophet of Allâh was more pragmatic than Jones. Suicide was of no use to him. He needed his followers alive so they could wage war for him, bring him booty and conquer the world for him. He glorified martyrdom and death on battlefields. The pragmatism of Muhammad can also be appreciated in the fact that while Jones and many other cult leader committed suicide and died along with their followers, Muhammad rarely took an active role in any battle.

While any sane person can easily see waging war and killing innocent people in the name of God is lunacy, no Muslim, not even the so called "moderate" ones can see that. Jihad is a vital pillar of Islam and any Muslim who disagrees with it is not a Muslim anymore. That is why the term "moderate Muslim" is an oxymoron. No one can be called moderate while he or she subscribes to an ideology that prescribes killing unbelievers. The difference between a terrorist Muslim and a so-called moderate Muslim is that the first wants to wage jihad now, while the latter thinks Muslims should wait until they become stronger and then wage jihad. In principle, no Muslim can disagree with the concept of jihad.

How can a billion, otherwise sane people, believe in this insanity? The answer can be found again in Jonestown.

Osherow writes: "After the Temple moved to Jonestown, the 'White Nights,' as the suicide drills were called, occurred repeatedly. An exercise that appears crazy was a regular, justifiable occurrence for the People's Temple participant."

The members of People's Temple were normal people. They were not insane or crazy. However, since they had placed their intelligence in the hands of a crazy man, they followed him blindly even in his madness.

Osherow writes: "The reader might ask whether this [the fake drills] caused the members to think that the actual suicides were merely another

---

[355] Winfrey, C. Why 900 died in Guyana. *New York Times Magazine*, February 25, 1979.

practice, but there were many indications that knew that the poison was truly deadly on that final occasion. The Ryan visit had been climatic, there were several new defectors, the cooks who had been excused from the prior drills in order to prepare the upcoming meal were included, Jones had been growing increasingly angry, desperate, and unpredictable, and, finally, everyone could see the first babies die. The membership was manipulated, but they were not unaware that this time the ritual was for real."

Osherow explains that under such conditions, people are apt to justify their actions, including when they engage in acts of violence in compliance to what their leader dictates. "A dramatic example of the impact of self-justification," he says, "concerns the physical punishment that was meted out in the People's Temple. As discussed earlier, the threat of being beaten or humiliated, forced the member to comply with Jones's orders. A person will obey as long as he or she is being threatened and supervised. To affect a person's attitudes, however, a mild threat has been demonstrated to be more effective than a severe threat [356] and its influence has been shown to be far longer lasting.[357] Under a mild threat, the individual has more difficulty attributing his or her behavior to such a minor external restraint, forcing the person to alter his or her attitudes in order to justify the action. Severe threats elicit compliance, but, imposed from the outside, they usually fail to cause the behavior to be internalized. Quite a different dynamic ensues when it is not so clear that the action is being imposed upon the person. When an individual feels that he or she played an active role in carrying out an action that hurts someone, there comes a motivation to justify ones part in the cruelty by rationalizing it as necessary or by derogating the victim by thinking that the punishment was deserved."[358]

This point is so crucial. In Jonestown believers themselves would condemn their fellow non-conforming, uppity members, especially their own family, and punish them. Acts of cruelty for normal people are traumatic. To alleviate the pangs of their own conscience, they try to rationalize their cruelty by derogating the victim and considering him or her, deserving of the punishment. Muslims are required to wage war against the unbelievers and even

---

[356] Aronson, E. , and Carlsmith, J. M. Effect of the severity of threat on the devaluation of forbidden behavior. *Journal of Abnormal and Social Psychology,* 1963, 66. 584-588.

[357] Freedman, J. and Long-term behavioural effects of cognitive dissonance. *Journal of Experimental Social Psychology, 1965,* 1, 145-155.

[358] Davos, K., AND Jones, E. Changes in interpersonal perception as a means of reducing cognitive dissonance. *Journal of abnormal and Social Psychology,* 1960, 61, 402-410.

against their unbelieving parents, and kin. These acts of violence and cruelty are justified and rationalized away. Believers are taught that their harshness and intolerance against unbelievers are in compliance with Divine Will, in accordance with the holy laws of Islam, and as such are not only acceptable but admirable. When Muslims raided innocent people and massacred them, Muhammad reassured them saying, "So you did not slay them, but it was Allah Who slew them, and you did not smite when you smote (the enemy), but it was Allah Who smote...." (Q.8:17)

BBC's correspondent, James Reynolds interviewed Hussam Abdo, the 15 year-old, semi retarded suicide bomber who was caught at the checkpoint in Israel. He was asked: "When you put on that belt did you really know that you were going to go and murder people, that you were going to go and cause great suffering to mothers and fathers, that you were going to be a mass murderer? Did you really know that?" Hussam' responded:

'Yes. Just like they came and caused our parents sadness and suffering they too should feel this. Just like we feel this - they should also feel it.'
'Were you scared of dying?' he was asked.
His response was identical to what the followers of Jones said in the last minutes of their lives.
'No. I'm not afraid of death.'
'Why not?'
'Nobody is going to live forever. We're all going to die.'

Among the saying of Muhammad there is this gem:

An intelligent person is one who is constantly thinking about and preparing for death.[359]

A story is told of Abu Hudhaifa a young Meccan believer who participated in the battle of Badr while his father was on the opposite side, in the ranks of the Quraish. It is reported that when Muhammad instructed his followers to spare Abbas, his own uncle, who was also among the Quraish, Hudhaifa raised his voice, "What? Are we to slay our fathers, brothers, uncles, etc., and to spare Abbas? No, verily, but I will slay him if I find him." Upon hearing this impertinent remark, Omar, in his usual sycophantic gesture of

---

[359] http://blog.mashy.com/blog/loly?page=2

When Sane People Follow Insane People

loyalty, unshielded his sword and looked at the Prophet for his signal to behead the ill-mannered youth at once.[360]

This threat had an immediate effect. A dramatic change happened in the behavior of Hudhaifa and we see him after the battle, a completely subdued and different person. When he saw his father slain and his corpse unceremoniously dragged to be dumped into a well, he was overwhelmed and started crying. "What?" asked Muhammad, "Are you saddened for the death of your father?" "Not so, O Allâh's Prophet!" responded Hudhaifa, "I do not doubt the justice of my father's fate; but I knew well his wise and generous heart, and I had trusted that the Lord would lead him to the faith. But now that I see him slain, and my hope destroyed! ---- it is for that I grieve." This time Muhammad was pleased with his response, comforted Abu Hudhaifa, blessed him; and said, "It is well."[361]

The displeasure of Muhammad at Hudhaifa's irreverence in defying his word and the swift reaction of Omar threatening to kill him on the spot, were such powerful stimuli that Hudhaifa immediately changed his attitude and a day later he even saw the "justice" in his father's murder. Once Hudhaifa lost his father, in whose killing he had conspired by ganging up with his murderers, there was no going back for him. He had to justify what he had done and rationalize the slaying of his father. Coming to his senses and facing his own guilty conscience would have been painfully mortifying. He had to continue in his chosen path and convince himself that Islam is true or face a lifetime of remorse.

Cult leaders have an uncanny ability to control the minds of their followers. As Hitler said, bigger lies are more easily believed by the masses, and the psychopathic cult leaders are masters of big lies.

There is a story narrated by Abdullah bin Ka'b bin Malik that demonstrates the kind of control Muhammad exerted upon his followers, both psychologically and socially. Ibn Ka'b says he was a devout believer and had accompanied Muhammad on all his raids and that thanks to the proceeds of those wars he had become a wealthy person. But when Muhammad called his followers to prepare for the war of Tabuk, it was a hot summer, the fruits were ripe, and so he procrastinated and stayed behind. Upon returning from the expedition, Muhammad called on those who had not gone and enquired the

---

[360] Muir; The Life of Mohammet Vol. III Ch. XII, Page 109.
[361] Muir; The Life of Mohammet Vol. III Ch. XII, Page 109; (Waqidi, p. 106; Sirat p. 230; Tabari, p. 294)

reason. Many had legitimate excuses and so were reluctantly forgiven, but ibn Ka'b and two other staunch believers did not dare to lie in order to excuse themselves. Ibn Ka'b continues:

'Really, by Allâh, there was no excuse for me. By Allâh, I had never been stronger or wealthier than I was when I remained behind you.' Then Allâh's Apostle said, 'As regards this man, he has surely told the truth. So get up till Allâh decides your case.' Allâh's Apostle forbade all the Muslims to talk to us, the three persons out of all those who had remained behind in that Ghazwa. So we kept away from the people and they changed their attitude towards us till the very land (where I lived) appeared strange to me as if I did not know it. We remained in that condition for fifty nights. As regards my two fellows, they remained in their houses and kept on weeping, but I was the youngest of them and the firmest of them, so I used to go out and witness the prayers along with the Muslims and roam about in the markets, but none would talk to me, and I would come to Allâh's Apostle and greet him while he was sitting in his gathering after the prayer, and I would wonder whether the Prophet did move his lips in return to my greetings or not. Then I would offer my prayer near to him and look at him stealthily. When I was busy with my prayer, he would turn his face towards me, but when I turned my face to him, he would turn his face away from me. When this harsh attitude of the people lasted long, I walked till I scaled the wall of the garden of Abu Qatada who was my cousin and dearest person to me, and I offered my greetings to him. By Allâh, he did not return my greetings. I said, 'O Abu Qatada! I beseech you by Allâh! Do you know that I love Allâh and His Apostle?' He kept quiet. I asked him again, beseeching him by Allâh, but he remained silent. Then I asked him again in the Name of Allâh. He said, 'Allâh and His Apostle know it better.' Thereupon my eyes flowed with tears and I returned and jumped over the wall.

When forty out of the fifty nights elapsed, behold! There came to me the messenger of Allâh's Apostle and said, 'Allâh's Apostle orders you to keep away from your wife,' I said, 'Should I divorce her; or else! What should I do?' He said, 'No, only keep aloof from her and do not cohabit with her.' The Prophet sent the same message to my two fellows. Then I said to my wife. 'Go to your parents and remain with them till Allâh gives His Verdict in this matter.' Ka'b added, 'The wife of Hilal bin Umaiya came to Apostle and said, 'O Allâh's Apostle! Hilal bin Umaiya is a helpless old man who has no servant to attend on him. Do you dislike that I should serve him?' He said, 'No you can serve him, but he should not come near you.' She

When Sane People Follow Insane People

said, 'By Allâh, he has no desire for anything. By, Allâh, he has never ceased weeping till his case began till this day of his.'

On that, some of my family members said to me, 'Will you also ask Allâh's Apostle to permit your wife to serve you as he has permitted the wife of Hilal bin Umaiya to serve him?' I said, 'By Allâh, I will not ask the permission of Allâh's Apostle regarding her, for I do not know what Allâh's Apostle would say if I asked him to permit her to serve me while I am a young man.' Then I remained in that state for ten more nights after that till the period of fifty nights was completed starting from the time when Allâh's Apostle prohibited the people from talking to us. When I had offered the Fajr prayer on the 50th morning on the roof of one of our houses and while I was sitting in the condition which Allâh described (in the Qur'an) my very soul seemed straitened to me and even the earth seemed narrow to me for all its spaciousness, there I heard the voice of one who had ascended the mountain of Sala' calling with his loudest voice, 'O Ka'b bin Malik! Be happy by receiving good tidings.' I fell down in prostration before Allâh, realizing that relief had come. Allâh's Apostle had announced the acceptance of our repentance by Allâh when he had offered the Fajr prayer. The people then went out to congratulate us. The people started receiving me in batches, congratulating me on Allâh's Acceptance of my repentance, saying, 'We congratulate you on Allâh's Acceptance of your repentanc[e] [362]

Muhammad refers to this story in the Qur'an:

(He turned in mercy also) to the three who were left behind; (they felt guilty) to such a degree that the earth seemed constrained to them, for all its spaciousness, and their (very) souls seemed straitened to them,- and they perceived that there is no fleeing from Allâh (and no refuge) but to Himself. Then He turned to them, that they might repent: for Allâh is Oft-Returning, Most Merciful. (Q. 9:118)

As we can see in the above story, Muhammad had a tremendous control over his followers. The atmosphere of Medina was extremely charged. He could order his followers to shun one of their fellows, their own relatives and even order them to abstain from cohabiting with their spouses. The psychological control was so intense that some dreaded lying or making excuses. Muhammad could not possibly know what was going on in their minds, whether the excuses

---

[362] Bukhari Volume 5, Book 59, Number 702

they made were true or not. But he made them believe his god was aware of their innermost thoughts and therefore rendered them helpless and thus brought them under his total control. This is the ultimate form of control. The invisible "Big Brother" is not only watching your actions, he is also monitoring your thoughts. There is nothing more crippling than this kind of control.

Muhammad used the most powerful system to control people and their thoughts, which has lasted for 1400 years. Unless it is challenged, it will continue forever, eroding and destroying the most vital of human rights – the freedom to think and decide for oneself.

Alluding to those who had legitimate excuses and were not punished like these three men, Muhammad wrote the following verses:

> They will swear to you by Allâh, when ye return to them, that ye may leave them alone. So leave them alone: For they are an abomination, and Hell is their dwelling-place, a fitting recompense for the (evil) that they did.

> They will swear unto you, that ye may be pleased with them but if ye are pleased with them, Allâh is not pleased with those who disobey. (Q. 9:95-96)

Muhammad had no way to verify the legitimacy of these men's alibis, so with these warnings, he threatened those who lied of severe divine punishment. This kind of mind control works as long as one is gullible enough to believe in the lies of the narcissist cult leader. Once one stops believing in the narcissist's lies, he loses his control completely. Today Muslims are still under the sway of Muhammad because they believe in him. The fear of hell has paralyzed their thinking ability. The very thought of doubting Muhammad sends shivers down their spines and they dismiss that thought at once.

Osherow explains: "Let's step back for a moment. The processes going on at Jonestown obviously were not as simple as those in a well-controlled laboratory experiment; several themes were going on simultaneously. For example, Jim Jones had the power to impose any punishments that he wished in the People's Temple, and, especially towards the end, brutality and terror at Jonestown were rampant. But Jones carefully controlled how the punishments were carried out. He often called upon the members themselves to agree to the imposition of beatings. They were instructed to testify against fellow members, bigger members told to beat up smaller ones, wives or lovers forced to sexually humiliate their partners, and parents asked to consent to and assist in the beatings of their children." (Mills, 1979; Kilduff and Javers, 1978). The

When Sane People Follow Insane People

punishments grew more and more sadistic, the beatings so severe as to knock the victim unconscious and cause bruises that lasted for weeks. As Donald Lunde, a psychiatrist who has investigated acts of extreme violence explains: 'Once you've done something that major, it's very hard to admit even to yourself that you've made a mistake, and subconsciously you will go to great lengths to rationalize what you did. It's very tricky defense mechanism exploited to the hilt by the charismatic leader.' [Newsweek, 1978a]

A more personal account of the impact of this process is provided by Jeanne Mills. At one meeting, she and her husband were forced to consent to the beating of their daughter as punishment for a very minor transgression. She relates the effect this had on her daughter, the victim, as well as on herself, one of the perpetrators:

> As we drove home, everyone in the car was silent. We were all afraid that our words would be considered treasonous. The only sounds came from Linda, sobbing quietly in the back seat. When we got into our house, Al and I sat down to talk with Linda. She was in too much pain to sit. She stood quietly while we talked with her. 'How do you feel about what happened tonight?' Al asked her. 'Father was right to have me whipped.' Linda answered. 'I've been so rebellious lately, and I've done a lot of things that were wrong. I'm sure Father knew about those things, and that's why he had me hit so many times.' As we kissed our daughter goodnight, our heads were spinning. It was hard to think clearly when things were so confusing. Linda had been the victim, and yet we were the only people angry about it. She should have been hostile and angry. Instead, she said that Jim had actually helped her. We knew Jim had done a cruel thing, and yet everyone acted as if he were doing a loving thing in whipping our disobedient child. Unlike a cruel person hurting a child, Jim had seemed calm, almost loving, as he observed the beating and counted off the whacks. Our minds were not able to comprehend the atrocity of the situation because none of the feedback we were receiving was accurate

> The feedback one received from the outside was limited, and the feedback from inside the Temple member was distorted. By justifying the previous actions and commitments, the groundwork for accepting the ultimate commitment was established.

Only months after we defected from Temple did we realize the full extent of the cocoon in which we lived. And only then did we understand the fraud, sadism, and emotional blackmail of the master manipulator.[363]

The testimony of Jeanne Mills is in many ways identical to those of ex-Muslims. Ex-Muslims admit that they were not aware of the abuse that they were subjected to when they were believers. It is only after they leave Islam that they realize the enormity of the abuse and mind control. A Muslim woman marrying a Muslim man is just as subject to domestic violence as a non-Muslim woman converting to Islam and marrying a Muslim man. However, the former is often unaware of the abuse. She is used to abuse because she grew up with it. She saw her mother, aunts, and other women she knew abused. This is normal to her and she resigns to her fate with no complaints. Non-Muslim women marrying Muslim men, often come from families where women are not denigrated, beaten and abused. For them, the marriage to a Muslim man is much more oppressive than for a woman born and raised as a Muslim, who may even defend the right of her husband to punish her.

Christians, Jews or Hindus also leave their faiths. However there is not much anger and resentment in them. When Muslims leave Islam, they leave it with bitterness in their hearts. It is because only then they see the extent of their victimization. This is not how the apostates of other religions feel about their prophets. Ex-Muslims hate Muhammad intensely. The awakening is terribly painful. What is hurtful is the bitter taste of deception.

Osherow explains: "A few hours before his murder, Congressman Ryan addressed the membership: "I can tell you right now that by the few conversations I've had with some of the folks, there are some people who believe this is the best thing that ever happened in their whole lives." [Cheers and applause can be heard in the background] (Krause, 1978). The acquiescence of so many and the letters they left behind indicate that this feeling was widely shared or at least expressed by the members."

Islam, like the People's Temple, attracts the most vulnerable members of the society, those who are downtrodden and in need of a sense of purpose. In western society, where individuality is taken to the extreme, there is a sense of loneliness. Islam gives the new convert a sense of community. It gives them an alternative way of viewing their lives, a direction, a sense of belonging, a sense of transcendence, but it does so at a terrible cost. The cost is alienation from their own culture and country to the extent that they disown their families and

---

[363] Mills, J. *Six years with God.* New York: A & W Publishers, 1979.

former friendships, and plot their downfall. Islam, like People's Temple, teaches its followers to fear anything and anyone outside of their faith and regards nonbelievers as "the enemy." Just like the followers of Jones, true Muslims hate the possibility of any other lifestyle. Islam to them is the only correct way and everything else must perish. Muslims are increasingly suspicious of non-Muslims and are fervent believers of the conspiracy theories about the "wicked West". I have heard many educated and otherwise intelligent Muslims say seriously that the attack on the Pentagon and the WTC in New York in September 11, 2001 was the work of the CIA and the Zionists. This level of intellectual paralysis is only possible if you are the victim of a cult.

Control of Information

Muslims, like their prophet, are conditioned to be paranoid. They are taught that non-Muslims are the enemy, out to destroy them. I recall myself glaring at a friend who was curious to read Salman Rushdie's Satanic Verses. This, I did without even having any knowledge of its content. But Rushdie's book is really just a literary novel. The Qur'an is far more damaging to Islam than any book any critic could ever write. Nonetheless, as a Muslim you are not allowed to read anything criticizing Islam. It is not that you fear being caught; you are afraid of Allâh and his sadistic punishments. Reading anti-Islamic material shatters your own self-concept of loyalty.

Compare that to the People's Temple. "Within the People's Temple, and especially at Jonestown," writes Osherow, "Jim Jones controlled the information to which members would be exposed. He effectively stifled any dissent that might arise within the church and instilled distrust in each member for contradictory messages from outside. After all, what credibility could be carried by information supplied by 'the enemy' that was out to destroy the People's Temple with 'lies?' Seeing no alternatives and having no information, a member's capacity for dissent or resistance was minimized. Moreover, for most members, part of the Temples attraction resulted from their willingness to relinquish much of the responsibility and control over their lives. These were primarily the poor, the minorities, the elderly, and the unsuccessful. They were happy to exchange personal autonomy (with its implicit assumption of personal responsibility for their plight) for security, brotherhood, the illusion of miracles, and the promise of salvation. Stanley Cath, a psychiatrist who has studied the conversion techniques used by cults, generalizes: 'Converts have to believe only what they are told. They don't have to think, and this relieves tremendous tensions.' (Newsweek, 1978a)"

The above, perfectly describes the condition of Muslims, especially in Islamic countries, where any information slightly contradicting the official, public Islamic creed is censored and the believers are allowed only one view, the one provided by the Islamic authorities. In fact Muslims try hard to censor any anti-Islamic message even in non-Muslim countries. If a book or an article is published that they do not like, they protest and try to force the "offender" to withdraw his publication and apologize. One can only imagine the kind of control and censorship that Muhammad exerted over his followers in his compound, Medina. On numerous occasions Omar would draw his sword looking at Muhammad for his signal to behead an impertinent person who had challenged the Prophet's authority.

Just as Mecca fell to Islam, and just as Persia, Syria, Egypt and over fifty other countries fell under the domination of Islam; the rest of the world is not immune. More than 2,000 years ago, the Chinese sage Sun Zi [Tzu] said: "Know your enemy, know yourself, and your victory will not be threatened." These words are just as true today as they were then. The question is, "Do we know our enemy, and do we truly know ourselves?" Sadly the answer to both questions is negative. Not only do we have no clue about Islam, there are many of us who in their hatred of their own Heleno-Christians culture, have chosen to side with anyone who shares with them that hatred.

Ibn Ishaq tells a story that helps understand the nature of Islam. It is about Orwa's observation of the treatment that the followers of Muhammad conferred on him. On behalf of the Quraish, he visited Muhammad in his encampment at Hudaibiyah, on the outskirts of Mecca to dissuade him and his 1500 armed men from performing pilgrimage to Mecca that year, which the Meccans thought was provocative.

Muhammad was calm and Abu Bakr was speaking on his behalf. Orwa, not heeding Abu Bakr, became more earnest, and in accordance to the Bedouin custom, stretched forth his hand to take hold of Muhammad's beard. This was a token of friendship and familiarity and not an act of disrespect. "Back off!" cried a bystander, striking his arm. "Hold off your hand from the Prophet of Allâh!" Orwa was startled at the youth's interruption and asked, "And who is this?" "It is your nephew, Moghira," responded the youth. "Ungrateful!" exclaimed Orwa (alluding to his having paid compensation for certain murders committed by his nephew), "it is but as yesterday that I redeemed your life."

When Sane People Follow Insane People

Orwa was impressed by the degree of reverence and devotion that Muhammad's followers showed their prophet. Upon returning to Mecca he reported that he had seen many kings, the Khosrow, Caysar, and Najashi, but never had witnessed such attention and homage as Muhammad received from his followers. "They rushed to save the water in which he had performed his ablutions, to catch up his spittle, or seize a hair of his if it chanced to fall." [364]

As these stories make clear, Muhammad had built a personality cult around himself. He was the personification of his god that he was preaching. Obedience to him was obedience to Allâh and disobeying him was disobeying Allâh. This is everything a narcissistic psychopath craves – to be God incarnate. Muhammad manipulated everyone until he ascended to the throne of Allâh and became the de facto God.

Jeanne Mills commented: "I was amazed at how little disagreement there was between the members of this church. Before we joined the church, Al and I couldn't even agree on whom to vote for in a presidential election. Now that we all belonged to a group, family arguments were becoming a thing of the past. There was never a question of who was right, because Jim was always right. When our large household met to discuss family problems, we didn't ask for opinions. Instead, we put the question to the children, 'What would Jim do?' It took the difficulty out of life. There was a type of 'manifest destiny' which said the Cause was right and would succeed. Jim was right and those who agreed with him were right. If you disagreed with Jim, you were wrong. It was as simple as that."[365]

Muslims follow two things, one is the Qur'an and the other is the Sunnah. The Qur'an is the words of Muhammad (claimed to be Allâh's)[366] and the Sunnah is what people reported of what he said and did. The details of the Sunnah are recorded in the voluminous books of Ahadith. The doctors of Islamic law study for years to master these details and believers do not do anything without consulting them and learning the correct way of doing things. Sunnah is in effect the Islamic "prescription for living" based on the examples set by Muhammad and how he lived. These are the details about Muhammad's life reported by his companions and wives. Everything is detailed. Every action is prescribed. All believers have to do is spend years learning these "important" prescriptions for living Islamically, in accordance with the examples set by their

---

[364] Sirat Ibn Ishaq, p.823

[365] Mills, J. *Six years with God.* New York: A & W Publishers, 1979

[366] There are also those who believe the Qur'an is the work of multiple hands. Among the is Denis Giron http://www.infidels.org/library/modern/denis_giron/multiple.html

Prophet and follow them meticulously in the fond belief that they will have fulfilled their duty as Muslims and will be rewarded for their "good" deeds.

Good and bad in Islam are not defined by right and wrong but by doing what Muhammad enjoined and prohibited.

How did Muhammad develop such an ability to manipulate people, a power that has taken psychologists years to unravel? Muhammad was a narcissist and whatever he did was an expression of his narcissistic personality disorder. It all came to him naturally, an ability that he shared with other successful narcissists such as Hitler, Stalin, Jim Jones and Saddam.

Osherow writes about this when he talks about Jim Jones: "Though it is unlikely that he had any formal exposure to the social psychological literature, Jim Jones utilized several very powerful and effective techniques for controlling people's behavior and altering their attitudes. Some analyses have compared his tactics to those involved in 'brainwashing,' for both include the control of communication, the manipulation of guilt, and power over people's existence,[367] as well as isolation, an exacting regimen, physical pressure, and the use of confessions.[368] But using the term brainwashing makes the process sound too esoteric and unusual. There were some unique and scary elements in Jones's personality paranoia, delusions of grandeur, sadism, and a preoccupation with suicide. Whatever his personal motivation, however, having formulated his plans and fantasies, he took advantage of well-established social psychological tactics to carry them out. The decision to have a community destroy itself was crazy, but those who performed the deed were 'normal' people who were subjected to a tremendously provocative situation, the victims of powerful internal forces as well as external pressures."

This definition explains how it is possible for a multitude of sane people to follow an insane man. This happened in Germany. Hitler was insane, but millions of Germans who believed in him were not. How could millions of educated and intelligent people fall prey to the manipulations of a psychopath? As we see this has happened more than once. Dictators are often psychopaths, yet they manage to control millions and fool very normal, sane people.

The grip these psychopaths have over the emotions of their victims is mind-boggling. Three months after this horrendous event in Jonestown, Michael Prokes, who was spared because he was assigned to carry away a box of People's Temple funds, called a press conference in a California motel room. After claiming that Jones had been misunderstood and demanding the release of

---

[367] Lifton, R. J. Appeal of the death trip. *New York Times Magazine*, January 7, 1979.
[368] Cahill, T. In the valley of the shadow of death. *Rolling Stone*. January 25, 1979.

When Sane People Follow Insane People

a tape-recording of the final minutes [quoted earlier], he stepped into the bathroom and shot himself in the head. He left behind a note, saying that if his death inspired another book about Jonestown, it was worthwhile. (Newsweek, 1979) Doesn't this shed light on the psychopathology of the suicide bomber?

Jeanne and Al Mills were among the most vocal critics of the People's Temple following their defection, and they topped an alleged "death list" of its enemies. Even after Jonestown, the Mills had repeatedly expressed fear for their lives. Well over a year after the People's Temple massacre, they and their daughter were murdered in their Berkeley home. Their teen-age son, himself an ex-People's Temple member, testified that he was in another part of the large house at the time. As yet, no suspect has been charged. There are indications that the Mills knew their killer. There were no signs of forced entry, and they were shot at close range. Jeanne Mills had been quoted as saying, "It's going to happen; if not today, then tomorrow." On the final tape of Jonestown, Jim Jones blamed Jeanne Mills by name, and promised that his followers in San Francisco "will not take our death in vain." (Newsweek, 1980)

Muslims consider it their duty to kill anyone who leaves Islam. Their hatred of apostates is unbelievably intense. There is nothing that a Muslim hates so feverishly as an apostate. Muslims will not relent or give up until they find and kill apostates. Those who dare to defy Islam do so at their own peril. Muhammad's orders are unequivocal:

> But if they turn renegades, seize them and slay them wherever ye find them. (Q. 4:89).

Understanding Muhammad

Chapter Seven

Ripples and Effects

*I*t was only a twist of fate, in fact a series of them that made Muhammad the phenomenon he became. He was born to an unloving mother and spent his formative years, the crucial years that a child has to receive unconditional love, in a foster home where he learned he was an orphan. Then, when the time came for him to learn discipline, his grandfather and uncle spoiled him.

Psychologists believe that narcissism may be genetic. Although we can't be sure whether Amina, Muhammad's mother, suffered from NPD, it is safe to say that she was an immature selfish, and loveless woman for abandoning her only child to be raised by strangers when there was no justification for her to do so. Lack of love during the first five years of a child's life and lack of discipline after that greatly contribute to the development of narcissistic personality disorder, a trait Muhammad evinced throughout his life.

Muhammad was a loner since his childhood. He kept himself aloof from other kids and did not have friends. He remained a loner till he married Khadijah, which greatly increased his prestige among the Meccans. Even after the marriage, he used to spend most of his time alone in a cave. He was not comfortable in the company of those who treated him as equal. The only times he felt comfortable were when he was the center of attention. He was only at ease among his followers whom he had made to revere him with bogus claims and empty promises of heavenly rewards.

Understanding Muhammad

About the year 9 A.H. (nine years after his arrival in Medina) a group of Arabs from the tribe of Bani Tamim came to visit him. In the tradition of Arabs, they started calling him out from outside the apartments (hujurat) of his wives. "Hey Muhammad! Here we are coming from far away to see you." Muhammad did not like their tone. He wanted to be treated with reverence and respect like a king. He did not respond to their calls and put the following words in the mouth of his invisible deity urging everyone to be respectful to him.

> O you who believe! Be not forward in the presence of Allah and His Messenger, and be careful of (your duty to) Allah; surely Allah is Hearing, Knowing. O you who believe! Do not raise your voices above the voice of the Prophet, and do not speak loud to him as you speak loud to one another, lest your deeds became null while you do not perceive. Surely those who lower their voices before Allah's Messenger are they whose hearts Allah has proved for guarding (against evil); they shall have forgiveness and a great reward. (As for) those who call out to you from behind the private chambers, surely most of them do not understand. And if they wait patiently until you come out to them, it would certainly be better for them, and Allah is Forgiving, Merciful. (Q.49:1-5)

These men were not being disrespectful to God, but treated Muhammad casually, not as he expected to be treated. These are not the words of God, but the petty concerns of a narcissist seeking recognition and respect.

As fate had it, Muhammad met a wealthy woman who suffered from her own quirk of personality disorder. Often narcissists find co-dependents as companions. Their sadomasochistic relationship satisfies both, and in a twisted way they form an amazingly "functional" and lasting relationship. They do not love each other as neither one has any understanding of this noble sentiment, but they NEED one another because each feeds the narcissism of the other.

There is also enough evidence to conclude that Muhammad suffered from temporal lobe epilepsy. Therefore, he was not lying when he claimed hearing bells ringing, seeing light, and having visions of angels and other ghosts. Several times in his life he had epileptic seizures, starting at the age of five, in adolescence and later in adulthood.

However, the seizures stopped as he aged. This is often the case with TLE. Nonetheless, convinced of his status as a messenger of God and impelled by his narcissistic thirst for grandeur, Muhammad continued fabricating verses even when his hallucinatory experiences ended. As a narcissist he believed he was superior being, licensed not only to lie, but to break all laws, and that whatever he did was acceptable and lawful. Narcissists do not consider themselves bound by any norms. Laws are made for ordinary people, not for them. They regard themselves as above the law, and any constraint. Narcissists think that they are the center of the universe, the reason for the world's existence, the best of creation, and whom everyone must love, fear and obey. They value others only to the extent that they are useful and contribute to their grandeur, providing them with continuous narcissistic supplies – and if they don't, they do not deserve to live. A narcissist is capable of killing millions of people with clarity of conscience and no qualms. Saddam Hussein, who gassed and massacred hundreds of thousands of Iraqis, remained defiant to the end of his trial, claiming that as the head of state it was his prerogative to kill in order to bring stability to the country. He showed no sign of remorse for his butcheries. Saddam, Hitler and Muhammad lied, but it is simplistic to call them liars, because they believed their own lies. They were psychopaths. Many of Muhammad's hallucinations were real to him. Yet he lied most of the time with the conviction he was entitled to do so because he was unique, special and above the law.

No one is always truthful or always a liar. Muhammad was no different. His experience in the cave was real. However, most of the time he lied and felt justified doing so. He considered himself so important, and his cause so august that he did not think he should be hindered by "minor details" such as being truthful. Those rules, he thought, were made for inferior beings and not for someone whom God had chosen to be his messenger, the best of the creation and through whom the universe had come to be.

Muhammad also had symptoms of obsessive-compulsive disorder. This explains his obsession with rituals, many of which he himself would observe even when no one was watching. His companions interpreted his obsessive-compulsive disorder as proof of his sincerity.

Muhammad was a superstitious man. He said many absurd and ridiculous things that his followers gobble up unquestioningly, such as:

> If anyone of you rouses from sleep and performs the ablution, he should wash his nose by putting water in it and then blowing it out thrice, because Satan has stayed in the upper part of his nose all the night.[369]

---

[369] Bukhari Volume 4, Book 54, Number 516:

Muhammad was not lying when he made these asinine statements. He believed in what he said.

To understand Muhammad we have to understand his psychopathology. He was not a liar but a psychopath who suffered from a litany of mental disorders. He lied, assured that he was entitled to lie and was annoyed if others did not believe him. He felt no need to give any proof for his claims. As far as he was concerned, the very fact that HE, such a superior being, made a claim was proof enough of the validity of that claim and everyone had to agree with him without hesitation or face annihilation.

Today, a billion sane and often smart people blindly believe and follow a psychopath. The signs of Muhammad's insanity are evident in the entire Ummah. Muslims lie shamelessly to advance the cause of Islam. Honest people who would never lie for their own sake will brazenly lie for Islam. On one hand they know what they say is false and on the other they say it with conviction and are offended if contradicted. "How dare you question the faith of a billion people?" Muslims are intolerant of dissent. They do not think that it is up to them to answer your questions in a logical way but rather attack you by calling you Islamophobic, hate monger and even racist, just as their prophet called those who did not believe in him, "blind, deaf and dumb, with no understanding."[370] He threatened those who doubted him saying, "On the Day of Judgment We shall gather them together, prone on their faces, blind, dumb, and deaf: their abode will be Hell: every time it shows abatement, We shall increase for them the fierceness of the Fire." (Q.17:97) Islam is not just a false belief but also a mental disorder. It is a disorder that reduces sane people into insane people.

The Socio-Political Factor

It is important to mention that a contributing factor to the success of Islam was the socio-political milieu in which Muhammad launched his prophetic career. Arabia of the seventh century lacked a central government. The society was tribal, where each tribe lived autonomously and independently from others. Rivalries often led to strife and warfare, to be settled after some blood was shed.

---

[370] (Quran. 2:18, 2:171, 6:39, 8:22)

Ripples and Effects

Various tribes formed alliances with each other for their own protection. Some made a living through waylaying and looting. This lack of a central power allowed Muhammad and his marauding gang to raid one tribe while making alliances with others, even inviting them to join him in his robberies, sharing with them the spoils, until their turn came and they became his victims.

He signed a treaty with the Jews of Medina so he could raid the Meccan caravans. Once he became powerful, he demanded the Jews pay the cost of his warfare. Then he overtook and exterminated them all. He signed a treaty with the Meccans in which he promised the cessation of hostility against them for ten years. This allowed him to direct his attention to the northern towns and raid Khaibar and Fadak. Then he broke his treaty with the Meccans and formed an alliance with the Bani Tamim, promising them a share of the booty and immunity, should they help him to raid Mecca. When Mecca fell, he felt secure and had no need for the Bani Tamim. He reneged on his promise and instead of paying them, demanded they pay him tithes or prepare for war.

After the conquest of Mecca, Muhammad felt so strong that he made his god reveal a sura saying:

> (This is a declaration of) immunity by Allah and His Messenger towards those of the idolaters with whom you made an agreement. So go about in the land for four months and know that you cannot weaken Allah and that Allah will bring disgrace to the unbelievers. And an announcement from Allah and His Messenger to the people on the day of the greater pilgrimage that Allah and His Messenger are free from liability to the idolaters; therefore if you repent, it will be better for you, and if you turn back, then know that you will not weaken Allah; and announce painful punishment to those who disbelieve. (9:1-3)

Thus Muhammad made it clear he was no longer bound by any treaty that he signed previously and that everyone had only four moths to convert, pay their tithes or face a painful punishment.

I hope that by now it is clear that Islam is nothing but a tool of domination that was invented by a psychopath narcissist and that any thought of reforming it is futile. Islam cannot be reformed, but it can be eradicated. You can't get rid of a lie by reforming it. This requires telling more lies. To get rid of a lie all is required is to tell the truth. Let not the size of Islam intimidate you. Islam is a tall edifice built on sand of lies. Once its foundation is exposed, those sands will wash away and this mighty edifice will crumble like a house of cards. The end of Islam is indeed at hand.

Dialogue between Civilizations?

Megalomania, bullishness, the sense of entitlement and all other narcissistic traits of Muhammad are present in each and every Muslim, to the extent that they emulate their prophet. From king to pauper, from president to janitor, Muslims consider themselves to be superior to the rest of humanity. They are convinced that one day Islam will dominate, mankind will submit to them, and they will be the masters of the world.

This feeling of self importance was expressed eloquently by Dr. Mahathir, the outgoing Prime Minister of Malaysia during an OIC (Organization of Islamic Conference) summit in 2003. He acknowledged that the early Muslims built their "civilization" by studying the works of the Greeks and other scholars before Islam and then boastfully added that the "*Europeans had to kneel at the feet of Muslim scholars in order to access their own scholastic heritage.*" In his speech he invited the Muslims to amass "*guns and rockets, bombs and warplanes, tanks and warships*" to subdue the non-Muslims detractors and again rule over them. [371]

All these riots, demonstrations and violence made by Muslims throughout the world are expressions of their narcissistic personality trait. It is their sense of inferiority exteriorized as megalomania and pretense of superiority. They try to hide their humiliation with arrogance and boastfulness. They want to establish their supremacy through threat, violence and terror.

Muslims claim to want "dialogue between civilizations." This term was coined by the ex-president of Iran, Mullah Khatami, in response to Samuel P. Huntington's theory of "Clash of Civilizations." What civilization? Islam is against civilization. However, dialogue is the last thing on their minds.

In September 2006, once again Muslims were up in arms - this time over a speech made by Pope Benedict XVI at the University of Regensburg in Germany. In this speech, entitled "*Faith and Reason,*" the pontiff delineated the fundamental difference between Christianity's view that God is intrinsically rational, as inspired by the Greek concept of *logos,* and Islam's view that "God is absolutely transcendent," who does as he pleases, is not bound by anything, including reason, and, therefore, his actions can appear irrational to humans.

Pope Benedict quoted a discussion that took place in 1391 between the erudite Byzantine emperor Manuel II Paleologus and an educated Persian on the subject of Christianity and Islam. "In that discussion," the Pope said, "the

---

[371] http://www.zionism.netfirms.com/Mahathir.html

emperor touches on the theme of the holy war and addressing his interlocutor says: '*Show me just what Mohammed brought that was new, and there you will find things only evil and inhuman, such as his command to spread by the sword the faith he preached.*' The emperor, after having expressed himself so forcefully, goes on to explain in detail the reasons why spreading the faith through violence is something unreasonable. Violence is incompatible with the nature of God and the nature of the soul. '*God,*' he says, '*is not pleased by blood – and not acting reasonably is contrary to God's nature. Faith is born of the soul, not the body. Whoever would lead someone to faith needs the ability to speak well and to reason properly, without violence and threats.... To convince a reasonable soul, one does not need a strong arm, or weapons of any kind, or any other means of threatening a person with death.... The decisive statement in this argument against violent conversion is this: not to act in accordance with reason is contrary to God's nature.*'"

The Pope then quoted Theodore Khoury, from whose book he had taken the above story who observed: "For the emperor, as a Byzantine shaped by Greek philosophy, this statement is self-evident. But for Muslims God is absolutely transcendent. His will is not bound up with any of our categories, even that of rationality." Here Khoury quotes a work of the noted French Islamist R. Arnaldez, who points out that Ibn Hazn stated that "God is not bound even by his own word, and that nothing would oblige him to reveal the truth to us. Were it God's will, we would even have to practice idolatry."

The Pope's speech offended Muslims. Their leaders protested angrily and denounced the Pontific. Some even called for his death. Needless to say that there were several riots and some innocent people were killed as the result. How can there be a dialogue when questioning Islam will result in violence and could cause the death of the questioner? If Islam is "misunderstood," shouldn't Muslims welcome questions and answer them to remove the misunderstandings?

There are many verses in the Qur'an that require clarification. "Slay the unbelievers wherever you catch them." (2:191) "Fight them, until there is no more dissent and religion is that of Allâh" (2:193) "The vilest of animals in Allâh's sight are those who disbelieve." (8:55) "I will instill terror into the hearts of the unbelievers: smite ye above their necks and smite all their fingertips off them." (8:12) "Verily, the unbelievers are unclean." (9:28) , etc.

How can Muslims explain these verses? Aren't these and many similar Qur'anic teachings, responsible for Islamic violence? Most religions have had violent histories. Islam is the only religion that teaches violence in its holy book. Why?

Understanding Muhammad

Emperor Manuel II Paleologus' question remains unanswered. "You have injured our sensitivity, you must apologize, you are a bigot, you are encouraging us to become violent," etc. are not logical answers. They are evasions. They are red herrings. If Muslims want dialogue, they must be prepared to answer some tough questions, particularly about the Qur'an and the deeds of their prophet.

In his speech, the Pope called on the West to affirm the faith in God built on reason. Then he said: *"It is to this great logos, to this breadth of reason, that we invite our partners in the dialogue of cultures."*

For too many Muslims, dialogue means you listen to what we tell you and then agree. If you ask tough questions to which we have no answers, we will be offended and you will be sorry. How can there be any dialogue between these two diametrically opposing approaches?

Isn't it reasonable to ask if there is no compulsion in religion, as one verse of the Qur'an says, why Muslims are asked to fight and wage jihad in so many other verses? Why are so many verses of the Qur'an intolerant of freedom of belief? Why does leaving Islam entail death penalty?

It's time to talk, but it must be a real dialogue based on real questions, tough questions, questions that have never been answered. Getting together for hugs and handshakes is not dialogue. Shoving 1400 years of dirt under the carpet is not going to bring us closer to each other. There are troubling questions about Islam that must be answered. The character of Muhammad must be scrutinized and his teachings reevaluated.

There have been too many wars, too much bloodshed and senseless killings. There is no need for more. We must talk. We must put aside religious zealotries, engage in a real dialogue and answer some tough questions.

It's then that we can see Islam, far from being a religion of peace is a doctrine of hate. It is a grave error to admit Islam in the pantheon of religions and grant it equal status. Islam is a fascistic political movement akin to Nazism invented by a mentally disturbed man. Islam is not created to unite the hearts of people, but to divide them and to instill hatred among them, forcing everyone into submission. It is created as his pretext for conquest. It brings nothing but misery upon its own followers and terror on others.

Assuming everyone converts to Islam, the killings will only increase as Muslims will continue fighting among one another, each group trying to impose its own version of true Islam, calling others heretics and worthy of death.

Islam must be abolished, for humanity to survive. It's truth that will destroy Islam. Confronted with truth, Islam is defenseless. Muhammad knew that. He prohibited criticism and decreed death for those who dissented.

Ripples and Effects

There is no place for Islam in the future of mankind. Islam must go, not only because it is false, but because it is violent, intolerant, and evil.

How Islam will end depends on us. If we do nothing, if we let it grow unchecked, Muslims will bring about the third world war and millions will perish in a nuclear Armageddon. Communism was evil, but communists loved life and because of that, the Cold War ended without a nuclear confrontation. Muslims love death more than we love life. This changes everything. You may call it insanity but to them it is faith in the afterlife.

A nuclear Armageddon will bring about the end of Islam, but only after a great portion of humanity is wiped out. If we act now and start this dialogue, questioning Islam and helping Muslims see the truth, Islam will be weakened and Muslims will be freed. These people are victims of a big lie. They do not need chastisement, but guidance. If dialogue fails, war is inevitable. Had Nazism been defeated ideologically before it gained power, 50 million people would not have perished. A nuclear war between Muslims and the free world will result in much more death.

One thing is certain, Islam's days are numbered. Will it end in a big bang, like Nazism did, after millions are killed, or will it fall into pieces on its own, like communism, after Muslims come to see the truth and leave it in large numbers? The answer to this question depends very much on what we do today.

Nature does not recognize good or bad; it recognizes force. Muslims are militant. They are actively promoting their faith through deception and terror. Deception and terror are the two strategies of jihad, a struggle all Muslims are part of, each in his or her capacity. Some wage this war with their lives through terrorism, others do it with their money by funding terrorism, and others by deceptively portraying Islam as a religion of peace. They are all part of the same campaign. Their objective is to take over the world and dominate it.

Non-Muslims are laid back, easy going and believe in multiculturalism and freedom of faith. This causes an imbalance of powers. This imbalance has given Islam the edge since its inception. Thanks to their militant ethos and tolerance of others, Muslims have overcome much more powerful nations. These victories have emboldened them and increased their arrogance. If non-Muslims do not rise up to confront the spread of Islam, Islam will win and the destruction of civilization will ensue.

It takes only a handful of determined militants to subdue and take hostage a large number of unwary civilians. Muhammad boasted, "I have been made victorious with terror,"[372] and Muslims follow his example. Non-Muslims are

---

[372] Bukhari, 4.52.220.

unwary and unprepared. Therein lies their vulnerability. Unless we see Islam as the enemy, a threat to our civilization, we must brace ourselves for very tough times ahead of us. Time is running out. If Islam is not defeated fast, we will be facing a future that will make the horrors of World War II look like child's play.

Islam is an epidemic of mental illness bequeathed from one man to his entire followers. This psychosis attaching itself to "God" makes it the most vicious threat against humanity that we have ever seen. Failure to see that threat and stop it soon, can result in the greatest calamity mankind has ever seen.

Where Are We Headed?

Muslims try to be like Muhammad in every way. The Mullahs study for years to learn their Prophet's sunnah (the way he lived), and then teach that to believers, who in turn, do their best to emulate him. Through the sunnah Muslims learn how Muhammad performed prayers, washed his face, hands and feet. They learn how he cleaned his teeth, nose and ears. They want to know how he ate, which fingers he licked after eating, which foods he liked or disliked, how he slept, dressed, and what was the shape and material of his clothing. How long was his beard? Did he perform ablution before going to his wives or after? With which foot did he enter the toilet? Did he urinate standing or squatting? Which direction did he face when answering the call of nature? On which foot did he placed most of his weight when squatting? With which hand did he clean his private parts? To a Muslim the meaning of piety is to do exactly what Muhammad did. Ibn Sa'd reports a hadith from a companion of Muhammad who tried to show off his piety by saying that he saw Muhammad liked squash and since then he, too, loves this vegetable.[373]

Muslims' thoughts reflect those of Muhammad and their actions mirror his. The moment one becomes a Muslim, one stops thinking. Muslims have lost their selfhood and have become clones of Muhammad. It is a fallacy to say Muslims are a diverse group of people. They are all mini replicas of their prophet. They differ in degree – some emulate him more and some less. This determines their level of violence. In essence all Muslims have the same mindset, values and attitude. There are also good people who call themselves Muslims. They are often denounced by real Muslims as hypocrites. These "soft" Muslims actually make up the bulk of the umma, but their voices are

---

[373] Tabaqat Volume 1, Page 374

often silenced because they find no support for their views in the Qur'an. In words they are moderates but in practice they sheepishly trail behind the zealot minority. In other words, the tail wags the dog.

The so called moderate Muslims are indeed hypocrites. If they do not believe in the violence preached in the Qur'an, why do they call themselves Muslims? Why do they not leave Islam and end this cycle of hate and violence? They are not innocent. They are guilty of compliance. They are silent accomplices of their jihadi co-religionists. These Muslims are ignorant of true Islam, but ignorance is not an excuse. Their adherence to Islam boosts the morale of the real Muslims who go about doing what Muhammad did, become terrorists, kill innocent people and try to take over the world by force.

The result is a hellish society that has little hope of improvement, in which everyone suffocates, and no one knows how to extricate themselves. Ironically, the more they suffer, the more they cling to Islam for their liberation. It becomes a vicious circle that gets worse, day by day.

More lives have been lost because of Islam than for any other cause. Billions suffered and continue to suffer because of Islam. If Hitler's insanity caused the death of fifty million people, the insanity of Muhammad bequeathed to his followers has cost hundreds of millions of lives, and we're still counting. The pain caused by Hitler is history. The wounds caused by Muhammad and his benighted followers have been bleeding for 1,400 years. They are still bleeding and will continue to bleed endlessly, until Islam is eradicated.

Just as in the People's Temple, the primary victims of Islam are its wretched believers. Their minds are filled with superstitions, their hearts with hatred, their lives with suffering, and their brains are paralyzed by fear of hellfire. They are the most pitiable people while they think others envy them. Muslim societies are dysfunctional, their countries are dictatorial and their lives are in shambles. It is up to them to end their denial and face the painful truth that Islam is a lie and the main cause of their miseries. If they fail to do so, they will be heading, just like the followers of Jim Jones, towards their doom.

Non-Muslims are guilty of naivety. They are the ones who inflame extremism when they validate Islam as a legitimate religion. They have allowed unrestricted propagation of this nefarious cult in their countries, unaware of what Islam really is. Islam does not recognize any other religion or system as legitimate. Wherever it comes to power, it abolishes all human rights.

Muslim immigrants are flooding Western countries with the intent of taking over these lands. Shortsighted, unscrupulous politicians bend over backwards to appease them and praise Islam as a "religion of peace" to vie for their votes. Some have gone so far as to pass "blasphemy laws" in order to ban criticism of Islam.

The number of Muslims in the West is growing fast. This is mainly due to immigration and their high birth rate. Large populations of Muslims in Islamic countries pose no threat to the world. For sure they will abuse the minorities among them and will make their lives hellish. As painful as this is, it does not pose a threat to mankind. But a large population of Muslims in non-Muslim countries is a serious threat. If Muslims multiply in their own countries they will only become poorer. They will fight among each other and will be weakened. They can only hurt themselves, but pose no threat to the peace and stability of the world. If however, they are allowed to grow in the West, democracy will be lost and this means the death of the Western civilization. If we let the West fall, humanity will revert to a dark age from which there would be no recovery. This is the most serious threat mankind has ever faced.

Also, keep in mind that Muslims in the West are more "evangelical" and militant than their co-religionists back home. Democracy provides them fertile ground to be virulent, something they can't even dream of in their native countries. Extremist Islamists will be jailed in most Islamic countries, while they roam freely in the West.

We must ask: Is Islam compatible with democracy and Western values? Are we going to be safe if Muslims are allowed to grow in our midst unchecked? Does multiculturalism mean that ideologies that are openly against multiculturalism, pluralism, and democracy should be allowed to be spread?

Multiculturalism assumes that every culture has something valuable to offer. It presupposes that all cultures can co-exist in harmony. Islam, however, has a proven record of creating isolated communities which often, if not always, are antagonistic and in conflict with those around them. Islam is not a culture, nor is it capable of meaningful integration with other cultures. Is there a benefit to recognize fascism and Nazism as legitimate ideologies and allow their proliferation in our schools and among our kids? Should we be tolerant of doctrines that are so clearly intolerant, promote inequality, foment hate and encourage terrorism? How rational is it to let a belief system thrive in our countries when the very tenets of that belief are intolerant of our beliefs and call for our subjugation and annihilation? Islam is not a culture. It is a doctrine that aims to subsume all other cultures. It is not another color in the rainbow of religions; it is the dark void of night that wants to devour all colors.

If any culture needs to be preserved, it is the Western, Helleno-Christian culture. It is this culture that is facing extinction. It is to this culture alone that we owe the Enlightenment, Renaissance, and democracy. These are the foundations of our modern world. It would be a terrible mistake not to preserve this culture. If we do nothing, we face a future where democracy and tolerance will fade and Islam's more primitive instincts will subjugate humanity.

All cultures are not made equal. A doctrine that advocates subjugation of women and minorities is not equal to a culture that promotes equality of all people irrespective of their beliefs, gender and race. Islam is not a culture. It is the antithesis of culture. It is barbarity, savagery and incivility. **Islamic civilization is an oxymoron, while Islamic terrorism is redundancy**. We owe our freedom and modern civilization to Western culture. It is this culture that is now under attack and needs protection.

I wrote this book with two goals in mind: to help Muslims see the truth and leave Islam, and to unmask the real face of Islam and warn of its threat, so the world can stand up and protect itself. Islam portrays itself as religion and uses religious terminology, but its goal is to subdue and dominate. This is the same goal pursued by Nazism and communism. Islam's ambitions are both worldly and political; its spiritual message is only a mask.

Islam must be confronted and defeated, not only on ideological grounds but also in the political sphere. Since the ultimate agenda of Islam is to topple democracy and establish its own totalitarian world order, it must be classified as a political ideology. Hence, it is the duty of politicians to fight it. Our politicians have a moral obligation to oppose any totalitarian ideology that threatens our democracy, whether it is Nazism, fascism, communism or Islam. Fighting against Islam must become the priority of every statesman. Islam is politics; its religious aspect is only pretence. Its method is to rouse foolhardy believers to action and make them eager to fight for its imperialistic objectives with bogus promises of an afterlife lustful and orgiastic reward. Without its political agenda Islam has no raison d'être.

I hope this book will increase the awareness of the threat of Islam. Most people are oblivious to this threat. They are in denial. Yet all one has to do to see this threat is to listen to what Muslims say. Listen carefully to their slogans during their angry protests. Read their placards. They are the writings on the wall. Freedom has never been so vulnerable to attack as it is today.

Freedom does not come free. Westerners enjoy freedom because their forefathers fought Islamic aggression. Had they been defeated, the Europe of today would have been just as dystopian a land as are the Middle East and the rest of the Islam infested world. They had two revolutions, one in America and the other in Europe and they fought in two world wars to gain their freedom. War is not pleasant but liberty has to be gained, sometimes through warfare.

Today, the jihadis are back with a vengeance; this time under the guise of immigrants and economic refugees. Muslim immigration is the Islamic Trojan horse. If Westerners do not detect this threat in time, they stand to lose everything. The danger is real and time is running out.

We have three alternatives before us:

a) Do nothing and let Muslims take over countries through immigration and demographic explosion. This could happen in a few short decades. Muslim immigrants on average produce four times more children than Europeans. These children are often raised with the tax money of their hosts in the hope that their "investment" in them will eventually pay dividends when these little Muslims grow up and support the pensions of those who paid for their upbringing. This is a grave illusion. Muslims will never pay to support non-Muslims. As soon as Muslims become the majority, they will take over power, scrap the pension plan, and replace it with Islamic "charity" where only Muslims benefit. Non-Muslims will be reduced to dhimmis – second class citizens – and will have to pay tribute to their Islamic rulers, in what WAS once their country. If Westerners think that one day Muslims will be working and paying for their pensions, they are in for a big unpleasant surprise. By letting Muslim immigrants in, they are nurturing their own nemeses. It is foolish to assume that those who riot today and cheer every time terrorists kill non-Muslims will one day become responsible citizens and work to maintain their hosts in their old age. Muslims in non-Muslim countries are not an asset, but a huge liability. They are the biggest threats these countries face.

b) The second alternative is to fight them now before they become stronger. This means mass deportation and even civil war. Even then Muslims will win because post colonial Westerners are guilt ridden and constrained by their conscience. They are unable to kill indiscriminately, while an alarming number of Muslims have no such qualms. Good Muslims can kill any number of non-Muslims, including their children with total freedom of conscience. Remember Beslan? They have divine sanction to do so.

Ripples and Effects

On Feb. 13, 2007, the CBC published the results of an Environics poll. According to this poll, fully 12% of Canadian Muslims said the aborted terrorist plot – that included kidnapping and beheading the Canadian prime minister and blowing up the Parliament and the CBC – was justified. 12% of 700,000 Muslims living in Canada means 84,000 Canadian Muslims support terrorism. On February 25, 2007, the UK Telegraph reported that Eliza Manningham-Buller, the director general of MI5, warned there were more than 1,600 "identified individuals" actively engaged in plotting terrorist attacks. There were 200 known networks involved in at least 30 terrorist plots. It is thought that the number of British citizens of Islamic persuasion involved in plots could be well in excess of 2,000. The situation is no different in other countries where there is a large Muslim conclave. The sunnah of Muhammad and the lack of conscience give Muslims an edge over their opponents. It was thanks to this lack of conscience that Muhammad and a handful of his warriors subdued much larger populations that were far more sophisticated. When civilization and barbarity collide, brute force always wins. History is full of cases where large empires were conquered by a bunch of swordsmen and robbers.

c) The third alternative is to fight Islam ideologically, before Muslims manage to eliminate public criticism and freedom of speech is lost for ever.

It is easy to see that the third alternative is the best. If Islam is defeated ideologically, many Muslims will turn against it. Ex-Muslims are the best allies the world has in this war. They know the evil of Islam, they know the value of freedom and they are determined to preserve it.

This would be a win/win war. We win because we convert the enemy into a friend, and our enemy wins over his demon and is set free. There is no need for bloodshed. No bullets need be fired. By destroying Islam we will eliminate the source of hate and will lay the foundation for a better world that is based on understanding and unity of mankind.

To defeat Islam ideologically we must talk about it openly and allow it to be questioned. Islam cannot stand criticism. It is held together like a house of cards and will fall just as easily. Those who oppose criticism of Islam are the enemy of mankind. These fools try to appease Muslims and by doing so dig their own graves and the graves of Muslims too. Isn't it better to wage this war through dialogue than wait and fight it with bombs? Isn't Neville Chamberlain's legacy of appeasement of Adolf Hitler and Nazi Germany with his signing of the

Munich Agreement in 1938, conceding Czechoslovakia to Hitler enough to know that we must never bend to the demands of bullies?

Dr. Vaknin says: "The narcissistic bully very often gets his way… his misdeeds are overlooked, his misbehavior tolerated. This is partly because, narcissists are excellent liars with considerable thespian skills - and partly because no one wants to mess around with a thug, even if his thuggery is limited to words and gestures."[374] Isn't this how Muslims behave? Aren't their riots, demonstrations and thuggeries designed to intimidate the world into not criticizing them?

The debate on Islam has begun, but the truth is hard to find and old beliefs die hard. Islamic apologists such as Karen Armstrong, John Esposito and Edward Said have taken it upon themselves to portray a one-sided and deceptively rosy image of Islam. The mainstream media finds this positive image far more convenient to promote. Whilst these misleading, but politically correct voices attempt to defend the indefensible, angry Muslims show the true face of Islam with their constant readiness to harass, intimidate, and assassinate anyone who slights their religion.

This is a crucial debate. Faith Freedom International (FFI) has been promoting this debate since 2001, while I have been doing it since 1998. I hope this book will help expand it. Dialogue, reason and intelligence can defeat Islam only if they are given a chance. Falsehood can survive through brute force and censorship, but it can't survive in a free and open discussion. Lies vanish when confronted with truth, like ice melting in heat.

To defeat Islam in the political sphere we need public awareness. Politicians are not leaders. They are followers. If the outcry from the public is loud enough, someone will step up to make those voices heard.

This is a war. The enemy is an ideology. We must take our gloves off and get tough with our enemy. Let's not be intimidated by its size; Islam stands on a very shaky ground. It rests on nothing but lies. All we have to do to demolish it is to expose those lies and this gigantic edifice of terror and deception will collapse. Muslims will be set free and the world will be saved from the venom of Islam. We owe it to our children. It is our responsibility to make their world safe and free.

---

[374] Narcissism in the Workplace: online conference transcript
healthyplace.com/Communities/Personality_Disorders/Site/Transcripts/narcissism_workplace.htm

Index

263

Y

Yahya (John the Baptist): 111
Yasir: 18.
Yathrib: 22, 45, 47, 48, 51, 86, 213, 214.
Yemen: 22, 219.
Yusuf Khattab (see Joseph Cohen)
Yvonne Ridley: 25.

Z

Zakat: 41, 215, 223, 224.
Zakariah: 122.
Zarqawi: 25.
Zeid: 95, 123.
Zeinab (daughter of Muhammad): 85, 91.
Zeinab (wife of Muhammad): 95, 197.
Zoroastrian: 19.

Printed in the United States
116110LV00002BA/176/P